D0927808

Comfort Women

ASIA PERSPECTIVES

ASIA PERSPECTIVES
History, Society, and Culture
Carol Gluck, Editor

Comfort Women

Sexual Slavery in
the Japanese Military
During World War II

Yoshimi Yoshiaki

Translated by Suzanne O'Brien

COLUMBIA UNIVERSITY PRESS
NEW YORK

Columbia University Press

Publishers Since 1893

New York   Chichester, West Sussex

Comfort Women: Sexual Slavery in the Japanese Military During World War II

by Yoshiaki Yoshimi

Copyright ©1995 by Yoshimi Yoshiaki

Originally published in Japanese by Iwanami Shoten, Publishers, Tokyo, 1995.

Translation copyright ©2000 Columbia University Press

Library of Congress Cataloging-in-Publication Data

Yoshimi, Yoshiaki, 1946–

   [Jugun ianfu. English]

   Comfort women : sexual slavery in the Japanese military / Yoshimi
Yoshiaki ; translated by Suzanne O'Brien.

      p.   cm. — (Asia perspectives)

   Includes bibliographical references and index.

   ISBN 0–231–12032–X (cloth)

      1. Comfort women—Asia.   2. World War, 1939–1945—Women—Asia.
   I. O'Brien, Suzanne.   II. Title.   III. Series.

   D810.C698 Y6713 2000

   940.54′05′082095—dc21

                                                              00–030305

Casebound editions of Columbia University Press books are printed on
permanent and durable acid-free paper.

Designed by Lisa Hamm

Printed in the United States of America

c 10 9 8 7 6 5 4 3 2 1

Contents

Comfort Women

Translator's Introduction

For more than sixty years now, women enslaved by the Japanese military during the Asia Pacific War have paid a terrible price to ensure the comfort of Japanese people. Between 1932 and 1945, untold thousands of women,[1] euphemistically known as "comfort women,"[2] were systematically rounded up and imprisoned in "comfort stations," brothels where they were repeatedly raped and abused by Japanese military personnel. In the years since Japan's defeat, these women have lived with the physical and emotional scars of their enslavement in silence. That silence, enforced by patriarchal power and discrimination in both Japan and their own countries, bought Japan a comfortable four-decade respite from facing its responsibility for these war crimes. Only in the 1990s, when survivors of the comfort stations began coming forward to speak about their ordeals, did the exorbitant human price they have paid for Japan's comfort become clear. Through their courage and activism, survivors have forced the Japanese government and public opinion throughout Asia to reconceive that price as a debt Japan must acknowledge and attempt to redeem.[3]

The suffering of comfort station survivors must be remembered, reflected upon, and enlisted in efforts to transform Japan's all-too-comfortable ways of remembering the war. In a number of public statements and in suits filed against the Japanese government, survivors have presented their own vision of how Japan should fulfill its responsibilities. They call on the Japanese government to investigate and reveal the truth about its wartime conduct, acknowledge its war crimes, punish those responsible, issue apologies and pay compensation to all its victims, and educate younger generations about Japan's war crimes so as to prevent their repetition. This vision demands that the Japanese government develop a habit of remembering its crimes and that it foster this habit among its citizens through educational initiatives.

Yoshimi Yoshiaki's *Military Comfort Women* (Jūgun ianfu, Iwanami shinsho, 1995; in this edition, changed to *Comfort Women*, as more commonly known in English) represents one Japanese historian's efforts to respond to comfort station survivors' demands and help realize their vision. Yoshimi, a professor of modern Japanese history at Chūō University in Tokyo, has been a leading figure in scholarly efforts to document Japanese war crimes. His work has been instrumental in forcing the Japanese government to admit some responsibility for the enslavement of comfort women. It has also prompted Japanese people to remember and to question their memories of the war. In *Military Comfort Women*, Yoshimi brings heretofore neglected accounts—those of the victims of the comfort station system as well as those of its designers and operators—to bear on Japanese recollections. By placing these disparate memories alongside commonly invoked Japanese memories of the war, Yoshimi reveals the prejudices that have allowed Japanese to regard comfort women as an inconsequential footnote to accounts of the war years and that lead many to dismiss the testimonies of comfort station survivors today. *Military Comfort Women* is not simply an investigation into previously understudied aspects of the Asia Pacific War but part of an ongoing struggle to restore the dignity of these women by acknowledging their fundamental human rights and compensating them for the gross violations of those rights during the war.

This struggle is being waged by victims and their supporters against those in Japan and other Asian countries who seek to minimize Japan's war responsibility or declare it adequately discharged. It is a struggle for recognition—of the suffering of comfort station survivors, of the comfort station system itself as a war crime, and of sexual violence against women during armed conflicts generally as a war crime and a crime against humanity. It is also a struggle over history and memories. Victims of Japan's war crimes have challenged Japanese accounts of the war and sparked intense conflicts over how Japanese history should be written and taught. While this struggle shows no signs of being resolved in the near future, it has already transformed the ways in which the Asia Pacific War is discussed and remembered.

NO TIDY ENDINGS FOR JAPAN IN THE 1990S

In the past decade, public discourse in Japan has been straining under the weight of a host of endings: the end of the Shōwa period with the death of Emperor Hirohito in 1989, the end of the Cold War, the end of the Liberal Democratic Party's monopoly on political power, and the end of the "postwar" period (hailed as the fiftieth anniversary of the end of World War II approached). However, a number of those who lived through the eras purportedly ending have refused to disappear quietly into the past. The most prominent of these have been victims of Japanese war crimes. They insist that no endings and, consequently, no new beginnings are possible so long as Japan refuses to acknowledge and assume responsibility for its crimes.

Leading the revolt against tidy endings have been victims themselves and Asian civic groups such as the Korean Council for the Women Drafted for Military Sexual Slavery by Japan.[4] With the support of members of this organization, three elderly Korean women filed suit in the Tokyo District Court in December 1991 demanding an official apology and compensation from the Japanese government for crimes committed against them during the Asia Pacific War. Their suit is one of dozens filed during the 1990s by victims of Japanese war crimes seeking redress. These plaintiffs range from former slave laborers to former colonial subjects drafted into the Imperial Army and then refused pensions after the war to survivors of biological experiments and chemical warfare in China. Refusing to remain silent or to wait any longer for their own governments to pursue their claims, the victims have come forward to demand that Japan acknowledge its crimes and make amends. Victims' determination to bypass their own governments and press individual claims for compensation directly through the Japanese courts has been a startling development in the process of coming to terms with the Asia Pacific War.

The confluence of victims' activism, new political alignments within Japan and among Asian nations, and the flurry of anniversaries and endings in the 1990s prompted the Japanese government to attempt to put to rest once and for all the charge that Japan had not properly apologized to its neighbors for its imperialism and wartime aggression in Asia. But rather than resolving questions of Japanese war responsibility, the apologies offered by the government in the 1990s have managed to incite both fierce opposition at home and greater suspicion of Japan abroad. Prime Minister Hosokawa Morihiro's 1993 apology for Japan's "war of aggression," which he characterized as a "mistaken war,"[5] was attacked by conservative legislators in the Liberal Democratic Party. In 1995, a group of these legislators sponsored a research association and published a volume of essays justifying the "Great East Asian War" and disputing the historical veracity of accounts of atrocities committed by the Japanese military, such as the Nanking Massacre.[6]

Similar revisionist groups sprang up outside government circles, such as the "Free History" (*jiyūshugishi*)[7] advocates led by University of Tokyo education professor Fujioka Nobukatsu, and echoed the claims that there is little historical proof of many Japanese war crimes and no need for Japan to apologize. These reactionary responses from Japanese politicians and academics, coupled with the government's subsequent retreat from the bolder language in Hosokawa's apology, have made victims and their supporters both in Japan and throughout the rest of Asia skeptical of Japan's verbal apologies, and have renewed their determination to secure an unequivocal acknowledgment of Japanese war crimes and official compensation.

THE COMFORT WOMEN ISSUE
AND PUBLIC MEMORY IN ASIA

By stepping forward to press their own claims for redress, survivors of the comfort stations have redefined not only their own role in public memories of the war (from prostitutes to survivors of sexual slavery) but also the limits of who can speak and whose memories matter in dominant accounts of the war throughout Asia. Until former comfort women came forward to tell their own stories in the past decade, they were largely relegated to the status of minor details, if they appeared at all. In Japan, they turned up in memoirs, histories, novels, and films, but their victimization was seldom regarded as criminal. In memoirs, Japanese veterans often relate fond memories of their experiences in comfort stations, which they viewed simply as brothels. Even some Japanese feminists who recognized the enslavement of comfort women as dehumanizing violence didn't consider it an actionable offense or cause for Japanese redress. Rather, the plight of comfort women seemed to be just one more example of how "women" are victimized in war.[8] The generic portrayal in Japanese recollections turns a blind eye to the specificity of comfort women's victimization in terms of gender, ethnicity, and class.

The dominant Japanese accounts of the war brand armed conflict as universally evil and equate the suffering of Japanese with that of other Asians, thereby obscuring the sexism, racism, and imperialism that spawned the comfort stations.[9] These accounts are founded upon a deliberate forgetting of the fact that Japanese aggression, often enthusiastically supported by Japanese citizens, was the direct cause of other Asians' suffering. This willful amnesia has enabled Japanese public memory to cast Japan in the roles of universal victim of and witness to the horrors of war (as the world's sole victim of atomic bombing)[10] and liberator of Asia from the yoke of Western colonialism.

These portrayals have, of course, been contested by other Asian nations. Yet even when the suffering of victims of the comfort station system has been invoked by Asian governments, it is often as just one more example of how their nations suffered under Japanese occupation or colonial rule.[11] In the role of victim, the South Korean government, for example, has arrogated to itself the right to represent the nation as a whole. The plight of comfort station survivors has seldom figured prominently in that representation, no doubt because it not only highlights the emasculation of Korean men under Japanese colonial domination (unable to protect "their" women from Japanese depredations) but also inevitably raises the issue of collaboration by Korean procurers. These painful aspects of Korea's colonial history undermine the masculinist myth of a uniformly victimized "Korea" by revealing the gender and class discrimination within Korea itself that inflected colonial domination and rendered young, impoverished women particularly vulnerable to exploitation.

Once again, the portrait of comfort women drawn by victimized nations erases survivors' status as members of an oppressed gender and/or class, and carefully sidesteps the discrimination they have been subjected to at home since the end of the war. Eager to attract or maintain Japanese development aid and investment, the postwar governments of Asian nations colonized or occupied by Japan during the war have often been reluctant to press issues of Japan's responsibilities to its victims. Not only the Japanese but other Asian governments as well would just as soon forget, for different but complementary reasons, that comfort women ever existed. Survivors' public testimonies have not only challenged Japanese public memory but also forced other Asians to reconsider the official accounts that have shaped their memories of the war since 1945.

Victims and women's groups have challenged the patriarchal privilege that empowers government leaders to waive the rights of "their" women to seek redress from Japan. In October 1998, for example, South Korean President Kim Dae-jung accepted the Japanese government's apology for inflicting terrible suffering upon Koreans during the period of colonial rule and pledged not to bring up issues related to Japan's colonization of Korea again. But Korean comfort station survivors have pressed ahead with their protests, lawsuits, and activism, insisting that the Japanese government officially acknowledge all its war crimes and pay them compensation directly from public funds. By refusing to cede the power to represent their experiences and demands, survivors have foiled government attempts to portray questions about Japan's war responsibility as largely resolved and to redirect citizens' attention to illusory visions of a prosperous future based on a congenial partnership with Japan and unencumbered by such historical burdens.

YOSHIMI YOSHIAKI'S RESEARCH AND THE DEVELOPMENT OF THE COMFORT WOMEN ISSUE IN JAPAN

Yoshimi Yoshiaki has been concerned with questions of Japanese war crimes and war responsibility throughout his career. He is a member of the generation of activists and historians who began in the late 1970s to challenge early postwar Japanese accounts that placed responsibility for the war squarely on the shoulders of the military establishment. Like independent scholar Kanō Mikiyo and children's book author Yamanaka Hisashi, Yoshimi challenged portrayals of average Japanese citizens as merely innocent victims of an expansionist military. Like-minded members of Yoshimi's generation sought to probe the question of Japanese citizens' war responsibility by taking up such topics as the role of women's groups in the war effort, the practices of "patriotic" wartime education, and the use of slave laborers by Japanese companies. Yoshimi examined Japanese soldiers' and civilians' experiences and memories of the war in his seminal work, *Grassroots Fascism* (Kusa no ne no fashizumu, Tokyo daigaku shuppanai, 1987). He is currently researching the Japanese military's use of poison gas during the Asia Pacific War. *Military Comfort Women* can therefore be read as one campaign in a struggle begun over twenty years ago by Yoshimi and other liberal Japanese scholars to clarify Japanese war responsibility.

In addition to his groundbreaking scholarship, Yoshimi has been an active participant in public discussions of the comfort women issue and in international groups seeking reparations for victims of Japanese war crimes. He has prepared evidence in support of comfort station survivors for use in Japanese courts. He is also a founding member of the Center for Research and Documentation on Japan's War Responsibility (*Nihon no sensō sekinin shiryō sentaa*), an independent research institute sponsoring and coordinating scholarly research on Japanese war crimes. Most recently, Yoshimi has been a tireless campaigner for the release of government-held documents and for the establishment of permanent committees in the Diet and prefectural assemblies to investigate Japanese war responsibility.

Yoshimi first became interested in issues of sexual violence and war while conducting research for *Grassroots Fascism*, but it was the testimonies of survivors that inspired him to take up the comfort women issue. Deeply moved by the courageous testimony of Korean comfort station survivor Kim Haksun, in January 1992 Yoshimi returned to the Japanese Self-Defense Agency archives, where he had previously come across documents pertaining to the comfort station system. There he located wartime documents attesting to the fact that the Japanese military planned, constructed, and operated comfort stations. Prior to the publication of these documents on January 11, 1992, the Japanese government had refused to acknowledge official military involvement, maintaining that comfort stations had been managed exclusively by civilian brothel owners and that the women had been "recruited" by private procurers. The government also dismissed the testimonies of survivors recounting kidnapping, coercion, and forced transport by Japanese military personnel as uncorroborated and therefore insufficient evidence of military participation.

In the wake of the publication of the documents in the *Asahi Shimbun*, one of Japan's major daily newspapers, the Japanese government finally admitted military involvement in the operation of the comfort station system and issued an apology to Korean survivors. Yet this move stopped far short of satisfying the demands of comfort station survivors. First, the government's admission of involvement remained ambiguous in regard to the roles of civilian brothel operators and procurers. While it acknowledged that the Japanese military set up or constructed comfort stations, conducted medical examinations of the women, and oversaw the management of comfort facilities, it still maintained that comfort women were rounded up primarily by civilian procurers, who were responsible for transporting them.

In addition, the apology the Japanese government offered was addressed only to Korean women; there was no attempt to address crimes against other Asian women. Finally, the government reasserted that it had no legal responsibility to pay compensation to the victims of its crimes because all claims to reparations had been waived in postwar treaties.

The ambiguities and half measures of the Japanese government's response to survivors' demands infuriated not only survivors' supporters but also anti-apology activists who seek to deny any Japanese obligation to apologize to or compensate women enslaved in comfort stations. Soon after these women began speaking out, attacks on the veracity and motives of their testimonies erupted in Japan, not only from the camps of right-wing extremists but also from government ministries and universities. Anti-apology activists assert that comfort women were in fact prostitutes; that they were not in the direct employ of the Japanese military; and that the way they were treated did not violate international law at the time. Therefore, Japan committed no crimes against them and has no responsibility to issue apologies or provide compensation. These assertions have become some of the main points of contention in the struggle over the comfort women issue.

Military Comfort Women is both a participant in and a product of this struggle. It refutes government and anti-apology arguments and illuminates such broader issues as the social institutions and attitudes that fostered the comfort station system, many of which persist in Japan today. This activist agenda informs the book's main arguments: 1) that the enslavement of comfort women was a systematic, orchestrated policy emanating from the highest reaches of the Japanese state; 2) that this policy violated international law and the women's human rights and therefore constitutes a war crime for which the nation is responsible; 3) that the coercion inherent in the system took many forms and must be understood in the context of gender, ethnic, colonial, and class oppression; 4) that Japan's crimes against comfort women did not end with the war and the dissolution of the comfort station system but continue today in the form of Japanese denials and evasion of responsibility; and 5) that Japanese responsibility does not rest only with the government or military but also extends to Japanese citizens who condoned imperialism and the sexual exploitation of women.

Integrating in-depth interviews with former comfort women, archival research, and a survey of countless memoirs written by former military personnel, *Military Comfort Women* provides a multifaceted account of the genesis, development, and operation of the comfort station system. At the time of its publication in 1995, this account was unique among the many recent works addressing the issue in that it drew not only on the testimonies of victims but also on military documents and memoirs written by the perpetrators of the system. By supplementing the insights and information provided by survivors' testimonies with information gleaned from documents produced by the military personnel who planned, managed, and frequented comfort stations, Yoshimi has been able to explicate the *systematic* nature of Japan's war crimes. His investigation of the perpetrators' perspectives also illuminates critical questions about comfort women's enslavement that cannot be addressed solely through survivors' testimonies, such as why a disproportionate number of comfort women were Korean and how the military's methods of populating comfort stations varied across Asia and over time in the course of Japan's imperialist expansion.

Military Comfort Women paints a chilling portrait of how women, many in their teens, were enslaved in response to directives from elite officers. Yoshimi traces the chains of command that linked officers in the field supervising the provisioning and operation of military comfort stations to the highest reaches of the War and Foreign Ministries, where the transport of comfort women was approved and organized. He also demonstrates that the coerced or duplicitous rounding up and transport of women to comfort stations was in direct violation of international law and was recognized as such by Japanese officials at the time. In light of this evidence, attempts to portray the comfort station system as anything other than a form of state-sponsored slavery are unconvincing.

Yoshimi's account demonstrates how the comfort station system came to be regarded by the military elite as necessary to the war effort. The comfort stations were in fact an attempt on the part of the military high command to prevent rapes committed by Japanese soldiers in occupied territories and the spread of sexually transmitted diseases among the troops. The comfort station system institutionalized sexual violence against comfort women in an attempt to curb unauthorized sexual violence. This strategy, however, failed miserably, based as it was on a simplistic conception of male sexuality (namely, that male sexual energy will build up and drive men to rape if it is not periodically released in sexual intercourse with women) and a deliberate ignorance about the nature of rape and the functions it serves in war. Yoshimi points out that rape came to be seen among the troops as one of the few "benefits" of military life, which was otherwise characterized by unrelenting surveillance, brutal discipline, meager provisions, and the constant specter of death from combat or disease. Some officers even condoned rape, believing that it improved troops' morale—a perpetual concern of military leaders. The reluctance of military commanders to try soldiers accused of rape enabled both authorized and unauthorized forms of sexual violence against women to proliferate under the auspices of the Imperial Japanese military.

While Yoshimi's analysis demonstrates that rapes in war zones and occupied territories were inextricably linked to the rapes that occurred in comfort stations, anti-apology activists refuse to acknowledge that comfort women were victims of sexual assaults or coercion for which Japan can be held liable. These activists have attempted to downplay the coercion inherent in the comfort station system in several ways. First, they maintain that comfort women were prostitutes servicing Japanese troops by choice. Second, anti-apology activists insist that the Japanese military did not use force in rounding up comfort women. Whatever coercion may have occurred, anti-apologists contend, was applied by civilian procurers and brothel operators and is therefore not something Japan can be held responsible for. Some activists even argue that the Japanese military treated comfort women "conscientiously."[12]

All of these arguments fly in the face of survivors' testimonies and ignore the coercive conditions in comfort stations themselves. Numerous Korean, Taiwanese, Filipina, and other Asian women forced to serve as comfort women have testified to the fact that Japanese military personnel or police officers were directly involved in their kidnappings. Anti-apology activists, however, claim that these women were in fact prostitutes plying their trade voluntarily in the war zones and occupied territories. This assertion brands the survivors' testimonies as false and survivors themselves as not trustworthy. Attacking the character of female victims of sexual assault is an age-old strategy for discrediting them by portraying them as somehow consenting to assaults. In addition, these activists reason that if comfort women were prostitutes, then whatever abuses they suffered in comfort stations were not crimes. Feminist supporters of the survivors, such as Yoshimi, reject this sort of reasoning and insist that all women enslaved in comfort stations, including Japanese women who had previously worked as prostitutes, were victims of human rights violations. Yoshimi emphasizes that regardless of how women were brought to comfort stations, once there, they lived in a state of perpetual coercion characterized by continual rape, confinement, and physical abuse. The means by which they were first recruited has no bearing on that fact and does not absolve the Japanese military and government from responsibility for the coercion to which comfort women were subjected.

Anti-apology activists have attempted to limit consideration of coercion in the comfort station system to the issue of whether Japanese personnel used force to round up comfort women. This perverse logic asserts that women rounded up by civilian procurers at the behest of the Japanese military can be labeled prostitutes, regardless of whether they were coerced or deceived, and therefore excluded from consideration as victims of war crimes. *Military Comfort Women* not only refutes this logic but also expands discussion of the coercion involved in the system far beyond these limits. Yoshimi draws on the testimonies of a variety of survivors to demonstrate not only that Japanese police and military personnel were directly involved in coercing women to supply the comfort station system but also that Japanese police, customs, and military personnel had every opportunity to recognize that women recruited by civilian procurers were victims of coercion and deception. In police interviews, at customs checkpoints, and in initial medical examinations for sexually transmitted diseases it was often clear to Japanese officials that the women were terrified, ignorant of what sort of "work" they would be doing, and sexually inexperienced. As *Military Comfort Women* demonstrates, the coercion used to round up and enslave comfort women was an acknowledged aspect of the comfort station system, pervading its operation at all levels.

At each stage of his investigation, Yoshimi asks how gender discrimination, racial and ethnic discrimination, and imperialist domination combined to facilitate the operation of the comfort station system and the victimization of young Asian women. Impoverished by Japan's exploitative colonial or occupation policies, many families were struggling to survive, and daughters were often the first to be sacrificed. In these circumstances, young women, who usually had little education and few economic prospects, often found procurers' false offers of good jobs irresistible. Yoshimi also points out that in occupied territories, "requests" from the Japanese military for a supply of young women were inherently coercive, as villagers were in no position to refuse. By exploring how different forms of discrimination interacted in the lives of women enslaved in comfort stations, Yoshimi broadens our understanding of the array of forces that made the comfort station system possible and extends the scope of inquiry into responsibility for the crimes committed in its name.

Anti-apology activists' denials that coercion was used by the Japanese military to round up women rest on a negative assertion of historical positivism: if there are no written documents proving that force was used by Japanese police or military personnel, then there is no irrefutable evidence that force was used and no need for Japanese people to accept survivors' claims. This is the essence of Fujioka's "Free History"—Japanese people should be free to think whatever they want about the past in the absence of written documents providing definitive evidence.

Yoshimi points out that insisting upon positivist standards of "proof" in regard to the comfort women issue is particularly perverse in light of the well-known fact that the Japanese military and government systematically destroyed documents as they withdrew from their overseas empire and prepared for the occupation of Japan. The hypocrisy of such a stance is illustrated by such prominent anti-apologists as former Justice Minister Okuno Seisuke. In 1996, Okuno declared to reporters that comfort women were simply prostitutes working in war zones, though he has admitted publicly that he personally participated in the incineration of Japanese government documents in advance of the arrival of American occupation forces. It is only by chance that the documents pertaining to the comfort station system uncovered thus far escaped this sort of destruction. Furthermore, many of the documents that did survive are still classified and have not been made public by the Japanese government. The insistence that former comfort women's testimonies be corroborated by written documents while even the few extant documents remain inaccessible starkly illustrates the resistance of anti-apology activists to considering survivors' demands for a full accounting of Japan's war crimes.

This privileging of written documents works to exclude from history and discussions of history the voices of the kind of people comfort women represent—the female, the impoverished, the colonized, the illiterate, and the racially and ethnically oppressed. These people have left few written records of their experiences, and therefore are denied a place in history and discussions of it by positivist gatekeepers. These "people without history" appear, then, only as they are represented in documents written by those in positions of power, and only these documents satisfy the gatekeepers' criteria for historical authenticity. As Yoshimi's research shows, comfort women often figure in official Japanese documents as just one more type of war materiel, whose supply and transport had to be attended to by military accounting officers. They never appear as human beings whose rights must be taken into consideration. It has only been through their testimonies that survivors have been able to challenge this portrayal. Anti-apology activists' insistence on written proof of victimization must be understood as an attempt to silence victims of the comfort station system before their version of history undermines the more comfortable one the activists cling to.

THE RECEPTION OF *MILITARY COMFORT WOMEN* AND THE STRUGGLES OVER JAPANESE HISTORY

Military Comfort Women has come to be regarded as required reading on the comfort women issue in Japan. It has sold more than 80,000 copies since its publication in 1995, and is often used as a textbook in college courses and by citizens' groups concerned with issues of Japan's war responsibility. It has also become a target for anti-apology activists' attacks. The *manga* artist and critic Kobayashi Yoshinori calls it the "Bible" of citizens' groups and singles out Yoshimi for vilification, branding him a fanatic who irresponsibly uses his authority as a professor to propagate his biased views. Kobayashi even compares Yoshimi to the lawyer Aoyama Yoshinobu, who vehemently defended Aum Shinrikyō, the cult responsible for the sarin gas attack on the Tokyo subway system in 1995 that killed eleven people and injured more than five thousand.[13]

Yoshimi, along with other scholars working on the comfort women issue such as Suzuki Yūko, has been criticized by the feminist scholar and critic Ueno Chizuko for fighting the battle against historical revisionists on their terms. In her article "The Politics of Memory,"[14] Ueno first articulates her critique of the modes that comfort station survivors' supporters have employed to combat the arguments of the anti-apology activists. According to Ueno, supporters' calls for more historical research and their belief that the historical "truth" produced by such scholarly endeavors will eventually win the day only play into the hands of anti-apology activists who demand documentary evidence of coercion. Ueno describes Yoshimi as "conscientious" but naive. She argues that Yoshimi shares with his anti-apology critics a positivist view of history that holds that for any historical phenomenon, a definitive truth exists and can be "discovered" if sufficiently searched for. What this view fails to recognize, according to Ueno, is that there is no single, objective historical truth. Rather, people have different experiences and views of history, each of which comprises "reality" for the people who lived through it. Only by bringing those disparate views into relation and dialogue with each other can history be understood, if not fixed and defined. Thus rather than trying to prove coercion took place by reference to existing documents, survivors' supporters should work on raising awareness of survivors' testimonies as part of the productive and ongoing process of remaking the past in the present.

Yoshimi has responded to these criticisms by rejecting Ueno's character-ization of his historical views and questioning her understanding of what's at stake in the comfort women issue.[15] He points out that, unlike anti-apology activists, he has always treated survivors' testimonies as uniquely valuable accounts of the past and as evidence just as valid as written documents. Fur-thermore, he recognizes the complexity and multiplicity of testimony: state-ments by the same survivor vary according to the occasion and interviewer, but this does not make them any less "true." Written documents and his-torical writing, he believes, are similarly complex and contextually deter-mined. Yoshimi also notes that the primary aims of activists on the comfort women issue have been to force the Japanese government to acknowledge direct participation in the operation of comfort stations and to take respon-sibility for its war crimes. It was only after the discovery and publication of Japanese government documents that the government finally abandoned its claims that comfort women were merely prostitutes in the employ of civil-ian procurers. Accumulating a wide array of evidence has also been critical in the prosecution of survivors' legal cases. Thus, Yoshimi argues, Ueno has misunderstood or overlooked the strategic and activist nature of much of the research into the comfort women issue.

The debates between Ueno and Yoshimi raise critical issues regarding survivors' testimonies and their status in discussions of the comfort women issue. The challenge for survivors' supporters is how to appreciate the varying and productive nature of survivors' testimonies without undermining their power and coherence when they are taken up as evidence in the context of legal proceedings. It is through their testimonies and activism that survivors have been able to create new identities for themselves, and each of their testimonies reveals a different aspect of their experiences. The variations illustrate that even an individual's or a group's memories of the past are plural. When this multiplicity is then brought to bear on the memories of people with a very different understanding of that past, it becomes clearer that all memories are necessarily limited and contextual, and that no one of them alone can suffice as historical truth. The question for discussion then becomes which memories, whose memories are given pride of place in history and accorded the status of truth.

THE COMFORT WOMEN ISSUE AND THE STRUGGLE OVER NATIONAL HISTORY

In many senses, conflict over the comfort women issue is a struggle among competing claims to victimhood and the right to represent the past. Through their testimony, research, and activism, survivors of the comfort station system and their supporters have challenged Japanese people to see themselves and their elders not simply as victims of the war but as perpetrators of systematic violence and war crimes as well. Anti-apology activists portray this challenge as an attack on those who fought and died to ensure Japan's current prosperity.

In fact, these activists turn the logic of victimhood on its head. First, they assert that survivors of the comfort station system are not victims at all but merely former prostitutes. Then they cast the elderly Japanese men who fought in the war and today's Japanese children as the true victims of the current debates about Japan's war responsibility. This view is illustrated most vividly in the work of Kobayashi Yoshinori. He contrasts stark images of Japanese soldiers fighting and dying in the war with images of Japan's current prosperity: young people drinking beer, snowboarding, and playing video games while older people enjoy golf or ballroom dancing. Accompanying text admonishes readers that "We, living tranquil lives today in an era of peace, have absolutely no right to condemn and make criminals of our grandfathers, who fought and died thinking that they were fighting for the sake of 'country and family.' "[16] According to this logic,[17] Japan's postwar prosperity retroactively absolves older Japanese of any responsibility for crimes committed in the service of (their own) country and family. Comfort station survivors' testimonies threaten to expose the criminal acts of older Japanese, and thus must be resisted.

One of the groups most actively espousing this view is the Japanese Society for History Textbook Reform.[18] The Society was founded in January 1996. Its most prominent members include Nishio Kanji, professor of German literature and philosophy; Fujioka Nobukatsu; and Kobayashi Yoshinori. The immediate inspiration for the group's founding was the announcement in 1995 that textbooks scheduled to be adopted for use in Japanese middle and high schools in 1997 would include mention of comfort women. Members of the Society object to the "masochistic" view of Japan's modern history that they claim pervades Japanese history education because it portrays Japan as criminal or evil and impedes the proper development of students' national identity. They argue that this "masochistic" view is an amalgamation of two anti-Japanese acounts of Japan's modern development foisted upon the nation after its defeat: one propounded by the Allied countries after the war and manifested in the Tokyo War Crimes Trials, and the other formulated by communists from the Soviet Union. The Society's main activities include the production of new history and civics textbooks for use in Japanese middle and high schools as well as a nationwide movement (thus far unsuccessful) to have the minimalist (one- to two-sentence) references to comfort women expunged from Japanese textbooks.

Comfort station survivors' testimonies have focused scrutiny not only on the wartime conduct of millions of older Japanese but also on postwar Japan's matter-of-fact acceptance of the exploitation of tens of thousands of Asian women. What is so objectionable to Society members about the testimonies is their forceful reappropriation of a heretofore commonly accepted "fact" about Japan's wartime experience, and that this reappropriation has been effected by women whose accounts were never expected to impinge upon Japanese public memory. Comfort women were considered to be mere prostitutes, and there was no reason to expect that they would ever lay claim to their "shameful" pasts in public.

Outraged Society members consider this reappropriation an infringement on Japan's proprietary rights to Japanese history and memory of the war. Fujioka Nobukatsu, for example, argues that it is only because Japanese people currently lack national pride that Japan is unable to defend its own view of history. "Since the end of the war, the Japanese have acquired a self-depracatory mind set that allows them to accept the 'testimonies' of Korean and Chinese nationals, the 'victims' of war and of Japanese militarism, as unquestionable fact."[19] Another Society member, Namikawa Eita, describes the mention of comfort women in Japanese textbooks in even more alarmist terms. "The inclusion of material describing 'comfort women' in textbooks is also evidence of this country's pathology. When we write our history textbooks, we weigh every word, fearful of the reaction of neighboring nations. This is the epitome of intellectual and volitional decadence, and of a nation ideologically and spiritually enslaved. . . . Japan is not a sovereign nation."[20] Anti-apology activists such as those in the Society oppose any demand that Japanese history take into account the experiences of non-Japanese. Efforts to do so in the writing and teaching of history are portrayed as the loss of Japanese independence and sovereignty. The real victim of the movement to rewrite Japanese history is, in the anti-apology view, the Japanese nation.

A HISTORY OF SUFFERING AND A LEGACY OF ACTIVISM

Many of the victims of the comfort station system did not survive their ordeals or have passed away since the end of the war, but the remaining survivors are living testaments to the fact that Japanese war crimes are still the cause of great suffering in the present. In the fifty years since Japan's defeat, former comfort women have struggled to cope with the physical and emotional consequences of their enslavement, which include disease, debilitating injuries, sterility, and psychological trauma. One Korean woman forced to serve as a comfort woman in China and Sumatra told interviewers that for decades after the war, "my abdomen used to hurt terribly, as if my womb was being cut away from me."[21] Ch'oe Myŏng-sun, another Korean survivor of the comfort stations, confessed that "When I turned 30, I began to . . . become mentally confused. . . . I stayed indoors for 30 years, crawling on my knees. It has only been in the last four years that I have started to walk properly. I still take medicine, tranquilizers, without which I would be restless."[22] These women have also faced discrimination and abuse in their families and communities on account of their victimization. For them, as for numerous other victims of Japanese war crimes, neither the end of the war nor the supposed end of the postwar era has brought an end to their suffering.

But after almost five decades of silence, these women came forward at great personal risk to demand justice. Their testimonies indict not only Japan's wartime conduct but also its continuing postwar failure to atone for that conduct by issuing an unambiguous, comprehensive apology and compensating victims and their families. The postwar national cultures that have silenced and despised former comfort women as "polluted" women or traitorous collaborators have also been the objects of scathing critiques by survivors of comfort stations. In this sense, the comfort women issue is not concerned exclusively with Japan's war crimes but also more broadly with the conditions and attitudes that fostered the comfort station system both in Japan and in the nations of its former empire.

Many women's groups contend that in the past fifty years Asia has not come very far at all in rectifying those conditions and attitudes. Flourishing prostitution industries have given rise to rampant trafficking in women and a never-ending flow of sex tourism.[23] Japan is the largest market for Asian women, with over 150,000 working in its sex industry,[24] and Japanese men constitute the majority of sex tourists in Asia.[25] Lured to Japan with the same promises of work and good pay that deceived young Korean women in the 1930s and '40s, many young Filipina and Thai women are brought in every year and forced into prostitution. Thus the sexual exploitation and abuse of Asian women both in Japan and by Japanese men abroad continues to this day.

The sexism, racism, and economic inequalities that underlie the trafficking in women to Japan are often repeated within other Asian nations, where women from rural and indigenous populations are disproportionately represented among prostitute populations in the urban centers. The large numbers of American military personnel stationed in Japan, South Korea, and the Philippines have also stimulated demand for prostitutes' services. Even in peacetime, militaries' "management" of the sexual desires of their soldiers creates conditions ripe for the sexual exploitation of disadvantaged women. The activism of former comfort women and their supporters has drawn attention to the historical precedents for that exploitation and energized groups fighting against it. In response, international alliances among women's groups throughout Asia have grown up to renew the fight against the sexual exploitation of women and violations of their human rights.

The effects of comfort station survivors' activism have also extended well beyond Asia. Their testimonies and protests succeeded in bringing the issue of violence against women in wartime to the attention of a variety of international bodies. Activists lobbied the International Commission of Jurists and the UN Human Rights Commission to take up this issue, and the reports of these bodies contributed to the recent recognition of sexual violence against women during armed conflicts as war crimes and crimes against humanity. Gay McDougall, Special Rapporteur to the UN Sub-Commission on Prevention of Discrimination and Protection of Minorities on systematic rape, sexual slavery, and slavery-like practices during armed conflict, notes that activism by comfort station survivors and their supporters was a "significant impetus" for the UN's commissioning of her 1998 report, which argues that sexual violence against women must be prosecuted as a crime against humanity.[26]

The chilling parallels between the Imperial Japanese Army's comfort stations and the rape centers set up by Serbian forces in the civil war in the former Yugoslavia are a bleak reminder that sexual violence against women has been just as potent and horrible a weapon in the 1990s as it was in the 1930s and '40s. Yet today, these war crimes are no longer going unnoticed and unpunished. The International Criminal Tribunals for the former Yugoslavia and for Rwanda have indicted numerous people on charges of torture and genocide for crimes involving sexual violence against women. Furthermore, rape and sexual slavery are explicitly mentioned as crimes against humanity in the statutes of the International Criminal Court (ICC). This permanent organization was established by international treaty in Rome in July 1998 partly in order to remedy the ad hoc nature of the international community's response to war crimes and crimes against humanity. Though the ICC will only have jurisdiction over crimes that occur after its founding, it will provide a mechanism for pursuing claims like those of former comfort women in instances when the offending government refuses to accept legal responsibility for war crimes and to prosecute those responsible.

In December 2000, women's groups from across Asia will gather in Tokyo to hold their own international tribunal on violence against women. At the legal proceedings, survivors and nongovernmental organizations will present evidence in support of charges against individuals, groups, and governments. The tribunal will address not only the cases of women who were enslaved in comfort stations but also the rapes of an estimated 200,000 women during the war for independence in Bangladesh in the 1970s and the use of rape as a method of torture by the military government during the internal conflict in Burma in the 1980s. Plans are also under way to try cases of rape and sexual enslavement of women in East Timor under Indonesian rule as well as cases of rapes committed by troops during the India–Kashmir conflict in the 1990s.

For many of these victims, the tribunal will provide their first chance to testify against their assailants and begin their struggle for justice. For survivors of the comfort stations, it will provide a forum for pressing the Japanese government to pursue prosecution of individuals responsible for war crimes committed against them. Survivors' courage and achievements have provided a model of citizen activism and inspiration to countless women throughout the world who are suffering as a result of sexual violence. Their efforts have brought to an end the impunity that perpetrators of sexual violence against women in war have enjoyed throughout history, offering the hope that such violence can be prevented in the future.

NOTES ON THE TRANSLATION

Japanese, Korean, and Chinese names are written in the native order, family name first followed by personal name.

Military terms have been rendered into English according to the translations provided in the *Handbook on Japanese Military Forces* by the U.S. War Department with an introduction by David Isby and an afterword by Jeffrey Ethell (Baton Rouge: Louisiana State University Press, 1991). This is a reprint of the classified handbook prepared by the U.S. War Department in 1944.

Text in [ ] are notes added to quoted materials by the author. Text in { } are clarifications and information added by the translator.

I would like to thank Professor Yoshimi for giving us *Jūgun ianfu* and for his support and patience during the translation process. I am also grateful to Okamoto Kōichi, who helped get the project going and read an early draft, and to Carol Gluck, who shepherded the project through to publication. Tanaka Miho's generous advice greatly improved the translation. Additionally, I would like to thank Nakahara Michiko and Gregory Pflugfelder for their close readings and constructive comments. Gustav Heldt, Dan O'Neill, and Indra Levy also provided invaluable suggestions and encouragement. I also want to express my thanks to Ms. Jennifer Crewe and Ms. Leslie Kriesel at Columbia University Press for their support and expertise.

Suzanne O'Brien
Tokyo, June 1999

Introduction to the English Edition

The "*jūgun ianfu*" or "military comfort women"[1] issue is an instance of war crimes committed by the Imperial Japanese military. The essence of the issue, as I make clear in this book, is the grave violations of human rights that combined sexual violence against women, racial discrimination, and discrimination against the impoverished. The salience and universality of these problems have attracted international attention to the issue of comfort women.

Four years have passed since the initial publication of this book, and in that time, fierce debate has sprung up around the issue both within Japan and in the UN Commission on Human Rights. An outline of the debates that have unfolded within Japan will probably be useful to readers of the English edition.

In the reports of Special Rapporteur Radhika Coomaraswamy (submitted to the UN Commission on Human Rights on January 4, 1996) and Special Rapporteur Gay J. McDougall (submitted to the UN Sub-Commission on Prevention of Discrimination and Protection of Minorities on June 22, 1998), the comfort women system was recognized as a system of military sexual slavery, and the necessity for the Japanese government to punish those responsible for it and to compensate its victims was confirmed. The Japanese government, however, has refused to accept these recommendations.

During the preparation of the Coomaraswamy report and following its submission, two activist movements arose, one consisting of victims demanding compensation from the Japanese government and those supporting their demands, and the other opposing those demands. Within this opposition movement there are three positions.

First, the Japanese government, in cooperation with a group of scholars led by then University of Tokyo professor Wada Haruki,[2] set up the Asian Women's Fund in June 1995. On August 15 of that year, on the fiftieth anniversary of Japan's defeat, the Fund called upon Japanese citizens to make contributions. This instance of cooperation among the conservative mainstream, social democrats, and progressive scholars was made possible by the existence of the coalition government of Prime Minister Murayama Tomi-ichi, which united the three major political parties at the time, the Liberal Democratic Party, the Social Democratic Party, and the New Party *Saki-gake* {Pioneers}.[3] The Fund raised 480 million yen ($4 million)[4] with the intent of disbursing to each former comfort woman 2 million yen (about $16,667) in "reparations." In addition to these publicly raised monies, the Fund would also distribute millions of yen worth of medical and welfare services ($25,000 each to South Korean and Taiwanese former comfort women and $10,000 each to Filipina former comfort women) paid for by the Japanese government. These attempts to compensate former comfort women ended up infuriating them and their supporters as well as the South Korean and Taiwanese governments. According to the Asian Women's Fund, more than one hundred former comfort women have accepted the payments. But it is likely that most of these women are Filipinas who have little hope of receiving any form of aid from their own government. The Asian Women's Fund has had no discussions with the governments of North Korea or China.

There are several reasons why the Asian Women's Fund's efforts caused such an uproar. First, the Japanese government still denies any legal respon-sibility vis-à-vis former comfort women and refuses to compensate them directly. Many suspect that, in order to preserve its official position and avoid being pressed by the UN Human Rights Commission, the govern-ment has come to rely on this vague means of "settling" the issue. The Japanese government is contributing funds to the effort, but these funds are not reparations. The reparation payments are made out of the money amassed through private citizens' donations. Thus the government has been able to maintain its position of not paying out even one yen in reparations. This also leaves the government free to emphasize in private that while it does have some "moral responsibility" to former comfort women, the brunt of that responsibility rests with private citizens. The government's acknowl-edgment of moral responsibility is merely the flip side of its insistence that it has no *legal* responsibility. This departure from the conventional use of this terminology indicates that the level of responsibility the government has acknowledged is very slight. There is no reason to doubt the good intentions of the progressive Japanese scholars who approved of the Asian

Women's Fund or those of the Japanese citizens who contributed to it. But those good intentions have come to naught.

Another reason for the uproar was the "letter of apology" {*owabi*} issued in the name of Prime Minister Hashimoto Ryōtarō (first made public on August 14, 1996) and sent along with the disbursements from the Asian Women's Fund. (By the time the fund-raising drive ended, Mr. Murayama was no longer prime minister, but Hashimoto, president of the Liberal Democratic Party, continued his policies). The expression "owabi" in Japanese denotes a sense of apology slightly more weighty than an "Excuse me" offered when one bumps shoulders with someone on the subway. But it is an expression with a wide scope for interpretation that can range from a very minor sense of being sorry to a serious acknowledgment of wrongdoing and proffering of an apology {*shazai*}. The Japanese government has not acknowledged any crime, though, so the Prime Minister's owabi can only be interpreted as something trivial. A further regrettable point is that, in the English translation, the letter is clearly identified as an expression of "my {the Prime Minister's} personal feelings." This locution seems an attempt to dilute the impression that the letter is an owabi offered by the Prime Minister in his official capacity.

The second position that has emerged in Japanese debates over the comfort women issue is that even the Japanese government's attitude is too apologetic. A movement advocating this view became active in the wake of the publication of the Coomaraswamy report. The immediate catalyst for its formation was the announcement in June 1996 that all of the new middle school textbooks approved by the Ministry of Education (from seven publishers, scheduled to come into use in 1997) included descriptions of military comfort women. These descriptions, however, each amount to only one or two brief lines of text, on the order of "Women were made to accompany the military as comfort women and were treated horribly." These descriptions are so simple that they don't even include an explanation of what comfort women were. (And textbook authors had to struggle to get Ministry of Education approval for even these simple descriptions.) To some educators, historians, and middle and high school teachers, these {descriptions} disgrace the history of their own people and cause people to lose pride in the Japanese nation. They began a movement that seeks to have the descriptions of military comfort women removed from middle school history textbooks. This movement, however, has been unable to alter the government's position, which insists on acknowledgment of Japan's "moral" responsibility in regard to the comfort women issue, and has not succeeded in forcing the removal of the descriptions.

Thereupon this group founded an organization called the Japanese Society for History Textbook Reform (*Atarashii rekishi kyōkasho wo tsukurukai*), headed by Nishio Kanji {a professor at the University of Electro-Communications specializing in German literature and philosophy}. The Society, in concert with conservative local politicians and religious organizations, began a very active movement attempting to create a "story of the Japanese people" that fosters "self-confidence as a Japanese person." In addition, one Society member, the comic book artist Kobayashi Yoshinori, produced two comic books (one in 1997 and another in 1998) that depicted comfort women as prostitutes whose goal was to earn money and emphasized that the Japanese government therefore had absolutely no responsibility toward them. Both these volumes became best sellers, and *On War* {Sensōron} (1998) in particular is said to have sold five hundred thousand copies. In Japan, where many young people no longer read books or newspapers, the influence of comic books cannot be ignored.

By 1995, a new group, centered on right-wing legislators in the Liberal Democratic Party and the New Frontier Party, began actively opposing the Diet's "apology resolution" regarding the invasion of Asia and the compensation of individual victims of the war. This group's influence began to be felt in 1996 and extended even to citizens who were not right-wingers. In the aftermath of the end of the Cold War, nationalism is gaining power in many countries. In Japan, this group was the forerunner of that trend.

Another new phenomenon is the participation of the heads of large corporations that represent Japan-such as Kaku Ryōzaburō, the honorary chairman of Canon Corp.; Yamamoto Takuma, the honorary chairman of Fujitsu Corp.; and Okamoto Kazuya, then executive director of Tokyo-Mitsubishi Bank (in 1998, he became the president of Tokyo-Mitsubishi Securities Corp.)—in the Japanese Society for History Textbook Reform.

In response to this movement, those seeking an apology and compensation for former comfort women from the Japanese government founded the Japanese Center for Research and Documentation on Japan's War

Responsibility in April 1993 (with Arai Shin'ichi as director and Yoshimi Yoshiaki as deputy director), and begun publishing a journal, *Research on War Responsibility* (March 1999 saw the twenty-third issue published). They have also uncovered historical documents, conducted interviews with victims, and formulated proposals for resolving the issue. The women's group VAWW-NET Japan (with Matsui Yayori as director) is currently organizing an international war crimes tribunal on violence against women in war to be held in Tokyo in 2000, the slogan for which is "Dignity and Justice for 'Comfort Women'!" The Japan Federation of Bar Associations repeatedly recommended to the Japanese government (on January 24, 1995; July 3, 1997; and March 6, 1998) that it establish legislation to provide for an investigation into the facts of the comfort women issue, an apology, and compensation. A civic group dedicated to the creation of fact-finding committees on war damages has also been active, and on September 30, 1998 it coordinated the founding of the League of Diet Members for the Establishment of a Fact-Finding Law for the Sake of Lasting Peace {*Kōkyō heiwa no tame ni shinsō kyōmeihō no seiritsu wo mezasu giin renmei*}, focused exclusively on the single issue of the establishment of fact-finding committees. The League includes members of the Liberal Democratic, Liberal, Clean Government, Communist, and Socialist parties. By April 1999, the League had 110 members.

These are the three main movements concerned with the comfort women issue in Japan. How Japanese people regard these movements, however, is a separate issue. In February 1997, a representative Japanese television network, JNN, conducted a telephone survey and asked respondents, "What do you think about politicians' and the government's response to the military comfort women issue?" The results of the survey are as follows:

50.7% replied that "{Politicians have} made many thoughtless remarks and should apologize properly to Asian countries and the victims"

27.4% replied, "I think Japan has apologized too much already"

14.1% replied that "The Prime Minister has apologized and they have already responded properly to the issue"

7.7% replied, "can't respond. . . don't know."

The survey shows that the most common answer from more than half of the respondents was that the government's apology was insufficient. We cannot ignore, however, that almost 30 percent were of the opinion that there have already been too many apologies. The impression some in Europe and America have that Japanese people who demand an apology and compensation are isolated and threatened in Japanese society is clearly mistaken. But this survey pointedly demonstrates that feelings of nationalism and ethnocentrism are permeating society. The recession and increased rates of unemployment Japan has experienced in the 1990s are a driving force behind this movement, fostering sentiments like "Japanese people! Regain your self-confidence! Have some pride!"

There are currently seven suits filed by former comfort women seeking an apology and compensation from the Japanese government pending in Japanese courts. By the end of 1999, Taiwanese women and Chinese women from Hainan Island are likely to file additional suits. Decisions have been reached in three of the cases.

The decision in the suit filed by three Korean former comfort women in the Shimonoseki branch of the Yamaguchi Prefectural Court was handed down on April 27, 1998. The court found that Japanese Diet members, especially since the government published the informal remarks of the Cabinet Secretary and acknowledged "moral responsibility" in August 1993, had a legal responsibility to establish legislation providing for compensation but had not fulfilled that obligation. So the court ordered that each woman be awarded 300,000 yen (about $2,500) in damages. This was a landmark decision, making it clear that Diet members have a responsibility to establish a compensation law. But both the victims and the government were dissatisfied with the court's decision and the confirmation of the duty of both the government and the Diet to create compensation legislation. The government filed an appeal that seeks to avoid paying any compensation, and the victims filed an appeal that claims they have not been properly compensated. As a result, the case has still not been settled.

The Tokyo District Court, on October 9, 1998 in a suit filed by forty-five Filipina former comfort women, ruled that the plaintiffs had no right to claim compensation for damages and rejected their suit without acknowledging the damages they had suffered. The decision in a suit filed by Dutch former internment camp inmates that included a former comfort woman

among the plaintiffs was handed down on November 30, 1998. It acknowledged that they were abused, but rejected their request for compensation
on the grounds that there was no basis in international law for individuals
to claim compensation.

Thus the chances that Japanese courts will hand down decisions that will
clear a path to redress are decreasing. So unless we find a means to create
laws mandating compensation for victims, resolving this issue will be difficult. The overwhelming majority of Diet members hold the opinion that
Japan has no problems with war responsibility, or that those problems have
already been resolved. So whether the League of Diet Members for the
Establishment of a Fact-Finding Law for the Sake of Lasting Peace is able
to pass a law mandating investigations into the facts of Japan's war responsibility, including the comfort women issue, is sure to have a great impact
on the resolution of this issue.

For the benefit of readers of the English edition, I'd like to note in advance
a few key points. First, the military comfort women system was a system
of military sexual slavery. This is not because the women were rounded
up by such violent means as forcible abduction. There were considerable
numbers of those sorts of abductions in China, Southeast Asia, and the
Pacific region, but not many instances in the Japanese colonies of Korea
and Taiwan. It is not clear whether Japanese policemen or military personnel (as opposed to civilians) did, in fact, round up women by violent
means in Korea and Taiwan. If too much emphasis is placed on extreme
cases in which officials used violence to gather women, the much larger
number of cases of deception and viciousness will be overlooked. The
essence of the issue lies in the facts that there was coercion in comfort stations, that minors were pressed into "service," and that many women were
rounded up by deception or under conditions of debt slavery, whereby
they were required to pay back sums advanced against their "service." And
in colonized areas, the fact that there was a system whereby officials did
not do the dirty work but had procurers do it for them is the real issue.

As of now, no documents have come to light that can give an accurate
figure for the total number of comfort women, so we can only fall back
on rough estimates. It is estimated that the total was between fifty thousand and two hundred thousand women. In terms of ethnic background,

Korean and Chinese women were the most numerous, followed by Southeast Asian women, and then Japanese women. The total number of comfort stations is also unknown, but even the lowest estimates put the number at more than a thousand.

In records written by people associated with the Japanese military, there are figures for the number of rapes committed by Japanese military personnel, but those figures are extremely low. While this merits reflection, it does not mean that rape was not a significant problem. For example, in February 1942 section chiefs at the War Ministry discussed the fact that fourteen rapes had been committed in the Philippines as a serious problem. The reason for this levity was that they knew that the number of reports of rape that reached the army central command was only a tiny fraction, the tip of the iceberg, and that behind those figures was a large number of incidents that went unreported. Rape was considered a dishonor for soldiers and officers in the field, so rapes were usually covered up and not reported to superiors.

I should also comment on the value of the yen during the Second World War. For example, one Korean comfort woman was sold for an advance payment of 300 yen and led off by deception. Though it is impossible to calculate exactly how much that 300 yen was worth, multiplying it by about 4,000 yields a figure approaching the value in today's yen. That is, 300 yen at that time is the equivalent of 1.2 million yen today {$10,000}. To give several figures for reference purposes, a beginning policeman's salary in 1935 was 45 yen per month, and a beginning elementary schoolteacher's salary in 1941 was 50 to 60 yen. In 1940, the highest price for a gram of pure gold was 4.61 yen.

In conclusion, I'd like to express my hope that the dignity of victims forced to become comfort women will be restored as soon as possible, that steps will be taken to prevent recurrences of this sort of violation of human rights, and that persistent Japanese memories of the war will break free from introversion and become open to the world.

In the English edition, a number of errors have been corrected. Full annotations have also been added.

Upon the publication of the English edition of this book, I'd like to express my profound thanks to the translator, Suzanne O'Brien, a doctoral candidate at Columbia University. I also received the support of Professor Carol Gluck of Columbia University and the mediation of Professor Okamoto Kōichi of Waseda University, for which I am deeply grateful.

Yoshimi Yoshiaki
Chūō University
May 15, 1999

The Emergence of the Issue

In December 1991, three South Korean former comfort women (*ianfu*) filed suit in the Tokyo District Court seeking an apology and compensation from the Japanese government. The shock their suit gave Japanese is still fresh in people's minds. I was particularly struck by the words of the one plaintiff who was willing to use her real name, Kim Hak-sun. In an interview given to NHK (the Japan Broadcasting Corporation) prior to her trip to Japan, Kim declared, "I wanted to sue for the fact that I was trampled upon by the Japanese military and have spent my life in misery. I want the young people of South Korea and Japan to know what Japan did in the past."[1] Those words inspired me to begin researching the comfort women issue.

Any military personnel with wartime experience knew of the existence of comfort women. In 1947, the writer Tamura Taijirō took up the issue of Korean comfort women in his novel *Shunpuden* (*A Prostitute's Story*), which was later made into a movie. But did we really recognize the system then as a violation of women's human rights, as a national or war crime? In 1973, Senda Kakō published *Military Comfort Women* (*Jūgun ianfu*), taking up the challenge to investigate the actual conditions comfort women endured. Thus it can't be said that people were completely unaware of the issue until recently. Rather, social concern about its gravity was never widespread. Korean women's movements, centering on the Korean Council for the Women Drafted for Military Sexual Slavery by Japan, were responsible for raising public awareness of the issue.

In May 1990, Korean women's groups issued a joint statement demanding an apology and compensation on the "*Teishintai*" or "volunteer corps" {refers to the many Korean men and women pressed into labor service by the colonial Japanese government; some of the women were forced to serve in comfort stations} issue to coincide with then Prime Minister Roh Te-woo's visit to Japan. At the time, the volunteer corps and the comfort women were considered to be two aspects of the same issue in South Korea.

The Japanese government, however, did not make any move to acknowledge state or military participation. At the June 6 meeting of the House of Councillors Budget Committee, the government issued the following statement.

> In regard to comfort women . . . it appears that the persons thus treated were led around by civilian operators following the military forces. We consider it impossible for us to investigate and make a definitive statement as regards the actual conditions pertaining to this practice.[2]

The reason that such issues as an official apology, the restoration of people's reputations, and individual compensation have remained unresolved in the fifty years since the end of the war is that the Japanese government has taken this position. It is well known that the government systematically destroyed official documents at the end of the war, and this has made it possible to maintain that no evidence of its participation exists.

The Korean women's groups, angered by the Japanese government's denial of historical reality, again issued a joint statement demanding that Japan become a "democratic country with a morality of truth." The statement demanded that:

1. the Japanese government acknowledge the fact that {the military} forced Korean women to accompany troops as comfort women;

2. the Japanese government issue an official apology for these practices;

3. the Japanese government disclose all acts of brutality {committed by the government or military};

4. a memorial to the people victimized be erected;

5. survivors or their families be compensated; and

6. in order to prevent the recurrence of these wrongs, the facts be taught as a part of history education.[3]

By March 1991, I had been studying in the United States for two years, so I didn't realize that the government response to these demands had become an issue. But the duplicity of the response was clear. In fact, before I left for my trip abroad, I had been confirming official documents in the Self-Defense Agency's National Institute for Defense Studies Library that attest to the fact that the Japanese army directed the setting up of comfort stations. After I heard Kim Hak-sun speak, I went back to the National Institute for Defense Studies Library and looked for relevant documents. I found six pieces of evidence that had survived the destruction of documents and was able to publish them in the newspaper.[4]

Why were these materials, which we would expect to have been destroyed, still extant? They were among a group of documents written prior to 1942 that had been stored in an underground warehouse in Hachiōji to protect them from the U.S. air raids. They were scheduled for incineration in the final days of the war, but the arrival of the Allied Forces preempted that plan. The documents were seized by the Allied Forces and brought to the United States, then later returned to the Self-Defense Agency's National Institute for Defense Studies Library. No one knew that this collection contained documents relating to the comfort women, so they were overlooked.

Since the discovery of these documents, many people have labored energetically to dig up more materials. I published a collection of these materials that contradicted the conclusions of the government's first survey of materials.[5] In 1993, I participated in an independent survey of documents sponsored by the Center for Research and Documentation on Japan's War Responsibility that resulted in the discovery and publication of sixty-two additional documents.

The public announcement of the first six pieces of evidence had a profound impact. On January 12, the day following the publication of the documents in the newspaper, then Chief Cabinet Secretary Kato Koichi publicly acknowledged the Japanese military's participation {in organizing the comfort station system}. On the 13th, he announced talks on formulating an apology. On the 17th, then Prime Minister Miyazawa Kiichi, who was visiting Korea, officially apologized at a meeting of top Korean and Japanese leaders.

WHAT DID THE GOVERNMENT ACKNOWLEDGE?

After these announcements, the government conducted a limited survey of official documents and hearings with some former comfort women from South Korea. The government announced the findings of its inquiry on August 4, 1993 (testimony from the hearings, however, was not made public). In that statement, the government acknowledged the following facts:

1. The Japanese military was "directly or indirectly involved" in the establishment and management of the comfort stations and in the transfer of comfort women.

2. As for the "recruitment" of comfort women, "in many cases they were recruited against their own will, through coaxing, coercion, etc." and "at times administrative/military personnel directly took part in the recruitment."

3. "They lived in misery at comfort stations in a coercive atmosphere."

4. The "recruitment," transfer, and control of comfort women born on the Korean Peninsula were conducted "generally against their will, through coaxing, coercion, etc."

5. The issue of military comfort women is "an act, with the involvement of the military authorities of the day, that severely injured the honor and dignity of many women."

6. To the former comfort women, "the government of Japan would like to take this opportunity once again to extend its sincere apologies (*owabi*) and regrets."[6]

Thus the government acknowledged military and police participation and the coercion of comfort women, and the issue came to be understood as one of a grave violation of human rights.

WHAT DIDN'T THE GOVERNMENT ACKNOWLEDGE?

The following points in the Chief Cabinet Secretary's statement appear problematic.

First, according to the statement, the comfort stations were operated "in response to the request of the military authorities of the day." The "recruitment" of comfort women was also conducted "mainly by private recruiters who acted in response to the requests of the military." The military's participation in the establishment and management of the comfort stations, as well as in the transportation of comfort women, is hereby taken to have been "indirect" in some cases. In short, the statement left room for an interpretation that cast civilian businessmen in the roles of "recruiters" of comfort women and actual operators of the comfort station system.

Yet, on the same day, in a document issued by the Cabinet Councillors' Office on External Affairs "On the Issue of Wartime 'Comfort Women'," was the statement "It is evident, at any rate, that in the war areas, these women were forced to move with the military under constant military control and that they were deprived of their freedom and had to endure misery." The only thing evident here, however, is that the nuance of this statement is quite different from that of the government's official statement. Whether the subject doing the forcing is the state/military or private operators remains ambiguous.

Second, the statement emphasizes the prevalence of women born on the Korean peninsula or of Korean ethnicity among those forced to become comfort women, making no reference to those of Chinese, Taiwanese, Southeast Asian, or Pacific island origin. In fact, the Japanese government held hearings with only a single group of former comfort women from Korea. While it is clear that Korean women were proportionately over-represented among comfort women, an inquiry into the issue cannot begin and end with a single round of hearings.

Third, while the statement admits that "grave injury [was done] to the honor and dignity of numerous women," the government response goes no further than an offer of "deepest apologies (owabi) and regrets." One would have expected the statement to engage with the issue of whether the practice was in violation of international law, whether the government had committed a war crime. The government's response certainly should have included a thorough explication of the truth, an acknowledgment of and apology for the crimes, compensation, and an outline of steps to be taken to prevent a recurrence of these crimes, but in all these it was lacking.

The government statement breeds many doubts. Yet even this sort of official acknowledgment on the part of the government is not widely shared by Japanese people in general. For example, when the Justice Minister in the Hata administration, Nagano Shigeto, declared that he "thinks the Nanking Massacre is a fabrication" and was forced to resign, he also stated that, "Comfort women were licensed prostitutes in that era, so we can't look at {that practice} through today's eyes and call it contempt for women or racial discrimination against Koreans."[7]

In fact, while we can say that the Japanese government has officially made apologies (owabi), it has not changed its stance that individual compensation cannot be granted and that the right to demand reparations on a nation-to-nation level has already been exhausted.

THE TASK OF ILLUMINATING THE ISSUE IN ITS ENTIRETY

The military comfort women issue encompasses various questions that must be addressed. The violation of the human rights of women is, of course, a primary one. But others include the nature of the Japanese military, colonial policy, and racial contempt for other ethnic groups. The most pressing task, however, is to establish the historical facts. This book aims at providing a cornerstone of certainty from which inquiry into all aspects of the military comfort women issue can proceed. Additionally, it will serve as the basis for what I would like to contribute to the discussion of this issue.

This work takes as its foundation three groups of materials. Generally speaking, all three have come to light since 1991:

1. foreign and domestic documents uncovered thus far;

2. records from interviews with former comfort women. I have recently interviewed scores of Korean, Filipina, and Dutch former comfort women;

3. the survey sponsored by the Center for Research and Documentation on Japan's War Responsibility of military unit histories and memoirs of war experiences in the National Diet Library's collection. The memoirs of former officers and soldiers are still being published today, and a wealth of important information can be found in them.

These documents, however, have considerable limitations, especially the first group. In addition to the fact that many documents were destroyed at the end of the war, many of those that remain (police records, documents of the Department of Overseas Affairs and Home Ministry relating to the colonies, the huge collection of diaries of officials and personnel accompanying the military held by the Defense Agency, materials relating to the war crimes trials held by the Justice Ministry and the Foreign Ministry, Welfare Ministry documents relating to demobilization and support) have not yet been made public. It is my hope that the government will declassify these documents immediately, but currently, we only have access to the tip of the iceberg. Yet from the shape of the portion we can see, we can estimate the outline of the whole. This book presents these materials with an eye to delineating those larger contours.

Before proceeding, I would like to consider the issue of terminology. The most prominent term is the one I've taken for the title of this book, "military comfort women" (*jūgun ianfu*). Many feel that the stark contrast between the original meaning of the term "comfort" and the coerced horror these women experienced renders the term utterly unacceptable. Dr. Gerand Jungslager, legal advisor to the Dutch Foundation for Moral Claims Against Japan, reports that Dutch former comfort women explicitly reject the term "comfort women" in their testimonies on the grounds that what they were subjected to bears no relation to the concepts of love, sympathy, warmth, and compassion that the term "comfort" connotes.[8] Furthermore, while the expression "{following the} military" (*jūgun*) did not originally imply voluntary action, it acquired those connotations in such expressions as "military reporters" (*jūgun kisha*) {reporters who covered military affairs and accompanied the military on its movements}. At any rate, some feel that because the term has this nuance of consent and willing participation, it should not be used to refer to comfort women.

"Military comfort women" were women restrained for a certain period with no rights, under the control of the Japanese military, and forced to engage in sexual activity with Japanese military personnel. These women can only be described as "military sex slaves" (*gunyō seidorei*). I agree that the term "military comfort women" is inappropriate, but it is already widely known, and a more acceptable alternative has not yet appeared. This book, therefore, uses the term "military comfort women" and investigates the conditions in which they lived. For the same reasons and with the same reservations, I also use the term "comfort stations" (*ianjo*). However, since this term was occasionally used to refer to civilian brothels as well, I use the term "military comfort stations" to distinguish those run by and for the military.

As for terms like "prostitute," "licensed prostitute," "serving woman," and "waitress" (*baishunfu, geigi/shōgi, shakufu,* and *jokyū,* respectively), I think they need to be redefined to mean "women who were exploited sexually." I would place all those terms, including "military comfort women," in quotes.

Text in [ ] are notes added to quoted materials by the author. Text in { } are clarifications and information added by the translator. I have also omitted the honorific titles usually added to people's names.

Chapter One

The Course and Conditions of the Establishment of the Military Comfort Station System

From the First Shanghai Incident to the Start of All-Out War in China

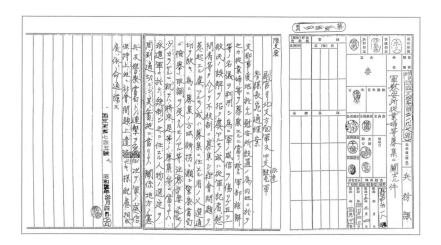

The Establishment of the First Military Comfort Station by the Navy During the Shanghai Incident

When were the first military comfort stations established, and how did the system expand? As noted above, since the materials that remain are only the tip of the documentary iceberg, it is very difficult to give a definitive answer. But according to reliable documents uncovered so far, the first confirmed military comfort station was established in Shanghai.

On September 18, 1931, the Japanese army blew up sections of track of the South Manchuria Railway in Liutiaohu in northeastern China (Manchuria). Claiming that the explosions were set off by Chinese troops, the army initiated the war against China. These events are known as the Manchurian Incident. The Chinese army refrained from resisting in order to avoid an all-out confrontation, so the Japanese army was able to bring the northeast under its control in a relatively short period of time. In January of the following year, the Japanese army opened hostilities in Shanghai, an assault that became known as the First Shanghai Incident. This attack was intended to draw the attention of Europe and America away from Japan's engineering of the founding of the puppet state of Manchukuo in March 1932. It was around this time that the Japanese army and navy units dispatched to Shanghai established the first military comfort stations.

According to the recollections of Okamura Yasuji, Vice Chief of Staff of the Shanghai Expeditionary Force (commanded by General Shirakawa Yoshinori), the army was schooled in the military comfort women system by the Japanese navy in Shanghai. It appears, then, that the first comfort stations were constructed by the navy.

In Shanghai, the Chinese government had been attempting to enforce a ban on licensed prostitution. For appearances' sake, the Japanese Foreign Ministry had to cooperate with this effort, so in 1929 the ministry abol-

Japanese army document, "Matters Regarding the Recruitment of
Women Workers for Military Comfort Stations" in *Rikushi mitsu dainikki*
(Secret documents on continental China), 1938, No. 10
JAPANESE SELF–DEFENSE AGENCY ARCHIVES

ished the *kashizashiki*, or house of assignation {a type of licensed brothel} system. However, the Japanese government created the "restaurant serving woman" (*ryōriten shakufu*) system as a loophole for itself, in effect retaining a form of licensed prostitution. In a document from late 1938 entitled "In regard to the current state of regulations on private prostitution in the concession and the regulation of special prostitutes reserved for Japanese citizens in Shanghai during 1938,"[1] the Consulate General of Shanghai remarks that "with the great increase in military personnel stationed in the area due to the sudden outbreak of the Shanghai Incident, the navy established naval comfort stations as a means to aid in supporting the comfort of those troops, and those stations have continued to operate up to the present."[2] It was at the time of the Shanghai Incident, then, that naval comfort stations were set up.

The naval comfort stations established at this time were large enough to occupy several buildings. A document from a slightly later period reveals that at the end of 1936, there were ten restaurants employing serving women (102 of those women were Japanese, while 29 were Korean). Of these ten establishments, seven were reserved exclusively for naval personnel.[3] The document reports that these were "reserved exclusively for naval personnel, and absolutely no local customers (civilians) were allowed. Furthermore, the serving women's medical examinations are performed twice a week by medical specialists in the presence of naval personnel or police officers from the consulate. Additionally, in cooperation with the navy, the regulations are strictly enforced, and no new establishments are allowed to open."[4] To prevent sexually transmitted diseases, the military and the consulate (the Foreign Ministry) conducted rigorous medical examinations in comfort stations. These seven restaurants were naval comfort stations. At this juncture, not just the military but the Foreign Ministry as well was taking part in overseeing military comfort stations.

Since this infrastructure was already in place when the full-scale war broke out in China, the navy was able to send military comfort women to China immediately. According to a report issued by Akamatsu Kotora, governor of Fukuoka Prefecture, and dated November 30, 1937, two Korean women received identity papers and permits from the Yawata police headquarters to cross from Fukuoka Prefecture to Shanghai to become "serving women in a naval comfort station" in Beisichuanlu in Shanghai.[5] Korean women living in Japan were quickly brought to China as military comfort women.

The Army and Comfort Stations

Okamura Yasuji, Vice Chief of Staff of the Shanghai Expeditionary Force, established comfort stations for the army in March 1932 modeled on naval comfort stations. According to his recollection, some acts of rape were committed by Japanese military personnel in Shanghai, prompting him to call on the governor of Nagasaki Prefecture to request a "military comfort women corps."[6] The army probably focused on Nagasaki Prefecture first because there were many women born there who became *karayukisan* {women sent to Siberia, Asia, and throughout the Pacific as indentured prostitutes}. It is essential to point out here that the justification given for this request is the prevention of rape. Okabe Naosaburō, a Senior Staff Officer in the Shanghai Expeditionary Force who worked with Okamura, wrote the following entry in his diary.

> Recently, soldiers have been prowling around everywhere looking for women, and I often heard obscene stories {about their behavior}. As long as conditions are peaceful and the army is not engaged in fighting, these incidents are difficult to prevent. Rather, we should recognize that we can actively provide facilities. I have considered many policy options for resolving the troops' sexual problems and have set to work on realizing that goal. Lieutenant Colonel Nagami [Toshinori] will bear primary responsibility in this matter.[7]

From this description, we can follow the chain of command through which Vice Chief of Staff for the Shanghai Expeditionary Force Okamura and high-ranking staff officer Okabe gave the orders to establish military comfort stations, and Nagami Toshinori carried them out. The most significant aspect of this account, however, is the logic behind the establishment of these facilities, the fact that they were set up in order to prevent rapes by military personnel. How did this idea arise? And, why, instead of investigating the outbreak of rapes, was the first reaction the swift establishment of military comfort stations?

We can only assume that the army already had some sort of plan. The army surely had in mind its experiences with troops sent to fight in Siberia between 1918 and 1922 (a war of intervention in the Russian Revolution). In 1921, Okamura was attached to the 14th Infantry Regiment and was sent to Europe and the United States. When he returned to Japan, he was very briefly made commander of one of the regiment's battalions. This regiment had seen combat in Siberia. Okabe was an expert on Russian affairs, and when troops were sent to Siberia, he was attached to the headquarters of the Vladivostok Expeditionary Force (Khabarovsk Military Secret Service). According to surveys of returning troops who had served in Siberia, "more than half of the soldiers didn't understand why they had been sent there." Because they didn't understand the purpose of the conflict, the soldiers were, by their own accounts, unruly. The troops' low morale and the slackness of military discipline were obvious, and there were many incidents of rape and of pillaging civilian houses for domestic animals or firewood.[8] As a primary impediment to military tactics, the troops' behavior became a considerable problem even for top military leaders.

Another characteristic of the troops sent to Siberia was a high rate of infection with sexually transmitted diseases. The number of soldiers found to have contracted sexually transmitted diseases between August 1918 and the end of October 1920 reached 1,109.[9] In the same period, there were 1,399 soldiers killed and 1,528 wounded in battle; thus the number of soldiers who contracted sexually transmitted diseases was quite high comparatively. Since contracting a disease was considered dishonorable, however, many who did hid their condition; the actual number afflicted was probably therefore significantly higher than the official numbers indicate. The figures for the military police corps dispatched to Sakhalin with jurisdiction over Northern Sakhalin and Nikolaevsk-na-Amure indicate that out of 331 soldiers who became ill, 33 had contracted sexually transmitted diseases, amounting to 10 percent of the total number of soldiers out of action due to illness. According to the military police headquarters' analysis, one reason for this high rate was that a large percentage of the prostitutes and serving women with whom the soldiers had intercourse were infected with sexually transmitted diseases (in 1921, 21 percent of these women were afflicted).[10] Tsuno Kazusuke, chief of military administration on Sakhalin, issued "rules and regulations on prostitutes and serving women" on September 1, 1920 requiring the women to obtain permission to work from the military police and submit to medical examinations as ordered by the military police.[11] This amounted to a licensed prostitution system under the control of the military police. Clearly, the Japanese military already had experience in these matters long before the Manchurian Incident.

The Case of Northeastern China

According to the documents we have, the first confirmed military comfort station was set up in March 1933. This was the "Disease Prevention and Hygiene Facility" established for the 14th Mixed Brigade, which was stationed in Pingquan. Thirty-five Korean serving women and three Japanese serving women were employed there. An army doctor was in charge of conducting regular medical examinations of these women.[12] While the term "military comfort station" does not appear in this document, it is clear that this "facility" was a de facto military comfort station.

One of the motives for setting up this facility was the prevention of sexually transmitted diseases. In Pingquan, there were three or four brothels in the licensed quarters, but many of the twenty prostitutes living there were infected. On this account, military personnel were forbidden to enter the licensed quarters in March and were invited to go to the military comfort station instead.[13]

The military was very anxious to prevent the spread of sexually transmitted diseases among the soldiers, and "the necessity of preventing the infection of the troops" became a major concern. Because some of the newly inducted Korean comfort women were found to have been infected with sexually transmitted diseases, the Brigade Headquarters relentlessly warned soldiers to check prostitutes' health certificates, to use condoms and "Secret Star Cream" disinfecting lubricant, and to wash their genitals with disinfectant after going to the comfort station. In addition, "Guidelines for Conducting Medical Examinations of Prostitutes and Serving Women" were issued, and all prostitutes in the area, including those in the licensed quarters, were to be subjected to medical examinations more than once a week.[14]

Later, when requests came in from units with soldiers who wished to go to the Chinese licensed quarters, the Brigade Headquarters decided that the military would conduct medical examinations of the prostitutes there as well. Subsequently, they lifted the ban on soldiers' trips to the Chinese licensed quarters. The brothels at which the military conducted examinations for sexually transmitted diseases were, in other words, those the military had designated as comfort stations. However, when the examinations revealed that more than 30 percent of the women in the licensed quarters were infected with sexually transmitted diseases, the Brigade Headquarters reported that "the results were extremely poor."[15]

There are not many documents relating to the establishment of military comfort stations in northeastern China in this period. It is beyond doubt, however, that the example of the 14th Mixed Brigade is merely the tip of the iceberg. Wherever the Japanese army went, sizable groups of comfort women were forced to accompany them. For example, there is the testimony of Nakayama Tadanao, director of the Nakayama Institute of Japanese-Chinese Medicine, who traveled from Jinzhou to Chengde, the provincial capital of Rehe Province, in June 1933. Nakayama reports receiving the following reply when he forcefully requested transport on a military airplane belonging to the Imperial Army Headquarters in Jinzhou.

> Coming to Manchuria, and especially to Chengde, I understood clearly how the "girl army" (*jōshigun*) was actually not a play on words, but was actually a part of the army, was really an "army." I grasped the truth of the Jinzhou headquarters' statement that "women are a necessity, so they are transported by airplane." When the Japanese army advances, the officers' primary concern is the transportation of the "girl army." The reason Japanese troops don't rape Chinese women is precisely because they have the "girl army." So they are not merely prostitutes![16]

The "girl army" generally referred to groups of prostitutes, especially those who traveled overseas. Nakayama writes that the "girl army" in this case was "really a part of the army," transported along with provisions "through a hail of missiles." Comfort women, he observed, became "nurses as tender as wives" to the wounded soldiers. These descriptions underscore the fact that comfort women were not an anomalous presence in the Japanese army, but rather were treated as essential to its functioning.

THE TRANSITION INTO THE PERIOD OF WIDESPREAD
ESTABLISHMENT OF MILITARY COMFORT STATIONS

The Era of the Nanking Massacre

In July 1937, Japan began its full-scale aggressive war against China. Within days, hundreds of thousands of troops were dispatched. From 1938 onward, more than one million regular army troops were deployed on the Chinese mainland. This was the first time that the Japanese army had had such huge numbers of men on active duty. Beginning at the end of 1937, the Japanese army began to build military comfort stations throughout China.

The setting up of such a large number of military comfort stations was intimately connected to the invasion of Nanking that gave rise to the Nanking Massacre. In November 1937, after ninety days of heavy fighting for control of Shanghai, the Central China Area Army (commanded by General Matsui Iwane) began to advance toward Nanking. It rampaged through the communities along the Yangtze River on the way, looting, massacring, setting fires, and raping. Like all war crimes, the rapes were hideous acts. But they were also particularly troublesome for the leaders of the Japanese army. Not only did the mass rapes earn the outrage of the international community, but Japanese military leaders knew very well that the Chinese looked upon rape with particular outrage. The general staff headquarters of the Kwantung Army made the following observations in 1932.

> The Chinese value honor very highly, and for appearances' sake treat their wives with respect. Among all immoral and violent acts, the Chinese regard rape to be the worst and consider it an extremely serious social problem. [Bandits and thieves] lie, deceive, loot, and steal with no compunctions; but they very rarely commit rape.[17]

As this report indicates, the mass rapes committed by Japanese troops were considered a serious obstacle to maintaining order in occupied China. On December 11, in the midst of its offensive toward Nanking, the Central China Area Army ordered the establishment of military comfort stations. Iinuma Mamoru, Chief of Staff of the Shanghai Expeditionary Force that participated in the invasion of Nanking, wrote in his diary that day, "On the matter of the establishment of military comfort stations, documents from the [Central China] Area Army arrived, and {I will} oversee the execution {of those orders}."[18] This diary entry was written just before the occupation of Nanking.

After receiving these orders, the Second Staff Section of the General Staff of the Shanghai Expeditionary Force drew up plans, and on the 19th, a staff officer, Colonel Chō Isamu, set about the task of building military comfort stations. The occupation of Nanking began on December 13. According to the diary of Vice Chief of Staff Uemura Toshimichi, "[December 28] It seems that the troops' lawlessness [illegal conduct] steadily increases. The Second Staff Section's plan for the establishment of military comfort stations is currently under consideration."[19] The establishment of military comfort stations was proceeding apace.

The 10th Army under the command of the Central China Area Army was also ordered to establish military comfort stations and immediately set about constructing them. In the diary of Major Yamazaki Masao, a 10th Army staff officer, we find a vivid description of the model for setting up military comfort stations in Huzhou.

> Lt. Colonel Terada was sent ahead to take command of the military police and establish entertainment facilities in Huzhou. At first, there were four women, and from now on there will be seven. Because the women are still terrified, it was difficult to gather seven women. I heard that they didn't "perform" their "tasks" very well. If we consistently assure them that their lives will not be in danger, that they will always be paid, and that they will not be treated cruelly, then more women who want to join up will come forward. The military police revealed that they are supposed to round up one hundred women. . . . There has been no special notice issued, and there isn't even a sign posted at the entrance. But the troops heard the news somehow, and [the comfort stations] have flourished. Soldiers must be warned about their tendency to lapse into abuse. Lt. Colonel Terada has more experience now that he has carried out this task. Major Ōsaka and Captain Sendō, who arrived today, couldn't wait to go once Terada told them about the comfort station. And they left imme-

diately with the commander of the military police. They returned about an hour and a half later, well satisfied.[20]

Immediately after the occupation of Nanking, Chinese women in the region were coerced into becoming comfort women. The army's General Staff ordered the military police to round up comfort women and set up comfort stations. That the women rounded up were terrified comes as no surprise; even today, the description of the "tendency to lapse into abuse" is horrifying. We cannot overlook the fact that commissioned officers took the initiative in going to military comfort stations.

Other documents confirm that Chinese women were forced to become comfort women during this period. On December 18, the 3rd Stretcher Company of the 3rd Division Medical Corps triumphantly entered the city of Yangzhou after the fighting around Zhenjiang and Yangzhou had ended. Shortly thereafter, a military comfort station was set up in Yangzhou as well. According to the recollections of Sugino Shigeru, a member of the group in charge of setting up the comfort station, he walked around with other members of the group and members of the Yangzhou Self-Government Association (organization for maintaining order) and gathered together forty-seven Chinese women. They were then set up as comfort women in a commandeered four-story wooden building called the Yangzhou Oasis Inn.[21] The direct management of the comfort stations by the army and the rounding up of women by the Chinese themselves deserve our attention.

Central China After 1938

Early in 1938, military comfort stations were being set up in rapid succession. For example, according to the "Situation Report" of Manba Shitomi, commander of the 2nd Independent Heavy Artillery Siege Battalion, two comfort stations under direct military management had been set up in Changchow by January 20, 1938. One was "managed by the line of communications unit" and the other was "managed by a unit under the direct control of the Shanghai Expeditionary Force."[22] Each unit had use of the comfort station "on a specified day, with the commanding officer's permission, and each unit was allotted about one hour." Precautions were taken against sexually transmitted diseases by "sending military physicians

beforehand to conduct hygiene examinations {of the comfort women}."[23]
The "Battlefield Diary" of the 2nd Company of the 2nd Independent Heavy
Artillery Siege Battalion attests to the fact that no matter how military leaders tried to keep the behavior of soldiers under control, problems kept crop-
ping up at comfort stations. Since the diary contains such warnings as
"always pay (for services rendered)"[24] and "exercise self-control at comfort
stations and don't commit violent acts,"[25] we can assume that these sorts
of problems occurred. Reports of a rape and an instance of looting, as well
as warnings about "soldiers who try to assault women" and "soldiers who
enter civilian homes uninvited in search of women"[26] attest to the fact that
soldiers continued to commit rapes even after the establishment of comfort stations.

According to the battlefield diary of Ogishima Shizuo, a corporal in the
2nd Battalion of the 101st Infantry Regiment, he first encountered a comfort station in January 1938 while quartered at the Toyota Spinning Mill
in Shanghai. His diary reads as follows:

January 8   In the evening, the captain told us about the opening of the
comfort station. Many of the men were happy about it.

January 9   Today, the first of the Chinese *pii* [comfort women] arrived.
Because the *shuho* {originally this term designated a PX, but later it came
to be used as a name for a comfort station} was set up near Headquarters, Corporal Furuya and Superior Private Tanaka went as the men in
charge. {note: *pii* is a vulgar term for the vagina in Chinese}

January 10   Today, the shuho opened.

January 11   In the afternoon, I went to the 7th Company with a military doctor to oversee the inspection of the shuho for its opening. It
really made me feel that a little neglect could have dire consequences.
In the evening, two more serving women came.

January 12   Tonight, all the noncommissioned officers went to the shuho
together.

January 13   Today, I was ordered to go to the shuho immediately
by the officers in charge. To troops at the front it was an interesting

place, probably because there were serving women at the shuho. There was only one thing for sale there at that point. People wanting to buy "it" besieged {the serving women}, and they were very busy all night.[27]

We would expect the shuho to be a military commissary, but in this case, "there was only one thing for sale." Clearly, the shuho was a military comfort station, and it seems to have been managed directly by the army.

According to the recollections of Asō Tetsuo, a military physician assigned to the line of communications hospital of the Shanghai Expeditionary Force, a military comfort station set up in Yangjiazhai in Shanghai sometime in the beginning of 1938 was also under the direct management of the military.[28] At that time, he conducted examinations for sexually transmitted diseases on about a hundred comfort women, 80 percent of whom were Korean. The remaining 20 percent were Japanese. From around this time, women from Japan and Korean began arriving in China in ever growing numbers.

If we try to deduce the numbers of comfort stations and comfort women in central China between 1938 and 1939 from the occasional Foreign Ministry document still extant (largely reports from the consulates in various areas), we arrive at the following figures.

Shanghai—army comfort women: 300 women (not including those at the 7 naval comfort stations)[29]

Hangchow—4 military comfort stations and 36 comfort women[30]

Jiujiang—24 military comfort stations and 250 comfort women (143 Korean women and 107 Japanese women)[31]

Wuhu—6 military comfort stations and 70 comfort women (22 Korean women and 48 Japanese women)[32]

Wuhan—20 military comfort stations and 395 prostitutes and serving women (but all of these women were not comfort women)[33]

Nanchang—11 military comfort stations and 111 comfort women (100 Korean women and 11 Japanese women)[34]

Zhenjiang—8 military comfort stations[35]

Yangzhou—1 military comfort station[36]

Danyang—1 military comfort station[37]

These figures are mainly taken from statistics on Japanese subjects (Japanese, Koreans, and Taiwanese) organized by occupation, so Chinese comfort women are not included. Comfort stations under the direct management of the military are not included either. These are only statistics compiled by the consulate, but they demonstrate that the proportion of Korean women was higher than that of Japanese women. Furthermore, comfort stations proliferated, not only in major cities but in small and medium-sized cities as well.

The Establishment of Large Numbers of Comfort Stations in Central China Begins

The expansion of military comfort stations proceeded first in the Yangtze valley but quickly spread to northern China. The reasons {behind the expansion} were the same—Japanese troops in northern China committed numerous rapes. As these acts inflamed the anger of the local Chinese, they could not be ignored even at the highest levels of the Expeditionary Force Headquarters.

Okabe Naosaburō, Chief of Staff of the North China Area Army, noted in his "Written Notification of Warnings on the Treatment of the Local Population by Military Units and Personnel" in July 1938 that public order was unstable in the occupied territories in northern China as a whole. He put forward the following reasons for the unsettled conditions and policies to address them. This is one of the documents I discovered. It happened to be included in the huge "Battlefield Diary" of the 9th Infantry Brigade. It is the type of document that we never would have found if we had not combed through this lengthy diary carefully.

According to various reports, the trigger causing such potent anti-Japanese sentiment is the widespread diffusion of news about rapes committed by Japanese military personnel in various areas. In fact, {these rapes} have fomented unexpectedly profound anti-Japanese feelings. . . . Naturally, such self-defense organizations as the Kōsōkai {Red Spear Society} or the Daitōkai {Big Blade Society} in places like Shandong, Henan Province, and southern Hopei, which have fiercely resisted the raping and pillaging of soldiers since time immemorial, were inflamed, but now it is the norm for the entire local population of each area to be so enraged, particularly by rapes, as to seek revenge even unto death. . . . Accordingly, not only are rapes illegal acts in each of these areas, but they also undermine public order and obstruct the combat activities of the military as a whole. We ought to call them acts of high treason that threaten the nation. . . . We must stamp out the outbreaks of these acts. Any commanders who disregard these orders can only be called disloyal subjects.

. . . Along with strict controls on soldiers' individual behavior of the aforementioned type, the provision of facilities for sexual comfort as quickly as possible is of great importance, {as it will} eliminate cases in which people violate the prohibition {on rape} for lack of facilities.[38]

The North China Area Army, which had command of all military units in northern China, acknowledged that rapes occurred frequently in all areas and so enraged the local population that the situation had become an obstacle to the maintenance of public order and to combat activities. As a countermeasure, the Area Army Chief of Staff ordered each unit under his command to build military comfort stations.

Compared to the cases of central and southern China, we simply don't know many concrete details about the establishment of military comfort stations in northern China. This is because the population statistics compiled by the consulate did not include "comfort woman" as one of the occupations. The only related material we have is a document called "A Table of Statistics on the Population of Subjects Organized by Occupation" from the North China Consular Police Department.[39] According to this document, the population of "geisha, prostitutes, and serving women" was 8,931. We can estimate the relative number of comfort women subsumed under that category. Of course, this figure only represents the number of Japanese subjects, that is, Japanese, Korean, and Taiwanese women. Chinese comfort women were not included. At any rate, it is undeniable that beginning in 1938, military comfort stations sprang up at an alarming rate all over northern China in accordance with the orders of the North China Area Army.

The Situation in Southern China

In October 1938, fighting spread into southern China. A report entitled "Wartime Report (Relating to Line of Communications)" issued in April 1939 by the Headquarters of the 21st Army in Guangzhou records information on military comfort stations and comfort women. According to this document, the 21st Army directly supervised 850 comfort women. An additional 150 comfort women were assembled by individual units under the 21st Army's command from their respective hometowns, bringing the total number of comfort women to 1,000.[40] This figure represents only those women in areas where the military police were stationed. Since military units not under the jurisdiction of the military police also had comfort stations, the actual number of comfort women was much larger.

The main areas where comfort stations were established were Guangzhou city, eastern Guangzhou, northern Guangzhou, Henan, Foshan, and Haikou (Hainan Island). But there were also comfort stations in Sanshui, Jiujiang, Zengcheng, and Shilong.[41] From the statements of Matsumura Takeshi, chief of the Medical Section in the 21st Army, we can conclude that the number of comfort women was increasing. He gave the following description of the situation in a meeting with the Ministry of War Medical Bureau.

> To prevent the spread of sexually transmitted diseases, we have been importing one comfort woman for every 100 soldiers. That amounts to 1,400 to 1,600 people so far. Treatment is being given at Hakuai Hospital, with comfort station operators bearing the costs. Tests for syphilis are conducted twice a week.[42]

The number of comfort women had climbed to 1,400 to 1,600. It goes without saying that this figure represents only the comfort women supervised by the 21st Army; there were also considerable numbers of comfort women coerced into service by small-scale units under the command of the 21st Army.

Plans to Transport Comfort Women in Northeastern China

In July 1941, the army was massing more than eight hundred thousand troops in northeastern China along the border between China and the Soviet Union in preparation for an invasion of the USSR (in order to disguise the fact that this deployment was in preparation for an invasion of the Soviet Union, the troops were mobilized under the pretext of "Special Maneuvers of the Kwantung Army"). It is said that in order to service these troops, the Kwantung Army (commanded by Lieutenant General Umezu Yoshijirō) planned to assemble twenty thousand Korean comfort women in northeastern China, in addition to those who were already there. Staff officer Hara Zenshirō was put in charge of this plan. He requested the assistance of the Government-General (the governor-general was General Minami Jirō). Minami assembled about ten thousand Korean comfort women (eight thousand women by some accounts) and sent them to the northern regions of northeastern China. Hara is said to have set up special facilities there and forced the women "to do business."[43]

At present, primary documents that corroborate this account have not been discovered. If this is true, one would expect that to assemble so many women in such a short period of time, officials of the Government-General were deeply involved in drafting them.

THE PARTICIPATION OF THE ARMY CENTRAL COMMAND AND THE STATE

Army Elites Were Involved

The preceding section has provided an overview of the establishment of military comfort stations from the time of the First Shanghai Incident through the period of full-scale war in China. Judging from the examples taken up so far, the names of the commissioned officers involved in setting up military comfort stations that have surfaced demonstrate that these officers were almost all members of the army elite.

Okamura Yasuji, Vice Chief of Staff of the Shanghai Expeditionary Force in 1932, became commander of the China Expeditionary Force in 1944. Okabe Naosaburō, high-ranking staff officer in the Shanghai Expeditionary

Force in 1932, became Commander of the North China Area Army in the same year. Lieutenant Colonel Nagami Toshinori, who directly managed the establishment of comfort stations, later became the commander of the 55th Division. Lieutenant Colonel Chō Isamu, who was in charge of setting up comfort stations in Nanking, was arrested at a *machiai* or geisha house for his involvement in the October Incident, a conspiracy among commissioned army officers to stage a coup d'état in 1931. Despite this stain on his record, he later became Chief of Staff of the 32nd Army in 1944 and took up a post in Okinawa. Tenth Army Staff Officer Terada Masao, who ordered the military police to establish a comfort station in Huzhou, later became director of the Army Armor Service Board, responsible for oversight of all factories producing armored vehicles for the Japanese military. From the simple fact that those responsible for setting up the comfort stations were all elite military personnel, it is clear that the establishment of military comfort stations was a systematic operation. The decision to set them up was never made arbitrarily by army units in the field. Even if the concrete measures to set up military comfort stations were determined by army units in the field, the authority that actively approved and promoted this policy was none other than the Ministry of War itself.

Documents Confirming the Participation of the Ministry of War

One of the key documents that attest to the participation of the Ministry of War is a notice entitled "Matters Concerning the Recruitment of Women to Work in Military Comfort Stations," issued on March 4, 1938 by an adjutant in the Ministry of War. As a consequence of the discovery and publicizing of this document, the government's stance {on the comfort women issue} changed. I quote it here in its entirety.

> Notice from the Adjutant to the Chiefs of Staff of the North China Area Army and Central China Expeditionary Force
>   In recruiting women domestically to work in the military comfort stations to be set up in the areas affected by the China Incident {the contemporary Japanese term for the expansion of hostilities in China into a full-scale ground war in August 1937}, it is feared that some people have claimed to be acting with the military's consent and have

damaged the honor of the army, inviting the misunderstanding of the general public. We are also afraid that, through the mediation of reporters following the military and people visiting soldiers, people are recruiting women unsupervised and causing social problems. There have also been instances where a lack of proper consideration resulted in the selection of inappropriate people to round up women, people who kidnap women and are arrested by the police. There are many things {about the rounding up of comfort women} that require careful attention. In the future, armies in the field will control the recruiting of women and will use scrupulous care in selecting people to carry out this task. This task will be performed in close cooperation with the military police or local police force of the area. You are hereby notified of the order [of the Minister of War] to carry out this task with the utmost regard for preserving the honor of the army and for avoiding social problems.[44]

According to this document, the Ministry of War was aware that the procurers entrusted by army units in the field with the task of rounding up comfort women were resorting to methods akin to kidnapping in Japan. If this continued, however, the people's trust in the Japanese army would be destroyed. To prevent this, both armies in the field (the North China Area Army and the Central China Expeditionary Force) were ordered to regulate the rounding up of women and be more selective about whom they chose to carry out this task. In addition, when procurers were gathering women together, they were ordered to do so only in cooperation with the local police or military police.

This document was drafted by the Military Administration Section of the Military Administration Bureau. Umezu Yoshijirō, Vice Minister of the Army, approved the plan. Vice Minister Umezu later became the Chief of the General Staff. He was a top member of the army elite, famous for signing the instrument of surrender aboard the USS *Missouri* at the war's end. The phrase "You are hereby notified of the order [of the Minister of War] to" is also very important. That phrase signifies that the document was issued with the authorization of the War Minister Sugiyama Hajime. That is, it demonstrates that the Ministry of War itself was involved in comfort women policies.

Another important document is "Measures to Enhance Military Discipline in Light of the Experiences of the China Incident," a report sent as educational reference material to each army unit by the Ministry of War on September 19, 1940. The following quote summarizes that document.

> Judging from reports since the sudden outbreak of the China Incident, behind the undeniably brilliant military exploits, many criminal acts contrary to the true nature of the Imperial Army such as looting, rape, arson, and massacres of prisoners of war have occurred. {Such acts} incur animosity toward the sacred war at home and abroad and regrettably impede the achievement of its goals. An investigation into the conditions that gave rise to these criminal acts confirms that they frequently occurred immediately after combat. . . . It is necessary to restore order in the areas affected by the China Incident, give careful consideration to the setting up of comfort facilities, and attend to restraining and pacifying savage feelings and lust. . . . The emotional effects of sexual comfort stations on soldiers should be considered the most critical. It must be understood that the competence or lack thereof in overseeing {the operation of comfort stations} has the greatest influence on the promotion of morale, the maintenance of military discipline, and the prevention of crimes and sexually transmitted diseases.[45]

In short, military comfort stations were considered essential to raising the morale of the troops; maintaining military discipline; preventing looting, rape, arson, and the massacring of prisoners; and preventing sexually transmitted diseases. The Ministry of War explicitly acknowledged that comfort stations performed those functions.

There is evidence that methods for setting up comfort stations were being taught at the army's accounting school sometime around 1939. Shikanai Nobutaka, an army accounting officer who became president of the Sankei Newspaper Company and Fuji Television after the war, described his studies at the school from April to September of 1939 in an interview.

> At that time [when comfort stations were being set up], we estimated the endurance of the women rounded up in local areas and the rates at which they would wear out. We analyzed which women were

strong or weak in those areas, and then had to go so far as to determine "how long they would be in use" from the time soldiers entered the rooms until they left-how many minutes for commissioned officers, how many minutes for noncommissioned officers, how many minutes for soldiers . . . (laughter). We set different prices for different ranks and prices for overstaying. They called stipulations about these sorts of things the "General Plan for the Establishment of Pii Facilities," and we were taught this at accounting school as well. Recently, a group of classmates from the accounting school got together, and we discussed our memories of this sort of thing.[46]

Since jargon such as the term "pii facility" was not used in official documents, the regulations were probably called "General Plans for the Establishment of Comfort Facilities" or "General Plans for the Establishment of Special Comfort Facilities." The fact that such things were taught at the army's accounting school means that the setting up of military comfort stations was even more systematic than it is generally thought to have been. During the course of the Asia Pacific War, Paymaster First Lieutenant Shikanai was dispatched from the army's Main Supply Depot to Kokusai Gomu Kōgyō (International Rubber Industries, the forerunner of condom producer Okamoto, Inc.) in Katsushika, Tokyo, where he directed the production of condoms for the army.

Relations Between the Army Central Command and the Expeditionary Forces

To begin, I'd like to trace the lines of command between the army's central command (the Ministry of War and the Army General Staff Headquarters) and expeditionary forces. Each expeditionary force was dispatched under the emperor's orders, and they engaged in combat in accordance with orders issued by the emperor based on the advice of the Chief of the General Staff. The authority to command each of the expeditionary forces rested with the emperor, but he delegated those powers. The Chief of the General Staff was endowed with the authority to order troops into combat, and the War Minister was entrusted with military government. This is called "partitioned" authority. The Chief of the General Staff and the

War Minister were not invested with the supreme authority of command; they each exercised only partial authority.

The commanders of the Korea Army (the name of the Japanese army stationed in Korea) and the Taiwan Army served directly under the emperor, followed orders from the Chief of the General Staff regarding military operations, and got their orders regarding military government from the War Minister. As for the military police, the War Minister commanded those stationed in Japan and had jurisdiction over the personnel and duties of those stationed in Korea and Taiwan. The commanding officer of the Korea Army gave orders to the commanding officer of the military police corps in Korea, while the commanding officer of the Taiwan Army gave orders to the commanding officer of the military police corps in Taiwan. Accordingly, responsibility for activities involving the Korea and Taiwan Armies extended to the War Minister.

Even if we assume for argument's sake that the armies in the field ignored the intentions of the Army Central Command in regard to the establishment of comfort stations and the rounding up of comfort women, we can't say that the Army Central Command was completely without responsibility for what happened. In matters concerning comfort women, however, we can say that the staffs of the respective armies, and especially the line of communications staff, were the ones in charge. And, as the occasion demanded, the War Ministry itself gave orders and exercised control over these matters.

In fact, when comfort women were sent to the battlefields on ships, military ships sailing under the Japanese flag and managed by the army were used. Without the consent of the Army Central Command, this sort of activity would not have been possible. According to international law, a Japanese ship is considered to be identical to actual Japanese territory. Sea transport was under the jurisdiction of the Inspector General of Lines of Communication in the Army Department of the Imperial Headquarters (a post held concurrently with that of Vice Chief of Staff). In special circumstances, comfort women were also transported by plane.

In the case of Korean comfort women transported over land routes to China, Japanese railways in Korea were used. In Manchuria, the South Manchuria railroad, capitalized with Japanese funds, was used. On the Chinese mainland, Chinese railroads that were in reality managed by the Japanese army were used. In instances when railroads could not be used, such as the transferring of comfort women to occupied areas of China or other countries, the Japanese army used trucks.

The Home Ministry, the Government-General of Korea, and the Government-General of Taiwan

It was impossible for the army to organize the efficient transport of comfort women on its own. Various government organs cooperated in rounding up and transporting comfort women.

Looking first at involvement of the Home Ministry, according to a notice entitled "Matters Regarding the Treatment of Women Sailing to China" (dated February 23, 1938),[47] the Home Ministry gave orders tacitly approving the transport of "women whose purpose {for going abroad} was the 'shameful calling' " (such as comfort women), but only in cases where their destinations were northern and central China. The Home Ministry was thus a party to the dispatch of comfort women overseas. These orders were issued by Tomita Kenji, Bureau Chief of the Home Ministry's Police Protection Bureau, to the governors of all prefectures in Japan. The term "shameful calling" referred to prostitution.

Moving on to the involvement of the governments-general of Korea and Taiwan, the testimonies of former comfort women have rendered virtually indisputable the fact that the police forces of Korea and Taiwan were involved in some fashion in the rounding up of comfort women. In the cases of Korean and Taiwanese women sent by ship to China, documents called "travel identity papers" were issued by the police stations under the respective governments-general. If the police issued these documents knowing that some of the women were minors or had been coerced, then this was a violation of international law (see chapter 5). If they issued the documents unawares, then it constituted gross dereliction of their duties. When the police of Korea and Taiwan issued travel identity papers, they inquired into the occupations, identities, employment histories, conduct, period of stay, and purpose of travel of all passengers. If passengers did not have a legitimate reason for traveling, then they would not be given permission to go. Therefore, the police had every opportunity to become aware of the fact that the coerced rounding up of women was taking place.

If illegal activities were taking place on a large scale in Korea and Taiwan, responsibility for them extends to the respective governments-general. Furthermore, in the case of Taiwan, this means that the Overseas Affairs Minister (after 1942, the Home Minister), who should have been supervising these procedures, bears some responsibility as well. (In the case of the governor-general of Korea, there are no detailed documents setting out provisions for the cabinet's oversight of Korea's Government-General. The Home Minister had the authority not only to make administrative decisions but also to exercise the emperor's command authority.)

As comfort stations evolved, consulates (the Foreign Ministry) lost their jurisdiction over comfort women attached to the military. According to the records of the Consulate of Nanking, in April 1938 there was a gathering of relevant officials from the army, navy, and Foreign Ministry at the Nanking Consulate. They jointly agreed on matters concerning the authority to license and regulate imperial subjects engaged in various businesses. It was decided in regard to the army's exclusive "stores" (*shuho*) and comfort stations that "consulates will not interfere with establishments managed and supervised directly by the army." Consulates were charged with the task of regulating "comfort stations and so-called 'shuho' used generally."[48]

The Participation of the Police in the Rounding Up of Comfort Women

There were two general methods of rounding up comfort women. The first entailed the expeditionary forces themselves gathering together women in the occupied territories. The other method entailed rounding up women in Japan, Korea, and Taiwan. The former will be dealt with in detail in the second half of chapter 3. Here, I would like to examine the second method.

There were two ways of rounding up women in Japan, Korea, and Taiwan. The first involved the army in the field appointing a director or private operator and sending him to Japan, Korea, or Taiwan to recruit comfort women. Generally, this process was overseen by the headquarters of the North China Area Army, Central China Expeditionary Force, or South China Area Army. But there are also cases in which divisions, brigades, or regiments under the army's command were charged with supervising the activities of the agent. For example, according to an exchange of telegrams between the Foreign Minister and the consular-general of Hankow regarding a document entitled "Matters Concerning the Transport to China of Comfort Women for the Comfort Stations of Amaya's Unit in the Hankow Army,"[49] in 1939 the Zentsūji 40th Division stationed in Hankow (under the command of Lieutenant General Amaya Naojirō) rounded up fifty comfort women in Kagawa Prefecture. There was also the 1st Infantry Regiment of the Taiwan Army stationed in Xian District in Guangdong Province, which brought along its comfort women into battle at Nanning in Guangxi Province. In the midst of combat, it dispatched the wife of the operator of its exclusive comfort station to Taiwan, where she gathered six underage girls and forced them to come back to Xian District.[50] Two of the girls brought back were just sixteen years old; one was eighteen, and another was fifteen. The two youngest girls were a mere fourteen years old.

The other method of rounding up comfort women in Japan, Korea, and Taiwan entailed armies in the field sending requests to army units in Japan or to the Taiwan or Korea Army. That army would then choose an agent to round up comfort women.

In any event, the military police and local police forces don't appear in any records. The military and local police did, however, aid procurers, and in certain cases cooperated with agents in rounding up comfort women. In any case, when rounding up comfort women, the procurers had to have permits issued by the army or by government offices abroad (consulates), or proper travel identity papers issued by the police.

It is clear that the Japanese army and the state were definitely involved in the establishment of military comfort stations and the rounding up of comfort women.

WHAT WERE THE CONSEQUENCES OF THESE OPERATIONS?

The Reasons for Establishing Comfort Stations and Their Effects

As we have already seen, according to the records of the armies and commissioned officers, the purposes behind the establishment of comfort stations were to prevent rapes in the occupied territories and to prevent soldiers from contracting sexually transmitted diseases. But did they achieve these goals?

Beginning with the goal of preventing rapes, we find that there were no occupied areas in which rapes stopped. For example, Okamura Yasuji, commander of the 11th Army in 1938, was in command of the occupation of Wuhan. Despite the fact that he was the man who had come up with the plan to establish comfort stations, he felt it necessary to make the following statement about the conditions in the units under his command.

> At present, almost all units are accompanied by comfort women corps. It has reached the point where {a comfort women corps} is just one more line of communication corps. But even though such units as the 6th Division march with a comfort women corps, there is no end to the rapes.[51]

The introduction of the comfort station system did little to prevent rapes from occurring. The comfort station system was a system of officially recognized sexual violence that victimized particular women and trampled upon their human rights. It is impossible to prevent rape on the one hand while officially sanctioning sexual violence on the other. There is no reason to imagine that there would be any relation between the comfort station system and a substantive solution to the problem of preventing rapes.

Fundamentally, what was necessary to prevent rapes was the severe punishment of soldiers who committed them. That is precisely the first step that had to be taken. The Army Penal Code itself, however, was lenient when it came to the crime of rape.

Rapes committed in combat areas or occupied territories were "punishable by at least seven years of penal servitude and at most life imprisonment when women are raped while the crime of looting is being committed," according to Paragraph Two of Article Eighty-six of the Army Penal Code. At first glance, this seems to be a quite heavy penalty. This regulation, however, appears in the midst of an article on looting. It was not meant to clamp down on rape itself, but only addressed rape when it was committed along with the crime of looting. (This eventually became an issue, though, and in February 1942, the crime of rape was treated in a separate article of its own).

At any rate, given the way the laws were used by those who were supposed to enforce them, anything was possible. Okamura recounts the following incidents that took place in August 1938. The Chief of Staff of the 11th Army reported that "looting and rapes were common" among the Hata Detachments. Since even the wife and daughter of the village headman who had been contracted to build an airfield had been gang-raped, the work was not progressing. When commanding officer Okamura, angered by this news, ordered that the offenders be arrested, the captain of the military police replied that the victims didn't personally file a complaint against anyone, so it couldn't legally be considered rape. The captain "calmly stated his opinion that since no one has filed suit, the case has been dropped." The Chief of the 11th Army Judicial Department shared this opinion. Okamura said he was dumbstruck by this.[52] There were also many instances in which soldiers who committed rapes killed the women they had assaulted out of fear of being prosecuted.

First Lieutenant Hayao Torao, a psychiatrist affiliated with the Kōnodai Army Hospital, was charged with the task of preparing a report on "Phenomena Particular to the Battlefield and Policies Toward Them" by the army's 11th Military Medicine and Judicial Departments upon his return to Japan from Shanghai in 1939. One section of the report was entitled "Sexual Desire and Rape." As this section depicts the conditions of the time quite thoroughly, I quote from it at some length.

> The line of communications unit had the good sense to suppose that restraining the sexual desire of soldiers at the front for long periods of time would naturally lead to violence against Chinese women, and they quickly established comfort stations in central China. The essential purposes of these stations are to pacify the soldiers through satisfying their sexual desires and to prevent rapes that damage the honor of the Imperial Army. . . . Still there are considerable numbers of rapes in the countryside, and we also see many behind the front lines. . . . Because the idea that {soldiers} are free to do things to enemy women that would never be permitted at home is extremely widely held, when they see young Chinese women, they are drawn to them as if possessed. Accordingly, those arrested are simply unlucky, and we can't tell how many more offenders remain anonymous in the shadows. . . . Further-

more, the unit commanders, on the contrary, consider them {rapes} necessary to build up the soldiers' morale. They even pretend not to know about rapes they witness and let it go at that. . . .

To go so far as to defile the bodies of the women and girls of enemy countries cannot be considered behavior appropriate to truly civilized people. As a citizen who takes pride in being from an Eastern country of propriety, I'm deeply ashamed of this behavior. . . . Why is it that Japanese soldiers are so unreasonable when it comes to sexual desire? This is something I deeply regretted from the moment I arrived on the continent. Throughout one year of battlefield life, I felt this very keenly.

The military leaders there, however, didn't think it strange at all. And I never once heard an admonition on this subject. . . . The military leaders there assume that the soldiers' sexual desires are impossible to restrain and set up comfort stations so that the soldiers will not rape Chinese women. Rapes, however, are committed quite frequently. The good people of China invariably fear this as soon as they see Japanese troops. Commissioned officers were the first to go to comfort stations and recommended to soldiers that they go as well. These officers decided that going to comfort stations was official business. Soldiers of conscience, knowing what goes on in comfort stations, laugh scornfully at these military leaders. But there are also some officers who insult soldiers who won't go to comfort stations, calling them crazy.[53]

The observations that there were commanders who silently condoned rape, considering it good for "building troop morale"; that the vast majority of military leaders did not intervene; and that commissioned officers took the lead in going to comfort stations are bitter indications of the conditions of the time. The fact that military comfort stations were not effective in preventing rapes is clearly demonstrated.

The Problem of Sexually Transmitted Diseases

As hospitalization and recovery periods for sexually transmitted diseases were lengthy, they were a serious issue for the military. According to the North China Area Army's "Procedures for the Hygiene Education of Key Officers" (1940), the average number of days required for recovery from gonorrhea was 91, from soft chancres (early-stage syphilis) 58, from syphilis 76, and from lymphogranuloma inguinale 1,012.[54] Therefore, head military doctors emphasized the necessity of paying careful attention to "how fighting power was affected by sufferers of sexually transmitted diseases."[55] And if soldiers were sent back to Japan while suffering from sexually transmitted diseases, it would result in the spread of diseases at home and become a huge social problem. The North China Area Army, therefore, would not send home soldiers suspected of being infected until they were cured. It also had a policy of notifying the city, town, or village leaders in the hometowns of soldiers in danger of having relapses of their illnesses.

The Japanese army would not allow troops to use civilian brothels in order to prevent the spread of sexually transmitted diseases. It considered the creation of comfort stations managed by the army to be a suitable alternative. The idea that the purpose of military comfort stations was preventing the spread of sexually transmitted diseases is clearly expressed in examples we've already considered, such as the 1939 report of Matsumura Takeshi, Chief of the Medical Branch of the 21st Army.

But did the importation of comfort women reduce the number of soldiers infected with sexually transmitted diseases? At a conference of chiefs of army medical branches held in Tokyo on February 14, 1940, the chief of the North China Area Army Medical Branch made the following statement.

> We do our best to gather together those who need special treatment and treat them in a special hygiene treatment facility. . . . Hospitals in Taiyuan, Jinan, Baoding, and Datong have been designated as special hospitals for the treatment of sexually transmitted diseases, and intensive treatment is given there. Those who require special treatment in Japan are gathered in Tientsin and sent home. In a six-month period, we commit 2,600 patients to hospitals and treat them.[56]

As before, there were many patients. The situation was grave enough to require special hospitals dedicated exclusively to the treatment of sexually transmitted diseases. The number of soldiers in the 19th and 20th Divisions of the North China Area Army who contracted sexually transmitted diseases during combat operations reached 985. That figure does not measure up to the 6,791 soldiers with enteritis or to the 1,895 with stomach disorders, but it is comparable to the 1,390 soldiers afflicted with beriberi, the 994 with contagious diseases, and the 829 with malaria.[57] At any rate, the number of soldiers with sexually transmitted diseases was not small.

Because of the seriousness of this problem, military leaders forbade soldiers to visit civilian brothels, ordered military doctors to conduct regular examinations of comfort women for sexually transmitted diseases, and lectured soldiers on such preventative measures as condom use. Yet even in military comfort stations, which one would expect to be managed carefully, they were not able to prevent the transmission of sexual diseases. In the "Procedures for the Hygiene Education of Key Officers" discussed above, the section entitled "Prevention of Social Diseases" {sexually transmitted diseases} begins with the statement that "social diseases damage the body, destroy the family, and ruin the country."[58] It goes on to declare that:

Social diseases are contracted primarily through sexual intercourse. Almost all *geigi/shōgi* [comfort women] are infected. Therefore, the following precautions should always be practiced when having sexual intercourse.

a) Don't have sexual intercourse after drinking alcohol.

b) Check the {woman's} health papers {proving that she has been examined for sexually transmitted diseases}.

c) Make the woman wash before having sexual intercourse.

d) Always use a sack [condom].

e) Use Secret Star Cream [a disinfecting lubricant].

Before sexual intercourse, apply a small amount to the penis, put on a condom, and spread a small amount over the surface of the condom. After sexual intercourse, squirt the remaining liquid up the urethra.

f) After finishing your business, promptly urinate or wash with disinfectant. If disinfection is not carried out within five minutes after sexual intercourse, the disinfectant has no effect.

g) After returning to the barracks, stop by the medical office and ask for treatment.

h) Anyone noticing any unusual symptoms should get medical attention in the early stages {of a condition} and be treated thoroughly.

i) Anyone with phimosis {an unretractable foreskin} is very susceptible to social diseases, so he should be especially conscientious about disinfection.[59]

The injunction to consider almost every comfort woman a carrier of disease is appalling. These preventative measures advocated by military doctors were quite elaborate; it's unlikely that anyone actually adhered to such cumbersome guidelines. Consequently, despite the establishment of military comfort stations, sexually transmitted diseases continued to spread. In fact, there were even some indications that the existence of military comfort stations may have helped spread sexually transmitted diseases among the troops. First Lieutenant and military physician Hayao Torao wrote in his opinion paper that:

Military comfort stations have been established on a large scale, and prostitutes have been provided for military personnel. These prostitutes have caused sexually transmitted diseases to spread among the troops. This, in turn, has given rise to the necessity of building line of communications hospitals to treat these problems. . . . While the enlisted men are strictly controlled, sexually transmitted diseases are in fact more common among the commissioned officers. Rather than among the young officers, the afflicted are among the field officers, and they are receiving treatment from military doctors in secret. While the military comfort stations were set up in order to prevent the contraction of sexually transmitted diseases from Chinese people, and women from the home islands and Korea were brought over as prostitutes, it's ironic that those women ended up spreading sexually transmitted diseases.[60]

Whether the comfort women brought to China were a source of infection or not is highly debatable. Women with no history of prostitution should be seen as victims who were infected {by troops} rather than as sources of infection.

In fact, to prevent sexually transmitted diseases, what was necessary was the quarantining and treatment of the infected, and regular monthly checkups of commissioned officers and enlisted men with "localized, minute examinations of their bodies."[61] While examinations of comfort women for sexually transmitted diseases were carried out regularly, examinations of military personnel were not conducted vigilantly. It was considered a dishonor when a soldier was diagnosed with a sexually transmitted disease, so many tried to conceal their ailment. Therefore, officers and soldiers themselves were often the sources of infection.

The naming of military comfort stations as a cause of the spread of sexually transmitted diseases is a critical point. Not only were military comfort stations ineffective in preventing the spread of diseases, but they actually facilitated the infection of many more soldiers. It is a scathing commentary on the Japanese army that there were high-ranking officers (of field officer rank) among those afflicted with sexually transmitted diseases and that they received medical treatment in secret. These facts manifest the corruption of the Japanese army.

When we inquire into the situation during the Asia Pacific War, we find that the numbers of army personnel who contracted sexually transmitted diseases in the field are as follows. In 1942, there were 11,983 newly infected men; in 1943, there were 12,557; and in 1944, 12,587.[62] Thus, even judging by the number of cases the army managed to document, the number of soldiers with sexually transmitted diseases was increasing.

The Provision of "Comfort"

The purposes of the establishment of comfort stations were not limited to the prevention of rape and sexually transmitted diseases. They were also intended to provide "comfort" to the troops and protection from spies.

The war Japan initiated was an aggressive and unjustifiable war. It was also a reckless war Japan had no prospect of winning. To wage this type of war, the Japanese army kept its troops in the field for long periods of time with an insufficient vacation system; therefore, it considered sexual comfort for the troops necessary.

The North China Area Army, for example, instructed commanders that in order to prevent the "deterioration" of soldiers' thoughts in a bleak environment, "it is necessary to improve hygiene facilities as much as possible" and "facilities for the comfort of the troops should be improved as much as possible."[63] Needless to say, included among these comfort and hygiene facilities were military comfort stations. The second article of the comfort station regulations of the 3rd Independent Mountain Artillery Regiment dated November 14, 1939 directly states that "The purpose of the establishment of special comfort stations is to pacify and moderate the troops' brutal temperament and to aid in the promotion of military discipline. Therefore, it is necessary to control strictly behavior that degenerates into encouragement or promotion of {this temperament}."[64] The army was trying to "pacify the troops' brutal temperament" with its offer of sexual comfort. Here the aim was to offer opportunities for sexual intercourse itself. The fact that comfort stations were considered necessary even in areas close to the front lines where there were few civilians and little opportunity to commit rape or threat of sexually transmitted diseases clearly demonstrates that comfort stations were considered necessary for "comfort" alone.

Aside from these facilities, the Japanese army provided almost nothing else that could be called comfort. Military doctors frequently suggested that wholesome comfort and entertainment facilities were necessary. Second Lieutenant Asō Tetsuo, a military doctor, proposed a plan in 1939 for the establishment of a different kind of comfort station, separate from military comfort stations. These new stations would be equipped with leisure facilities for music, libraries, movies, and sports.[65] This plan, however, was never really implemented. Facilities for the amenities of daily life remained extremely crude. In addition, soldiers were not even granted leave. The European and American armies, in light of their experiences during World War I, made it a policy to grant their troops regular leave. But the Japanese army and navy did not grant leave during wartime, with the exception of a few special cases. Moreover, in the barracks, the human rights of the soldiers were not respected, and they were subject to the strict supervision and arbitrary discipline of their commanding officers on a daily basis.

In this bleak environment, trapped in the quagmire of the battlefields and wondering whether they would ever be able to go home again or not, it is no surprise that noncommissioned officers and senior enlisted men would only grow more profoundly discontented. As army ranks swelled precipitously, many officers were unable to supervise their men adequately. Miyazaki Shōichi, a staff officer in the 11th Army, describes the conditions in which the military comfort station system expanded. "Young officers, drafted officers, and the like had poor command over their men. We can't ignore the fact that they were unable to assert their authority over older enlisted men."[66] That the army was increasing the number of military comfort stations in order to maintain officers' will to fight and to prevent their dissatisfactions from boiling over is a fact that cannot be overlooked.

This was the reality behind soldiers' pursuit of a fleeting sense of liberation and peace of mind at military comfort stations. During the period of the Asia Pacific War, an army doctor posted to Burma described the military comfort station as "the sole pleasure" in an army that granted no freedoms.[67] One soldier candidly recounted his experiences in comfort stations in China as follows.

> The times when we (the men we were during the war) would be holding down our penises as we ran in {to the comfort station} were, after all, when we had just come back from a long battle jumping for joy and headed immediately over there. When we arrived at the rooms where the women were quartered, the soldiers would line up with numbers in hand. They all wanted to be freed from the stress of the singular experience of having walked the line between life and death. They stood there waiting, with their pants unbuttoned, fumbling with loincloths long since turned a dingy gray and fidgeting— is it my turn yet? is it my turn yet? . . . We thought there was no sense of fulfillment that burned so intensely as this.[68]

Thus it was that tragic scenes of soldiers trying to grasp a fleeting sense of fulfillment and to release the stress of the battlefield and their repressed feelings in comfort stations took place wherever the Japanese army went.

Protecting Against Spies

Finally, I'd like to examine the prevention of spying and the protection of army secrets. The danger that military secrets would be leaked to local prostitutes would grow if soldiers visited local brothels in occupied areas. Therefore, the Japanese army thought that building its own comfort stations and conducting regular supervision and surveillance of them was the best policy. For example, the General Staff of the 25th Army, stationed in Singapore in 1942, gives "the enforcement of military discipline, {the conduct of} anti-espionage {operations}, and the prevention of contagious diseases" as reasons for establishing comfort stations in an army report. Then on July 4, 1942, the General Staff issued orders banning soldiers thenceforth from visiting civilian brothels.[69] This example demonstrates that the aims of the establishment of military comfort stations included prevention of espionage as well as of rape and of the spread of sexually transmitted diseases.

Military police or inspection officers went to military comfort stations regularly to conduct examinations of management practices and of relations between military personnel and comfort women. For anti-espionage purposes, the army wanted comfort women to be Japanese subjects (Japanese, Koreans, or Taiwanese). But there were not sufficient numbers, and importing women from Japan, Korea, and Taiwan required time and effort. So the army quickly turned to rounding up comfort women locally. This practice made the supervision and surveillance of military comfort stations all the more essential.

Even as military comfort stations failed in their purported aims of preventing rape and the spread of sexually transmitted diseases, their numbers continued to increase, as did the number of comfort women. Thus as Japan rushed headlong into the Asia Pacific War, a new phase of expansion in the comfort station system was planned.

Chapter Two

Expansion Into Southeast Asia and the Pacific

The Period of the Asia Pacific War

Plans Immediately Before the Beginning of the War with the United States

In December 1941, Japan embarked on the war against the United States, Britain, Holland, and their allies, and proceeded to occupy vast tracts of Southeast Asia and islands in the Pacific. At the start of 1942, the Japanese army began setting up military comfort stations one after another throughout the occupied territories.

This was an operation studied and planned before the Asia Pacific war even began. There are important records demonstrating that this was the case. One is the *Diary of Official Duties at the Ministry of War*, compiled by Kinbara Setsuzō, Chief of the Medical Affairs Section in the Medical Affairs Department of the Ministry of War (and a staff member of the Medical Affairs Section until November 8, 1941), who took careful notes of the proceedings of various sorts of internal Ministry of War meetings.

For example, a military doctor who toured the Dutch East Indies (Indonesia) immediately before the start of the war made the following report (July 26, 1941).

> It is necessary that we take care to conduct ourselves in such a way as to cultivate a sense of trust among the native inhabitants that we love them and are acting sincerely toward them. Even though there are many Muslims who practice polygamy, their sense of virtue is strong. We must be extremely careful to give them no reasons to distrust the discipline of the Japanese army, by committing rapes, for example. On the one hand, there are many people among the native inhabitants who engage in prostitution out of economic necessity. Many of these in Bandung and other places are afflicted with sexually transmitted diseases. It is necessary that village headmen be

---

Comfort women taken into protective custody by the Allied Powers in Burma, August 1944.

assigned the task of building comfort stations and strictly administering syphilis tests to women.[1]

Major Fukada Masuo probably participated in the second round of Japan-Holland negotiations held in Batavia (today's Jakarta) between September 1940 and June 1941, and then secretly conducted the hygiene inspections necessary for the Japanese occupation of the Dutch East Indies. One of his conclusions was the proposal that, in order to prevent rape and the spread of sexually transmitted diseases by Japanese army personnel, comfort stations should be built. Local women should be rounded up to work in them and subjected to thorough examinations for sexually transmitted diseases. The expression "village headmen be assigned" appearing here clearly shows that the army would become involved in the forced rounding up of women who were not prostitutes.

The Start of the War and the Incidence of Rapes

In fact, when the Japanese army invaded Southeast Asia and islands in the Pacific, rapes were committed in all the occupied territories. At a meeting of section chiefs in the Ministry of War held on February 12, 1942, the Judicial Department reported that, "In Tomi's group, there were 112 cases of fleeing from the enemy, 3 rapes, and 3 instances of looting. . . . In the Philippines Area Army as well, there was a considerable number of rapes (14), and there were even cases of noncommissioned officers assaulting women."[2] "Tomi's group" refers to the 25th Army, which coordinated the invasion of the Malay Peninsula. It was the 14th Army that invaded the Philippines.

Actually, only a small proportion of the reports on crime ever reached the army's Central Command. Therefore, we can be certain that considerable raping and looting took place from the outset of the invasions of the Philippines and the Malay Peninsula. At a meeting of Ministry of War bureau chiefs held on May 2, Ōyama Ayao, chief of the Judicial Bureau, and Tanaka Ryūkichi, chief of the Military Administration Bureau, had the following exchange.

ŌYAMA: The captain currently in command of the 1st Independent Anti-Tank Regiment [actually, a battalion] of the 25A [25th Army] raped a married Malaysian woman in Kuala Lumpur and stole five or six watches from her husband. Then in Johol, he tricked the third princess of the royal family and defrauded her of a camera. In short, he committed the crimes of rape, looting, and fraud.

TANAKA:　The 25A had a reputation for those tendencies before it came to Kuala Lumpur. The 25A used this incident as an opportunity to completely remake that reputation.

ŌYAMA:　In the Philippines Region, there were also many rapes, but as a result of strict controls, there was a marked drop in crimes.

TANAKA:　(Rapes) were comparatively numerous in the Philippines, compared to other regions. Compared to the China Incident, however, we can say that there were not very many.[3]

From the statement that the 25th Army "had a reputation for those tendencies" before coming to Kuala Lumpur, we learn that the 25th Army had already committed a considerable number of rapes before arriving on the Malay Peninsula. The 14th Army, which invaded the Philippines, is also singled out as having committed many rapes there as "compared to other regions." This is surprising because the number of rapes that occurred during the invasion of the Philippines is said to have been small compared to the number committed during the China War. Clearly, the Army Central Command was well aware that an extremely large number of sex crimes occurred near the front lines in both China and the Philippines. Here we find military leaders saying that, as a result of strict controls, battalions were able to "completely remake {their} reputations" and that "there was a marked drop in crimes." But was this really the case?

This official diary shows that, rather than these problems being resolved, they were becoming ever more serious. In another report to Ministry of War bureau chiefs on May 9, Judicial Bureau Chief Ōyama gave the following account.

The number of crimes committed by the Southern Army comprised 237 incidents. In general, this figure is small compared to the number of crimes committed during the China Incident. The 14A [the 14th Army] committed many rapes. This is because the women are more appealing to Japanese.[4]

The explanation that "the women are more appealing to Japanese" is shameless. Judicial Department Chief Ōyama further noted in another report to the department chiefs on May 27 that the Southern Army had committed seventy-six acts of looting and rape after the opening of hostilities. The armies that committed the most crimes were the 14th Army, the 15th Army (stationed in Thailand and Burma), the 16th Army (stationed in Indonesia), and troops under the direct command of the Southern Army, in descending order by the number of crimes committed. In addition, a June 3 report states that in May, there were eight incidents of violence against women of Chinese descent on the Malay Peninsula. The following statement was made in a report to the department chiefs dated August 12.

> There were 610 crimes committed by the Southern Army. Many of these were rapes. Many crimes were committed by units transferred from China. They resulted from insufficient comfort facilities and insufficient supervision. There are 2,000 men confined in various detention centers, with three or four judges to deal with them.[5]

It must be pointed out that there were as many rapes occurring as ever. We should take note of the fact that among the armies committing these crimes, those previously stationed in China were singled out as being responsible for a large number. This was probably because they had committed similar crimes in China.

The Establishment of Comfort Stations by the Southern Army

The Southern Army (commanded by General Terauchi Hisaichi) directed the deployment of the army divisions in various areas of Southeast Asia. The Headquarters of the Southern Army planned and carried out the construction of comfort stations in each division under its command. The first document that confirms this fact is a telegram from the Taiwan Army (com-

manded by Lieutenant General Andō Rikichi, with Chief of Staff Major
General Higuchi Keishichirō) dated March 12, 1942.

> Taiwan Army Telegram No. 602
> In regard to Secret Army Telegram No. 63, we've been requested
> by the Southern Army General Command to dispatch as soon as pos-
> sible 50 native comfort women to "Borneo." As per Secret Army
> Telegram No. 623, we request travel permits for the 3 operators
> named below, who have been investigated and selected by the mili-
> tary police.[6]

The Taiwan Army received a request from the Southern Army for fifty
Taiwanese comfort women to be sent to Borneo (Kalimantan), and then
the Taiwan Army requested travel permits for three operators chosen by
the military police. The telegram was addressed to the War Minister. This
request was granted by a Ministry of War adjutant on March 16, and the
plan carried out. The three operators traveled to Borneo with fifty comfort women. On July 13, the Taiwan Army sent another telegram request-
ing permission to "dispatch an additional 25 comfort women" because
"when they [the first 50 comfort women] arrived, there were not enough
of them, and some of them became unable to bear the work."[7] All of these
telegrams were marked "secret" and were encoded.

The next document is a report on a survey of 20 Korean comfort women
sent to Burma and on the husband and wife who operated the facility and
looked after the women. This report appears in the "Psychological Warfare Interrogation Bulletin, No. 2," issued by the Allied Forces' South-East
Asia Translation and Interrogation Center in November 1944. According
to this report, on July 10, 1942, a fleet of ships carrying 703 Korean comfort women and 90 operators and their family members left Korea heading for Singapore.[8] These comfort women were rounded up by the operators at the "suggestion" of the Headquarters of the Korea Army, but the
impetus behind this "suggestion" was probably a request sent by the Southern Army to the Korea Army. These ships stopped in Taiwan and took on
board 22 Taiwanese women.

Also in July 1942, Katsuki Kyūji, whose father-in-law operated a military comfort station in Nanking and requested his help, and Inoue Kikuo,

who had responded to the drive to recruit operators for military comfort stations in Shanghai, rounded up groups of comfort women and sailed from Shanghai to Singapore aboard the SS *Atlas*. When they reached Singapore, they were split up and sent to different areas on the orders of the army. Inoue, who had rounded up twelve Korean women in China, remembers that the colonel in charge of gathering together operators in Shanghai told them that, "In accordance with a request from the Headquarters of the Southern Expeditionary Forces, the General Headquarters of the China Expeditionary Forces is exerting itself in this matter."[9] It is clear that these women were rounded up at the request of the Southern Army.

The Ministry of War Exercised Jurisdiction Over Travel

As discussed in chapter 1, from 1938 onward, consulates (the Foreign Ministry) no longer had the right to exercise authority over military comfort women. After the start of the Asia Pacific War, authority over the travel of comfort women and comfort station operators in Southeast Asia and in islands in the Pacific was exercised by the army and navy. It became possible for people to travel with only army or navy identification papers, without involving the Foreign Ministry. Foreign Minister Tōgō Shigenori issued the following instructions in January 1942 in response to an inquiry from the Foreign Affairs Section Chief in the Taiwan Government-General.

> In regard to this sort of travelers, I am uncomfortable issuing them passports, so I would like to have them travel on military ships with military identity papers.[10]

In fact, the phrases "I am uncomfortable issuing them passports" and "on military ships" in the text of this telegram were eventually crossed out because the Foreign Ministry determined that they would irritate the army and navy. Other phrases were rewritten to make the language gentler. In the phrases that were erased, we can almost hear the discomfort of the Foreign Ministry, stemming from its desire not to be involved in the dispatching of comfort women {to occupied territories}. The Foreign Ministry had officially cooperated with the policy of freeing prostitutes in

Singapore in the 1920s, had forced Japanese *karayukisan* to stop working and return to Japan, and had taken the step of not approving any further dispatches {of prostitutes}. It was natural, given this history, that the Foreign Ministry thought that the army and navy should take all responsibility for the overseas dispatch of comfort women.

After the start of the Asia Pacific War, the Ministry of War tried to have the Central Command supervise all dispatches of comfort women to Southeast Asia and the Pacific region. In a telegram from the Vice Minister of War to the Chief of the General Staff of the Southern Army and the Chief of Staff of the 23rd Army dated November 18, 1942, the Vice Minister confirmed that procedures for the dispatch of "both necessary personnel for military '*shuho*' and comfort women" would be in accordance with Article 1, Item 7 of Secret Army Document No. 1283 issued on April 23, 1942.[11] "Secret Army Document Concerning Asia, No. 1283" dealt with "matters relating to the procedures for the advance of personnel connected with the army to southern occupied areas (including Hong Kong)" (Adjutant's Notice) as approved by War Minister Tōjō Hideki. Article 1 laid out the "procedures for advance" for "army personnel and and other necessary civilian subjects connected with the army" traveling from Japan, China, and "Manchukuo" to "the South." It specified that the army would "select and furnish identification papers" to these travelers. Item 7 included regulations for the category of "other" essential personnel. These people were defined as "those selected by the Ministry of War," and the article stipulated that "The Ministry of War (Management of Political Affairs Section in the Southern Area) will issue identification papers." Since people without army identification papers would not be allowed to travel, it became impossible for comfort women to go to Southeast Asia and the Pacific region without the permission of the Ministry of War or the navy. As we saw previously in the case of comfort women rounded up and sent to Borneo by the Taiwan Army, the Headquarters of the Taiwan Army applied to the War Minister (Tōjō Hideki held the post of Prime Minister concurrently) for permission to send comfort women and comfort station operators overseas. That fact, as well as the fact that the Vice Minister of War granted these requests, clearly demonstrates that the Army Central Command was, without a doubt, actually controlling overseas travel.

The Prevention of Sexually Transmitted Diseases and the Ministry of War

In the area of the prevention of sexually transmitted diseases as well, the Ministry of War intensified the supervision of comfort stations. In a notice from an adjutant general in the Ministry of War entitled "Matters Relating to the Treatment of Sexually Transmitted Diseases Among Military Personnel Serving in the Great East Asia War"[12] dated June 18, 1942, the Ministry of War gave new instructions on preventing the spread of sexually transmitted diseases in all army units. The document mandates thoroughness in the hygienic management of comfort stations in all army units in the field. This was proposed by the Hygiene Section of the Medical Bureau, whose officials actively acknowledged the necessity of comfort stations in the management of sexually transmitted diseases. In this new phase of the war, the Army Central Command reconfirmed this necessity. Though this document was issued as a directive in the name of the adjutant general as authorized by the Minister of War, the official who actually approved it was Vice Minister of War Kimura Heitarō.

In fact, the spread of sexually transmitted diseases, which had been distressing the Army Central Command from the start, continued to be a serious problem. Lieutenant Colonel Yasuda Tsuneo, a military doctor, pointed out in a Medical Affairs Bureau report dated December 22, 1942 that the number of Southern Army personnel suffering from sexually transmitted diseases had reached 2,774.

> There is a trend toward that number increasing gradually in the future. At this juncture, it is necessary to formulate a fundamental policy, and we are making steady progress in preparations. It is time to increase the number of comfort stations. Key officers are not exercising self-discipline. Both preventative equipment and preventative medicine are scarce. . . . It is easy for the treatment of sufferers to be given up half-finished, but treatment must be administered thoroughly. On this account, hospitals devoted to the treatment of sexually transmitted diseases should be built and patients treated in a timely and thorough manner. At the same time, we should implement outpatient treatment for personnel on duty, and educate them about appropriate treatment.[13]

As the number of military personnel afflicted with sexually transmitted diseases in the Southern Army continued to rise, the army was working to increase the number of comfort stations as a means of addressing this problem. Yet key officers were not exercising "self-discipline," and preventative equipment and medicines were lacking. Under the pretext of preventing rape by soldiers and the spread of sexually transmitted diseases, we see the specter of key army officers trying to satisfy their sexual desires.

In a Medical Affairs Bureau report dated April 11, 1943, the new bureau chief, Kamibayashi Hiroshi, announced that "taking heed of the reality that the Southern Army has 5,000 people suffering from sexually transmitted diseases, we must give instructions on the urgent handling of this problem,"[14] and ordered a study of fundamental policy for preventing sexually transmitted diseases.

The Establishment of Military Comfort Stations Under the Direction of the Army Central Command

To deal with the chronic problem of rapes committed by army personnel, the Army Central Command did not limit its policy considerations to comfort stations. For example, in a report to section chiefs on July 30, 1942, Chief of the Army Affairs Section Nishiura Susumu made the following statement.

> Since {soldiers} are called up as many as two to three times, we should implement a special holiday program. It is not much, but we are trying to mitigate the problem even a little bit. The same goes for the mediation of marriage. We want to implement a policy immediately that will allow officers to bring their families along with them.[15]

There were many problems with soldiers on their second or third tour of duty who, never knowing when the war would end, had become nihilistic and lost sight of their life plans. Nishiura proposed the introduction of a furlough system to ameliorate some of their dissatisfactions. In a report to department chiefs dated October 31, Prime Minister Tōjō Hideki announced that, "In light of the national population problems, a program providing furloughs at home for soldiers at the front must be researched and put into practice"[16] and expressed his support for this policy. Thus a limited furlough system that served the dual purposes of mitigating soldiers' dissatisfaction and producing the children who were to become the next generation of soldiers was put in place. This program targeted mainly veteran soldiers, providing them with vacations that would also be "(re)productive." This system, however, fell far short of a comprehensive furlough system.

In the end, the Army Central Command tried to solve its problems by promoting ever more actively the establishment of military comfort stations. In a September 3 report to Ministry of War section chiefs, Chief of the Awards Section Kuramoto Keijirō detailed the completion of the "establishment of comfort stations for enlisted soldiers {those below the rank of officer}." He reported that 100 military comfort stations had been built in northern China, 140 in central China, 40 in south China, 100 in the Southern Region, 10 in the South Seas, and 10 on Sakhalin. There were comfort stations in a total of 400 different locations.[17] In order to prevent rampant rapes by Japanese soldiers, the Army Central Command itself ultimately embarked on a program of setting up military comfort stations during the Asia Pacific War.

Why was the Awards Section the bureaucratic entity to launch this program of building comfort stations? The Awards Section was originally in charge of the army's comfort and entertainment facilities, but after a limited reform of the army bureaucracy in March 1942, its duties were clarified. Thereafter, it was in charge of "matters concerning the welfare" of army personnel in general. The Construction Section of the Ministry of War's Intendance Bureau and the army's Main Supply Depot cooperated in sending "hygienic sacks" (condoms) as necessities for troops in the field to the armies overseas. According to Hayashi Hirofumi's research, 32.1 million condoms were sent to armies in the field in 1942, and that figure represents only those that have come to our attention.[18] The army did supply condoms, but these figures break down to fifty thousand condoms per division per month, which works out to two condoms per month per soldier (assuming each division had twenty-five thousand men).

At any rate, from 1942 onward, the Ministry of War, which had previously left the establishment of military comfort stations to the armies in the field, began to take charge of that task itself. It is clear, however, that this policy was never effective in tightening up military discipline. In a Ministry of War section chief report dated February 4, 1943, the Judicial Bureau had to report that the number of army personnel being punished for crimes was increasing, from 3,300 in 1941 to 4,332 in 1942 (actually, this figure only includes those charged up through November 1942). Crimes such as rape and desertion, in particular, were increasing.[19]

The Case of the Navy

In the navy, comfort women were called *tokuyōin* (special essential personnel). It was the Navy Ministry (Admiral Shimada Shigetarō was Navy Minister at the time) that originally decided on the practical policy of sending comfort women to Southeast Asia and the Pacific region. On May 30, 1942, the Chief of the Navy Ministry's Military Affairs Bureau, Rear Admiral Oka Takazumi, and Chief of the Military Preparations Bureau, Rear Admiral Hoshina Zenshirō, issued a joint report entitled, "Inquiry Into Matters Concerning the Second Dispatch of Special Essential Personnel."[20] According to this document, when the navy transported forty-five "special essential personnel" to the island of Celebes (Sulawesi), forty to Barikpapan on Borneo (Kalimantan), fifty to Penang on the Malay Peninsula, and thirty to Java in the second phase, the Chief of Staff of the Southwestern Regional Fleet, Rear Admiral Nakamura Toshihisa, was notified. (The number sent to Anbon and Singapore at that time is uncertain, but there were thirty restaurant "staff workers.") Nakasone Yasuhiro, who became Prime Minister after the war, was involved in the management of military comfort stations at this time as an accounting officer (with a rank of first lieutenant). In December 1941 he served in Dabao in the Philippines, and then in January 1942 he was transferred to Barikpapan on the island of Borneo. He records in his memoirs, "Commander of 3,000 Men at Age Twenty-three," that in the interim, he himself was in charge of setting up military comfort stations as the Chief Accounting Officer for the 2nd Construction Corps.

> It was a large unit of over three thousand men. Before long, there were soldiers and naval civilian employees who attacked local women or who gave themselves over to gambling. For these men, I went to great lengths and even built comfort stations. In fact, they packed into them like sardines.[21]

Construction corps were units that built facilities like airfields and employed many civilians. Since there was not enough time to build a comfort station in Dabao, this episode is thought to have taken place in Barikpapan.

When the navy sent comfort women to the front by ship, it used battleships or other military vessels. The command and supervision of these vessels was handled by the Navy Ministry or by specific naval stations or fleets.

According to the Navy Civil Administrator's "Report on Matters Concerning Demobilized Members of the Second Demobilization Corps of the Civil Administration Department of Celebes"[22] dated June 1946, in the period of defeat and demobilization, there were 281 Indonesian comfort women rounded up in the southern region of the island of Celebes, 250 of whom were attached to naval units. Naval officers rounded up the comfort women and directly managed three military comfort stations. We learn from this document that there were twenty-three military comfort stations built with the permission of the Chief of the Navy Civil Administration Department, supervised through the Political Affairs Department, with the actual rounding up of women and employment contracts and regulation carried out by civilian employees of the Civil Administration Department.

The comfort stations under direct naval management were overseen by the Kendari Naval Force. The costs of the comfort women's food, clothing, bedding, utensils, and utilities, as well as the salaries of servants, were all borne by the unit. In comfort stations supervised by the Civil Administration Department, those costs were paid by the Civil Administration Department.

In short, we can see that there was stronger centralized control in the navy than in the army and that comfort stations were also more directly regulated. At least in the case of the island of Celebes, comfort stations were officially under the direct management of the navy or were, in actual practice, directly managed by naval forces.

THE DIFFUSION OF MILITARY COMFORT STATIONS AND THE TOTAL NUMBER OF COMFORT WOMEN

The Types of Military Comfort Stations

In order to avoid confusion, I have not thus far raised the issue of the different forms that military comfort stations took, but I would like to consider that issue here. Military comfort stations can be divided into three types based on how they were managed. The first type is military comfort stations directly managed by the military for the exclusive use of military personnel and civilian military employees. The second type is comfort stations formally managed by civilian operators but supervised and regulated by military personnel or civilian military employees. The third type is facilities designated as comfort stations that were open to the general public but at which military personnel were given special priority.

The Malay Inspectorate of Military Administration, for example, drew the following distinctions between "comfort facilities" (restaurants were also included in this category along with comfort stations). These distinctions coincide perfectly with types 2 and 3 described above.

1. Exclusive Military Use—Entrance and use by the general public is not permitted.

2. Military Use—Entrance and use by the general public is also permitted. Military personnel and civilian military employees given special priority.[23]

Of course, these three types are only rough distinctions. Needless to say, there was in fact a broad range of forms, from directly managed comfort stations to civilian brothels. The original military comfort stations fall into the categories of type 1 and type 2. Type 3 forms occupy positions somewhere between military comfort stations and civilian brothels. During the China War, military comfort stations and comfort women reserved for the use of military personnel were to some extent under the control of the consulates and even the military police. But during the Asia Pacific War, comfort stations came under the exclusive control of the military, and the military character of their management became all the more pronounced.

Next I'd like to address the important differences that arose depending on the location of the comfort station. One of these was that comfort stations located in large cities were used not only by the military units stationed there but also by those merely passing through the city. The military comfort station district in Hankow (Sekkeiri), with thirty buildings all clustered together, is a representative example of comfort stations in large cities. Another type was comfort stations attached to a particular unit. These comfort stations often traveled among the various posts where companies from the same unit were stationed. Some even accompanied their units to the front. According to the recollections of an adjutant to the 8th Infantry Regiment stationed in central China during the full-scale war in China, there were ten Korean comfort women in the town where the regiment's headquarters were located. At the request of units stationed on the front lines, comfort women were put aboard trucks, accompanied by guards, and often forced to go to the front.[24]

A third distinction to be made is based on the character of the users. Comfort stations and restaurants reserved for officers were usually called "officer's clubs," and the comfort women at these clubs were primarily Japanese (when there weren't enough Japanese women, Korean, Taiwanese, or women from occupied territories were provided). In Yangon (Rangoon) or Meimyo in Burma, for example, there was an officers' club called the Suikōen. This was a special branch of a famous, high-class restaurant in Kurume, Japan (also called Suikōen). Its branch in Burma served only military personnel, and its comfort women were Japanese.

While there were comfort stations for noncommissioned officers and enlisted men with Japanese comfort women, in many cases the women in these comfort stations were Korean, Taiwanese, Chinese, Southeast Asians, or Pacific islanders. Also, in regions such as Southeast Asia and the Pacific, Japanese civilians living in the area and working on behalf of the military as company employees and the like were sometimes permitted to use military comfort stations. There were also cases of comfort stations being built for local men mobilized as auxiliary troops (*heiho*) to supplement the strength of the Japanese army. For example, in Mandalay, Japanese company employees and other civilians were permitted conditionally to use the comfort station after 12:30 at night. And among the four "quasi-reserved military comfort stations" with Burmese women, one comfort station called the Shinmenkan was reserved for the use of Burmese auxiliary troops. There were nine comfort stations in Mandalay: the officers' comfort station, the Uminooya, with Japanese comfort women; three comfort stations with Korean comfort women; one comfort station with Chinese women; and three comfort stations with Burmese women. Those comfort stations with non-Japanese women were for the use of noncommissioned officers and enlisted men (though after 9:00 pm they were reserved for officers' use).[25]

The Locations of Comfort Stations
and the Overall Number of Comfort Women

I'd like to set out once more an overview of military comfort stations. At present, Japanese, American, and Dutch official documents have confirmed the existence of military comfort stations in the following areas: China, Hong Kong, French Indochina, the Philippines, Malaysia, Singapore, British Borneo, the Dutch East Indies, Burma, Thailand, New Guinea (in the eastern Pacific), the Japanese Okinawan archipelago, the Bonin Islands, Hokkaidō, the Kurile Islands, and Sakhalin.

Yet it is clear that comfort stations were not limited to these areas. According to the memoirs of veterans of the Japanese army and navy, for example, there were also comfort stations on the Japanese protectorates of the Truk Islands, Koror Island, Taiwan, and Saipan, as well as on American-occupied Guam and the Indian Nicobar Islands.[26] Considering only confirmed locations, the area in which comfort stations were built stretches from the northernmost tip of the Kuriles in the north to Indonesia's Sumba Island in the south, and ranges from the Truk Islands and Rabaul on New Britain (Papua New Guinea) in the east to Akyab (Sittwe) in Burma in the west. We should assume that they were built everywhere Japanese troops were sent, excluding only the very front lines. In regions where many troops were sent, large numbers of comfort stations were built. They were also set up on the mainland in Kyūshū and Chiba Prefecture where many troops were stationed in preparation after the decision to resist the U.S. invasion of Japan's main islands was made. It should be mentioned in this connection that in the case of Okinawa, where research has progressed furthest, as of February 1994, 126 sites have been identified (adding possible locations brings the total to 131).[27]

Estimates of the total number of comfort women range from 80,000[28] to "approximately 170,000 to 200,000" Korean women alone.[29] While I think the latter figure is too high, the actual number of comfort women remains unclear because the Japanese army incinerated many crucial documents right after the defeat for fear of war crimes prosecution, and the Japanese government has not made public the bulk of the documents that have survived.

Hata Ikuhiko has attempted to estimate the number of comfort women as follows. He assumes that there were 3 million troops stationed overseas during the Asia Pacific War, and if there was one comfort woman for every 50 soldiers and they were never replaced during the war, then there were about 60,000 comfort women. If we assume there was a 50 percent turnover rate, then the total number of comfort women climbs to 90,000.[30] In 1942, there were 2.32 million men stationed overseas; in August 1945, that figure was 3.51 million. If we take into consideration regions where there were no comfort stations as well as domestic comfort stations, the round number of 3 million troops seems appropriate. But what about the estimate of one comfort woman for every 50 soldiers? As mentioned in chapter 1, it is said that the army tried to round up 20,000 comfort women for the more than 800,000 troops participating in the "Special Maneuvers of the Kwantung Army." If this figure is accurate, it works out to approximately one comfort woman for each 40 soldiers. In 1939, however, the 21st Army estimated the appropriate ration at one comfort woman per 100 soldiers. Since there are no reliable materials on which to base an estimate of the total number at present, these figures are products of only one of several methods for estimating the total.

One problem {in making these estimates} is how to determine the rate at which comfort women were replaced. To assume that they were never replaced is unrealistic. The turnover rate among comfort women due to death, suicide, flight, illness, injury and death during battles, as well as to returning home after the expiration of contracts, is estimated to have been quite high. According to a collection of testimonials by Korean former comfort women, five out of nineteen returned home before Japan's surrender. One fled, one was released due to illness, one was saved and returned home by a civilian military employee, and one boarded a repatriation ship.[31] If we include those who died overseas and those who left comfort stations but could not return home, the replacement rate climbs even higher. According to a study by the Taipei Women's Rescue Foundation, among forty-eight confirmed former comfort women, only sixteen remained in comfort stations until Japan's surrender. Even if we add to that number the seven comfort women who were repatriated because of the deteriorating military situation, the number who endured until Japan's surrender still amounts to less than half the total.[32] It must be assumed that there was considerable turnover among comfort women.

Given these conditions, if we tentatively assume a turnover rate of 50 percent and the lower ratio of one comfort woman per every 100 soldiers, at the absolute lowest, the total number of comfort women comes to 45,000. However, the ratio of one comfort woman to every 100 soldiers represents the number of comfort women under the control of the 21st Army in 1939 and does not include the comfort women whom the smaller units under its command procured at their own expense. Therefore the total number of comfort women was at the very least approximately 50,000 women.

I'd like to estimate the upper limit of that number, assuming a ratio of one comfort woman for every thirty soldiers. At the time, the term "*ni-ku-ichi*" was popular among comfort station operators. This term translates to "twenty-nine to one" and meant that the appropriate ratio was one comfort woman for every twenty-nine soldiers.

In fact, Japan even investigated the option of providing comfort women for the forced Chinese laborers it drafted. According to "Matters Concerning the Impressment of Coolies," a report by the Coal Control Association's Eastern Department Chief on October 21, 1942, it was the hope of the Asia Development Agency (the central agency in charge of governing the occupied areas of China) to provide "20 to 30 {women} for every 1,000 {laborers}."[33] An October 24 report on "Matters Concerning the Impressment of Coolies" records the orders of the offices involved, such as the Planning Agency and the Asia Development Agency, to provide "between 40 and 50 {comfort women} for every 1,000 {laborers}."[34] Both of these, however, were merely proposals on the drawing board. In the summer of 1943, one plan called for 9 comfort women to be dispatched to the Fushiki Harbor Company in Toyama Prefecture where 224 Chinese laborers were working. Five comfort women and one hostess were actually brought in to serve the laborers.[35] Fushiki was the only company that kept imported comfort women for the use of Chinese workers, and thereafter the program was abandoned. At any rate, it was assumed that one comfort woman for about every 30 laborers (estimates ranged from one for every 20 to one for every 50) was the necessary ratio. If we assume a 100 percent turnover rate, then the total number of these comfort women amounts to approximately 200,000.

These estimates of the upper and lower limits are meaningful in and of themselves, but we must reconsider how closely they approximate actual conditions. This is particularly crucial because in the occupied areas, cases of kidnapping or imprisonment for the purpose of gang rape, as well as of the short-term rounding up of women, were common. According to the written complaint filed by forty-six Filipina former comfort women suing for compensation in Tokyo District Court, nearly all of them experienced this sort of treatment. Eighteen were held for periods from a few days to about one month, fifteen were held for periods ranging from two months to six months, and ten were held for periods lasting from eight months to one year and several months. Those in captivity the longest were held for more than two years.[36] I expect that the number of victims of these sorts of crimes among Chinese, Southeast Asians, and Pacific islanders living under Japanese occupation was extremely high. Whenever the Japanese army moved, it required new comfort women. These locally rounded up comfort women were in demand for relatively short periods of time, until the army moved on and rounded up new ones. When we include this type of victim in our calculations of the total number of comfort women, the turnover rate in occupied territories rises to several hundred percent.

What Were the Ethnic Backgrounds of Comfort Women?

Including only those confirmed in official documents, Japanese, Korean, Taiwanese, Chinese, Filipina, Indonesian, Vietnamese, Burmese, and Dutch women were all rounded up as comfort women. It is clear from official Australian documents that Australian nurses were forced to serve as comfort women.[37] (The nurses maintain that they refused the Japanese army's request and avoided being forced to serve as comfort women.) From the recollections of military veterans, however, we learn that Indian women and women of Chinese descent in Singapore and Malaysia were also found among military comfort women. Thus we can assume that elsewhere as well local women were forced to serve in territories occupied by the Japanese army and navy.

What were the proportions of various ethnic groups among comfort women? There are no documents that address this issue directly. We can guess at relative trends from statistics related to sexually transmitted diseases. According the Research Team of the Army Department of the Imperial Headquarters report, "Sexually Transmitted Diseases from the Perspective of Military Discipline and Public Morals During the China Incident,"[38] between 1937 and 1940, 14,755 soldiers stationed in China contracted sexually transmitted diseases. The report gives the following figures for those soldiers' "female partners" at the time they contracted their diseases (these leave out those who became infected in Japan or Korea, as well as partners who fall into the categories of "public and private prostitutes whose nationality is unknown" and "unidentified"): 4,381 (51.8%) of the female partners were "Korean women," 3,050 (36%) were "Chinese women," and 1,031 (12.2%) were "Japanese women."

While not all of these "female partners" were comfort women, it is probably correct to assume that the vast majority of them were. At least in the cases of comfort women who had not worked as prostitutes, it was the soldiers who infected their partners. These figures are truly horrible to contemplate. The Research Team of the Army Department of the Imperial Headquarters asserts that "the activity of Korean women surpasses the others. This should be taken into account in future battles." According to this report, the largest proportion of comfort women were Korean, followed by Chinese women, who also made up a large percentage.

There are also other statistics, such as those found in the "Essential Hygiene Operations Report"[39] produced by the Medical Branch of Tsuruga's 15th Division. According to this report, the number of comfort women examined on one round by the Medical Branch averaged as follows.

LOCATION	JAPANESE	KOREAN	CHINESE	AVE. NO. PRESENT
Nanking	237	13	139	389
Wuhu	32	26	40	98
Zhenjiang	3	0	36	39
Jintan	0	5	6	11
Chao Xian	0	4	30	34
Lishui	0	0	10	10
Totals	272	48	261	581

If we exclude Nanking, where Japanese comfort women were concentrated, there were 122 Chinese women, 35 Korean women, and 35 Japanese women. The percentage of Chinese women was overwhelming. Japanese comfort women were concentrated in the large cities, while Korean women were brought to cities like Jintan and Chao Xian, where there were no Japanese comfort women. There were also towns like Lishui where all the comfort women were Chinese. Looking at these statistics, we can conclude that the number of Chinese comfort women was probably larger than is usually supposed.

In Southeast Asia and the Pacific region, transport was difficult, so the proportion of local women among comfort women was much higher. At a January 7, 1943 meeting of section chiefs, Chief of the Awards Section Kuramoto noted in regard to comfort stations built on orders from the Ministry of War that "large numbers of comfort facilities have been built, but {women} imported from Japan are not well liked. Locals trained on site are more popular."[40] This statement implies that professional prostitutes sent from Japan were not popular, while local women who were not prostitutes but were rounded up to be comfort women were preferred by Japanese troops. From statements like this, we can infer that the trend toward using local women as comfort women was gaining momentum.

From the evidence presented thus far, it is clear that the primary agent operating the comfort station system was the Japanese military. Furthermore, comfort stations were built and managed under the direction of the military.

Next, I would like to address the questions of how the women forced to work in comfort stations were rounded up, and under what conditions they were required to perform sexual services. In the following chapter, I will approach these questions through the women's testimonies and soldiers' recollections.

Chapter Three

How Were the Women Rounded Up?

*Comfort Women's Testimonies
and Soldiers' Recollections*

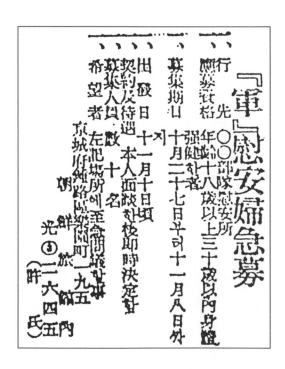

WOMEN FROM JAPAN

The Significance of the Testimonies

In this chapter, I would like to clarify the conditions under which comfort women were rounded up. What kind of women were forced to become comfort women? Where did they come from? We can infer some answers to these questions from military and government documents, but, as we have seen, there are significant limits to what we can know about what actually happened. This was a situation in which the military and the government themselves repeatedly warned those responsible for recruiting comfort women that they were not abiding by accepted standards.

This chapter is mainly comprised of the testimonies of former comfort women, verified as much as possible by reference to other documents. Many of these statements are products of recently conducted interviews. Needless to say, these recollections of events that occurred over fifty years ago are not without lapses. In fact, many of the Korean and Filipina women, perhaps because they did not have opportunities to receive sufficient education, gave statements that were full of contradictions or confusion about the timing of events. The Korean Council for the Women Drafted for Military Sexual Slavery by Japan and the "Volunteer Corps" Research Association held hearings at which the women related their experiences, and published the accounts of nineteen women (vol. 1) whose testimonies were considered reliable. An Byong-jik, a Seoul University professor who participated in the inquiry, describes the difficulties faced in trying to sort through the testimonies.

> One of the extremely difficult things about conducting this research is dealing with the many logical contradictions in the witnesses' testimonies. The events are already fifty years old, so there are probably lapses in memory {reflected in the statements}. There are also things the witnesses don't want to recall, so they abbreviate those

events, revise them, or confuse them with other events. In addition, it is conceivable that events occurred in that era that are beyond the imagination of our generation.[1]

I have also often experienced this sort of dilemma. Yet these testimonies, if we set aside lapses in memory and omissions concealing facts, are extremely important–not only because the information they contain does not exist in written form, but also because these intense experiences sometimes gave rise to strikingly vivid memories, and as the questions are repeated, facts and relationships that can only be narrated by those involved come to light. Only through these women's testimonies can we discover the stark realities that never appear in military and government documents, reports, or statistics. Here I will take up the testimonies considered to be the most reliable to reconstruct the facts about the rounding up of comfort women.

Japanese Comfort Women

When Japanese comfort women were to be sent overseas, they had to be over the age of twenty-one and chosen from among groups of prostitutes. These restrictions were imposed by the police. In the notice issued by the Home Ministry's Chief of the Police Bureau on February 23, 1938, "Matters Concerning the Handling of Women Sailing to China," the following regulations were established.

> In regard to the travel of women intending to engage in the shameful calling, the women must be currently working as prostitutes, at least twenty-one years of age, and free from sexually transmitted and other infectious diseases. Only those headed for north or central China will be allowed until further notice . . . they should be issued identification papers in accordance with the notice of the Vice Minister of the Foreign Ministry.[2]

As we will see in greater detail in chapter 5, these regulations were adopted because Japan was a signatory to an international treaty that forbade the buying and selling of women and children, and this had to be taken into consideration. Japanese comfort women were chosen, accordingly, from among the prostitutes working in brothels. Let's examine several examples.

A woman with the professional name Keiko, who continued to work at a Fukuoka brothel after she had paid off her debt to the brothel owner, was recruited to work as a comfort woman. She received a payment of 1,000 yen from an agent and traveled to Shanghai for the first time in 1938 to work in a military comfort station.[3] This agent was said to be a procurer for the army, rounding up comfort women on the orders of the Line of Communication Headquarters in Shanghai.[4]

Takanashi Taka, who worked as a prostitute on the South Seas islands of Saipan and Palau, returned to Japan in 1939, and worked in a geisha house in Osaka at the request of a friend.[5] Sick of the work and free of any debts to an operator, she was solicited by a Yokohama employment agency. Thinking, "Well, if there's good business, I'll go make some money," she went to China with a group of five or six other comfort women (among whom she was the oldest),[6] where they worked in a comfort station for officers in Nanking.[7] Since she was already thirty-six years old, she seems to have worked as a waitress and comfort woman. She had a status somewhere between comfort woman and proprietress, so her case was somewhat different from that of the average comfort woman.

A woman with the professional name Kikumaru, who worked as a geisha in Nishikoyama in Tokyo, went to the Truk Islands in 1942 to work in a comfort station for naval officers. Since the military agreed to pay off her debt of close to 4,000 yen to the brothel owner, she is said to have volunteered.[8] This military comfort station was directly managed by the navy. Comfort women were referred to as "special nurses" and treated as civilian military employees.[9] Contracts were for a period of one and a half years. Comfort women kept 40 percent of their earnings, while 60 percent went to the navy. Apparently, they were told that if they died, their spirits could be enshrined at Yasukuni Shrine {the Japanese national shrine where spirits of the war dead are enshrined and worshipped}.[10] This certainly can be seen as the mobilization of young women by manipulating their patriotism. At the time, Kikumaru was all of eighteen years old.

Ignoring the Age Rules

As the case of eighteen-year-old Kikumaru demonstrates, the police standards for obtaining permission to travel overseas were not strictly enforced. Sasaki Takayoshi, the Vice Consul in Shanhaiguan, made the following report to the Foreign Minister on May 12, 1939, and asked what sort of countermeasures should be taken.

> [According to the Home Ministry Police Bureau Chief's notice] women traveling to China for the purpose of engaging in the shameful calling are supposed to be twenty-one years of age or older . . . but [a restaurant manager who came through Shanhaiguan on her way to Peking] had with her four geisha, the following three of whom [names omitted] were all under the age of twenty-one. In spite of the fact that it was patently obvious, considering the manager's occupation, that their purpose in traveling overseas was to engage in the shameful calling, since they had been issued identification papers by the Chief of the Asahikawa Police Department, I was obliged to let them continue on their way. There have been two or three other cases like this. I request that you please investigate the facts of this incident and advise me how to deal with such situations.[11]

Four geisha whose purpose in traveling was to engage in prostitution were being led by a female restaurant manager. They passed through Shanhaiguan on their way to Peking. Even though three of the four were minors, they had identification papers issued by the Chief of the Asahikawa Police. There were several other incidents similar to this one, but the officials in Shanhaiguan did not know how to handle them. In this case, the girls brought from Asahikawa were aged fifteen, sixteen, and seventeen. It is clear that there were not a few cases in which, at the police's discretion, the travel of minors for the purposes of prostitution was tacitly approved.

Especially in the case of Korean women living in Japan, these standards were not enforced. The women and girls rounded up in Kyūshū by the army procurer who solicited Keiko included seven Japanese and eleven Koreans. While all of the Japanese were working as prostitutes, all of the Korean girls are said to have been tricked into going along.[12] A soldier from the 18th Division relates the following account of a Korean woman with the Japanese name Mariko whom he met in a comfort station called the Kōmyōsō in the Burmese city of Meimyō. While living in Shimonoseki, she heard that women were being recruited to work as orderlies in army hospitals in Tsushima, Japan. Since the woman who gave her the introduction was a Korean midwife she felt she could trust, she responded to the offer. In fact, she and about one hundred other women were taken to Hainan Island and put to work in military comfort stations.[13]

Isozaki Takako, an accounting typist at a munitions company called Osaka Hemp, boarded the SS *Mizuho* as a civilian military employee, headed for the branch office in Java in August 1944. The ship, however, was attacked by an American submarine and sunk. Approximately seventy female civilian military employees were rescued and found their way to Luzon in the Philippines. But they were treated by the military units there as hangers-on. Around October, the remaining thirty women were told by a soldier on duty, acting on orders from the adjutant, that the "adjutant said that if you become comfort women, we will take care of you. So how about it? As we told the others, you'll be guaranteed food, clothing, and housing. And, of course, you can be driven around in trucks!"[14] The women immediately refused, but this episode demonstrates that there were instances in which Japanese women who weren't prostitutes were requested to serve as comfort women.

WOMEN FROM KOREA

Examples of Deception

Cases of women being deceived and led off are much more common among those rounded up in Korea. Let's examine a representative example. According to the testimony of Song Shin-do, a Korean former comfort woman living in Japan who has filed a suit seeking compensation, she was forced to have intercourse with soldiers in a military comfort station in Wuchang just as it was about to be occupied at the end of 1938. The circumstances leading to her being held there were as follows.[15]

Song was sixteen years old by Japanese reckoning (fifteen years by Western), and was betrothed to a man her mother had chosen. But Song hated him and found the prospect of life wih him unbearable. So on her wedding day, she pretended to go to the bathroom and ran away. When she had been working as a nanny in Dejon for several months, Song was asked by a beautifully dressed Korean woman, "Won't you go to the front and work for your country?" She was a procurer rounding up comfort women. There was no explanation of what sort of work Song would be doing. Song was taken to Pyongyang and sold to a Korean man. They traveled overland to China, passed from Tientsin to Hankow, and arrived in Wuchang. This is a typical example of the solicitation of women, particularly underaged girls, by fraud.

We see many similar cases among the women's statements in the testimonies gathered by the Korean Council. Seventeen of the nineteen women whose testimonies appear in the book were rounded up in Korea. Of those seventeen, twelve were victims of this sort of deception. Li Yong-suk was making her living working as a maid in other people's homes, as both of her parents had died.[16] She was looked down upon by everyone, and in whatever household she worked, she endured being screamed at by both adults and children. She survived "crying tears of regret."[17] Around this time, a Korean husband and wife approached her, asking if she wouldn't like to go to Japan and work; she accepted their offer. Along with some other girls in similar circumstances, the Korean couple took her to Pusan.[18] There the girls were turned over to a Japanese man, who put them on board a ship. They made stops at Shimonoseki and Taiwan before being taken to Guangzhou. These events took place in December 1939, when Li was just seventeen years old.[19]

After the Start of the Asia Pacific War

Mun Pil-gi's parents owned a grocery store and some fields, so they were perhaps somewhat better off. Mun entered regular school (comparable to Japan's elementary schools, but attendance was not mandatory) at age nine.[20] Her father, however, withdrew her from school and burned all her textbooks, saying that "women who study become foxes." After she was forced to quit school, she had to do all kinds of work, such as housework, working in the fields, spinning thread, and helping out in the store.[21] She suffered from the discrimination against women that pervaded Confucian morality. Another critical factor was that for Koreans, Japan did not maintain a compulsory education system. Since Mun longed to study, when a Korean man told her that he would "take her to a place where she could study and earn a lot of money," she agreed to go.[22]

The year was 1943, and Mun was just eighteen years old. She left her village in a truck, but the truck stopped in an out-of-the-way spot. It is significant that she remembers that a Japanese policeman posted to the village's police box was standing there.[23] It seems likely that the police were secretly aiding agents in their efforts to round up comfort women. Mun was then taken to Pusan, put on a train to northeastern China, and forced to work in a military comfort station there.

As is clear from these testimonies, the vast majority of these girls came from poor families, so they were forced into a life of struggle with no hope. On account of Japan's colonial policies in Korea and general discrimination against women, these girls were unable to receive an adequate education. According to a 1930 survey of the state of the nation in Korea, 36 percent of Korean men were literate, while a mere 8 percent of Korean women were.[24] Trapped in these circumstances, the girls were deceived by procurers' appealing offers of good work in factories and such and then led off. Li Yong-suk made up her mind to go with a Japanese man after he "showed her a red dress and leather shoes."[25] Agents took advantage of these girls' feelings of oppression. Even if the girls realized something was amiss along the way, they had no means of escaping. Since they couldn't just go home, they gave up trying to escape, assured themselves that the work waiting for them couldn't be so bad, and tried to figure out what they would do in the future. In the end, they were forced to face the bitter reality of life in a military comfort station.

Women Who Were Sold

The Kitamuras, a husband-and-wife team of comfort station operators, related a typical story of buying women when they were taken prisoner by the American army in Burma. Their depositions are included in the English-language publications "Japanese Prisoner of War Interrogation Report" (No. 49), compiled by the U.S. Office of War's Psychological Warfare Team attached to the U.S. Army Forces in the India-Burma Theater, and "Psychological Warfare Interrogation Bulletin" (No. 2), produced by the South-East Asia Translation and Interrogation Center.

This Japanese couple bought twenty-two unmarried Korean women in 1942. They paid the girls' parents between 300 and 1,000 yen, depending on the girls' characters, appearance, and ages (200-300 yen, according to the former report). Before the Kitamuras were captured by the Americans, two of those girls were killed in a bombing raid. The remaining twenty women stated that their ages at the time they were sold ranged from seventeen to twenty-nine, with twelve girls under the age of twenty-one. It seems that they were not told that their work would entail sexual services. U.S. Army Sergeant Alex Yorichi made the following remarks during the first interrogation of the prisoners.

> The nature of this "service" was unspecified but it was assumed to be work connected with visiting the wounded in hospitals, rolling bandages, and generally making the soldiers happy. The inducement used by these agents was plenty of money, an opportunity to pay off the family debts, easy work, and the prospect of a new life in a new land—Singapore.[26]

It is clear that, for many women who were sold and forced to become comfort women, the economic fetters of a sum advanced against their labor and deception about the nature of the work were intertwined.

There is just one other similar case of a woman being sold among the testimonies collected by the Korean Council. Park Sun-e (fictitious name) was born the third daughter of an independent farming family and finished only two years of elementary school.[27] She married at age sixteen, but the couple was so poor that they could not make a living, so Park ran away.[28] When she married again at age eighteen, her husband was wealthy and the son of a good family but was often violent. When her child was three years old, Park took her to an "employment agency" and sold her.[29] When the child was transferred to another "employment agency" in Seoul, Park's debt already amounted to a huge sum.[30] Just as she was thinking that she wanted to pay off her debts and live with her child, she heard about good jobs "washing soldiers' uniforms in hospitals at the front and treating injured soldiers." She was told that if she worked for three years she would be able to pay off her debts and maybe even save some money, so she accepted.[31] She went by ship from Pusan to Shimonoseki and was then taken to Rabaul.[32] Park Sun-e was twenty-three years old when she was led off, but her story shares with the previous examples the combination of trafficking in people and deception.

Cases of Women Led Off by Violent Means

If we limit our discussion of violence used to lead women off to cases of women taken from Korea, we have the following testimonies. Mun Ok-chu was born in 1924.[33] Her father died young, and her mother was able to make ends meet by sewing and peddling goods. Occasionally, they were forced to get grain from her mother's parents.[34] Mun occasionally worked in a slipper factory managed by a Japanese man, but since it was not steady work, she sometimes hung around at home with nothing to do.[35] She often went to the home of a Korean friend who was given the Japanese name Haruko.[36] Her friend's family ran a cremation business, and before the bodies were burned there were often various ceremonies, so Mun was often treated to meals of the offerings made at these ceremonies.[37] This was during a time when she was hungry every day. She described how she was taken away in the fall of 1940 as follows. She was just sixteen at the time.

> One day, I went over to Haruko's house to visit. As the sun was going down, I left her house and headed home. Before I'd walked very far, a Japanese man in a military uniform approached me. Suddenly, he grabbed my arm and pulled me, saying something to me in Japanese. That was a time when even hearing the word "policeman" was a scary thing, so I was led off without saying a word. . . . I thought I was being taken to the military police.[38]

She was taken to a military comfort station in northeastern China. It is impossible to determine whether the Japanese man who kidnapped her was a soldier, a policeman, or a civilian dressed in khaki-colored clothing. But from the facts that the kidnapping occurred at sunset, that he was unaccompanied, and that he then passed her along to a procurer who appeared to be a civilian, there is a strong possibility that the kidnapper was a civilian. Of course, it is possible that these kinds of crimes went unnoticed or were ignored by the police because of the army's urgent requests for comfort women.

The Participation of the Government-General of Korea and the Korea Army

Since the Ministry of War ordered that the cooperation of the military police and local police be sought when comfort women were being rounded up, even in Japan, we can only assume that the cooperation between procurers and the military or local police in Korea and Taiwan was even closer.

It grew ever closer, especially after the start of the "Special Maneuvers of the Kwantung Army" in 1941. As we have seen, in preparation for the "Special Maneuvers," the Kwangtung Army is said to have attempted to round up twenty thousand Korean comfort women. It appealed to the Government-General of Korea, and eight thousand Korean women are said to have been rounded up and sent to northeastern China. If this was the case, those women were gathered in a very brief period of time, which would have been impossible without extensive assistance from the Government-General.

There were three different methods or levels of impressing laborers: "recruitment" (*boshū*), "official mediation" (*kan assen*), and "requisitioning" (*chōyō*). In the rounding up of comfort women, the most common method was probably "official mediation," in which bureaucrats and the police played prominent roles.

How did things develop after 1942? As the example of Taiwan demonstrates, the Southern Army probably just requested, through the Ministry of War, that the Korea Army round up comfort women. One piece of evidence supporting this assumption can be found in the statement of the Kitamuras, which appeared in the "Psychological Warfare Interrogation Report" (No. 2) discussed above.

The Kitamuras paid a huge sum of money for the twenty-two Korean women they bought. They reported paying between 300 and 1,000 yen per woman; if we assume an average of 500 yen per woman, the figure amounts to approximately 11,000 yen.[39] Business was so slow at the Seoul restaurant the Kitamuras managed that they decided to leave the restaurant's management to a sister-in-law and go to Burma. So how could they have possibly raised such an enormous sum of money? It is inconceivable that they came up with it themselves. They stated that the management of military comfort stations was mediated by the Headquarters of the Korea Army, so they may have been provided with considerable amounts of money from secret funds. Also, around the time they departed, the Headquarters of the Korea Army offered "to furnish any assistance they might require, such as transportation, rations, medical attention, etc." and gave them a letter (to this effect) addressed to various army units.[40] The Korea Army gave these procurers their most comprehensive support.

Conditions in the Last Years of the War

From 1943 onward, the mobilization of Koreans for war intensified sharply. According to Home Ministry documents, the number of Koreans impressed into labor service in 1943 through the mediation of the Government-General alone reached 138,438. In 1944, in addition to the 405,000 Koreans impressed by the Government-General and the 30,000 mobilized by the army, apparently there were another million "new necessary personnel." As the conscription system for Korean men had just gone into operation, the labor shortage became even more acute. In 1944, the Government-General decided to mobilize women on the pretext of "putting to practical use the idle labor power of women." It attempted to institute a comprehensive mobilization system encompassing all new school graduates and unmarried girls and women fourteen years of age and older. The Home Ministry reports that the following situation arose as a result of this program.

> The dispatching of patriotic labor corps is not the same as impressment. Do not follow the example of those who flee from the general recruitment of labor or who take part in unlawful violent riots. The conscription of unmarried women is considered necessary. It is said that some of those mobilized will be made into comfort women and such, but these are absurd rumors. On account of these pernicious rumors, we can expect the labor situation to become increasingly difficult.[41]

From this document we learn that not only were all unmarried girls fourteen and older to be mobilized, but that the rumor that they would be made into comfort women was widespread in 1944.

Between April and August of that year, the first round of conscription examinations were conducted on Korean men. In August, the "female volunteer labor corps order" was issued to put single Korean women between the ages of twelve and forty to work in munitions factories, and this was enough to spread the rumor that all unmarried Korean women were to be made into comfort women. This rumor caused many young women to panic. Families of some economic means withdrew their daughters from school and sent them into hiding in the countryside or hurriedly married them off. In families without means, the rumor gave rise to the following situations.

Kim De-son (a fictitious name) was separated from her parents while still a baby and grew up in her uncle's house. In September 1944, when she was just eighteen years old, her uncle told her that, "it is rumored that recently there have been many people taking away young women."[42] One day, when she arrived home, he told her to hide up under the roof. She hid there for a week. She became very hungry, and when she finally came down to get something to eat, a Japanese man and a Korean man came by. The Korean man told her, "If you go to Japan and work for one year, you can save money." Thinking that this was better than being impressed into service as a comfort woman, she accepted the offer.[43]

However, she was taken to Yangon in Burma. As the rumor that women in the "volunteer labor corps" would be forced to become comfort women spread, many single women from poor families thought getting a job was better than going into the labor corps. In this difficult situation, Kim De-son was deceived and forced to become a comfort woman.

Were There People Who Were Recruited of Their Own Free Will?

As a licensed prostitution system had been introduced into Korea, there were cases of licensed prostitutes becoming comfort women. Among the twenty women taken prisoner in Burma by the U.S. Army, the vast majority had no experience with prostitution, but there were a few who had been prostitutes. In Sergeant Alex Yorichi's report, he notes that only "a few had been connected with {the} 'oldest profession on earth' before."[44]

Yet, as was the case in Japan as well, licensed prostitution was an important source of income for operators. Thus while there were instances in which operators brought their prostitutes with them to the battlefields, they were generally loath to part with their prostitutes. We can't say that unlicensed prostitutes never became comfort women, but this was probably rare because so many of them were afflicted with sexually transmitted diseases. For example, the Inchon branch of the Temporary Line of Communication Headquarters for the Korea Army, which was engaged in transporting troops from the Korea Army to the battlefields in China, reported that, "Since 'social diseases' are wide-spread in Korea, it is essential that {soldiers} be instructed never to have contact with unlicensed Korean prostitutes." The Headquarters ordered all of the units in their barracks to strictly forbid any contact with unofficial Korean prostitutes.[45]

Even if we assume that there were a considerable number of cases in which prostitutes who had finished their periods of service and paid off their debts became landlords, waitresses, or comfort station operators, cases in which women became comfort women of their own free will were rare. And even supposing that they were common, it must be emphasized that, under the system of de facto sexual slavery that went by the name of *kashiza-shiki* (licensed houses of assignation), many women were rendered incapable of making a living any other way. If these women had had opportunities to become workers, professionals, or self-employed businesswomen, there is no reason to expect that any would have chosen to become comfort women. Even when it appears that a woman chose that path of her own free will, that "choice" turns out to have been the result of some form of coercion originating in colonial policies, poverty, or unemployment.

So did the recruitment ad, "An Urgent Call for 'Military' Comfort Women," discovered by a high school teacher in Nagoya, Takahashi Shin, and others really demonstrate that women were recruited of their own free will?[46] This ad stated that they were recruiting tens of able-bodied people aged eighteen to thirty years old "for the Military Comfort Station." The *Mainichi Shinpō* {in which the ad appeared} was a Hangul newspaper (written in the Korean syllabary), so it was unquestionably directed at a Korean audience. We do not, however, find this same type of ad appearing in the paper again, either before or after these two dates. Thus it is impossible to assert that this method of recruiting was a common one. Also, since we can't assume that poor women read newspapers, we should see these ads as directed at brothel operators who had women in their employ. The conclusion we should draw from the fact that these ads appeared in the paper is that the Government-General sanctioned the dispatching of comfort women.

Orders Regarding Travel Permits

To what extent was the Government-General of Korea aware of the illegal activities engaged in by civilian procurers who were rounding up comfort women at the request of the army? Since the local police, in cooperation with the military police, supported procurers when they were rounding up comfort women, the government could not have been unaware. According to criminal law as it was practiced in Korea, it was a serious crime to capture, kidnap, or traffic in people with the intent of sending them overseas or to transport kidnapped or purchased people overseas, so we would expect that the Government-General would have had to exercise strict controls {over travel}. But were these kinds of laws actually enforced?

On August 31, 1937, Vice Minister of the Foreign Ministry Horiuchi Kensuke required that the chiefs of police in each jurisdiction in Korea and Taiwan as well as in Japan issue travel permits to people traveling overseas to prevent "undesirable elements" from going to China in order to profit from the war. The application process for these travel permits generally proceeded as follows.

1. Japanese, Koreans, and Taiwanese hoping to travel to China from Japan or the colonies submit requests for identification papers to the local chief of police.

2. Upon receipt of these requests, the Chief of Police in Japan, Korea, or Taiwan will inquire into each person's nationality, current address, status, occupation, personal history, purpose in traveling, period of stay, and attitudes and behavior in the past. Identification papers will not be issued to people suspected of improper conduct.

3. Except for "people with legitimate reasons needing to get to China immediately," police are directed to withhold their approval of overseas travel.

4. The Chief of Police at the point of departure will not allow people without identification papers or passports to board ships headed for China.[47]

Each woman forced to become a comfort woman was subjected to these inquiries. If the police had investigated in earnest how these women had been rounded up at this juncture, they could not have failed to discover illegal activities. This means that they issued identification papers to these women aware of the illegal activities of procurers.

Frequent Kidnappings

Police controls were extremely haphazard. Yun Myong-suk's research paints the following picture of police enforcement of the relevant laws.

In March 1939, the police of the Government-General of Korea apprehended a man for kidnapping. He had been traveling through farming villages along the Gyongsang Nambuk-to and the Jonra Nambuk-to, claiming that "if the daughters of impoverished farm families struggling to make ends meet" went to Seoul, there was good work for them there. Misleading the young women and their families, he would then sell the women to Korean brothels or to brothels in Peking, Tientsin, Shanghai, or Mudanjiang.[48] He was linked to an organized network buying and selling people, and the number of people he sold into slavery is said to have reached 150. One of his victims received 20 yen and was told to mark the travel documents with her fingerprint because the documents were necessary for her to find a job.[49]

In another kidnapping incident detected around the same time, the kidnapper specialized in seventeen- and eighteen-year-old girls from Korean farming villages. In four years, he succeeded in deceiving approximately 250 girls and selling them in northern and northeastern China. It was also discovered that he had sheaves of blank forms granting him power of attorney for the women in order to acquire identification papers for them.[50] In a separate kidnapping incident discovered in July, official copies of family registers and other required documents had been forged with the cooperation of officials from the Pusan City Family Registry Office and the Notary Office.[51] There were also cases of these kidnappers dispatching prostitutes overseas. Thus only the most egregious criminals were arrested. And in the case of the dispatch of comfort women, since the police had been urgently requested to cooperate by the army, they probably issued identification papers as long as the necessary documents were in order.

Cooperation with the Dispatch of Comfort Women

Not only were police inquiries haphazard, but the Government-General of Korea, responding to the situation in the field, actively encouraged and coordinated the dispatch of comfort women. Local police departments also regulated the movement of comfort women and other travelers through the issuance of identification papers. In giving priority to the army's requests, the police could not also rigorously enforce regulations designed to prevent illegal activities.

During the period of full-scale war in China (1937–1941), the system of regulation operated as follows. First, consulates in each region of China conveyed the requests of the army units in their jurisdictions to the Foreign Ministry. The Foreign Ministry would then send these requests on to the Overseas Affairs Ministry, which would inform the Government-General of Korea. From the Government-General, these requests would be passed down to police departments and then on to provincial governors and police chiefs.

Let's examine the example of a comfort station in Wuhan. On September 14, 1938, with the invasion of Wuhan imminent, representatives from the army, the navy, and the consulate in Shanghai held a meeting and decided on a "General Plan for the Emergency Management of Imperial Subjects Dispatched to Hankow After the Invasion." This document reveals that the return to Wuhan of civilian merchants who served the army was given the highest priority, as was "the dispatch of people to set up military comfort stations." It also notes that travel permits for these people would be issued by army units or by the Special Duty Branch of the army and navy.[52] These guidelines made their way to the Government-General of Korea by the aforementioned route, permission from the police in Korea was received, and comfort women were sent off. Song Shin-do, whose experiences are recounted above, was one of these women. Shortly thereafter, however, a saturation point was reached. At that point, the Consulate General issued the following notice on February 3, 1939.

At present there are 214 bar-restaurants, 19 "cafes," 17 tea houses, 8 high-class restaurants, 220 shops selling sundries. In addition, there are 20 military comfort stations (these figures represent the number of establishments with permission to operate from the line of communications unit, the military police, or this consulate. There are also businesses that haven't opened yet). The trend from now on will be for this number to increase exponentially with each ship that arrives, and we request guidance on this issue. . . . As the aforementioned list of businesses shows, the market is already saturated. . . . You are advised not to allow haphazard travel to China by people yearning for open economic conditions. You are duly requested to make appropriate arrangements {to attend to this matter}.[53]

By the start of 1939, large numbers of imperial subjects thronged to Hankow hoping to strike it rich, and the markets quickly became saturated. The number of military comfort stations reached as high as twenty. The above notice followed the same route through the bureaucracy. Hagiwara Hikozō, Chief of the Korea Section in the Ministry for Overseas Affairs, received the notice from the Foreign Ministry and sent a notice to the Chief of the Foreign Affairs Department of the Government-General of Korea, Matsuzawa Tatsuo, on February 20, 1939, stating that "recently, the governors from each prefecture in Japan received separate copies of a notice to this effect from the Foreign Ministry, so please make the appropriate arrangements."

Upon receiving this notice, the Chief of the Foreign Affairs Department of the Government-General of Korea sent a notice to the Chief of Police of the Government-General of Korea. Thus from March 1939, the dispatch of comfort women to the Wuhan region was controlled by the police.

COMFORT WOMEN DISPATCHED FROM TAIWAN

The Report on Investigations in Taiwan

According to a report on Taiwanese former comfort women, by the end of 1992, fifty-six women who reported that they were comfort women (or were reported by their families, in cases where the women had passed away or disappeared) are considered likely to have been comfort women after investigations by the Taipei Women's Rescue Foundation. It has been confirmed that forty-eight of those fifty-six were, in fact, comfort women.[54] On the whole, these investigations are reliable. Yet even in the testimonies of women whose experiences as comfort women have been confirmed, there are still some problems, as in the case of one woman who testified that there was a television on the ship that transported her.[55] It has been impossible, until recently, to conduct hearings with victims in Taiwan. So keeping the limitations of these materials in mind, I'd like to explore the report in greater detail.

Twenty-eight of the forty-eight comfort women in this study were rounded up between 1942 and 1943. Thus the period immediately after the start of the Asia Pacific War was most active (ten women were rounded up between 1938 and 1941, while six were rounded up in 1944 or 1945).[56] Twenty-four of the forty-eight were between the ages of sixteen and twenty when they were rounded up; seventeen were aged twenty-one to twenty-five, and six were older than twenty-five.[57] Even in Taiwan, the majority of women were minors. Twenty-two women, almost half of the total, were rounded up in the province of Taipei.[58]

Excluding the three women rounded up on the continent and one rounded up in Korea (a Korean woman), twenty-two of the remaining forty-four women were deceived about the nature of the work they would be forced to do.[59] The vast majority of those deceived were told by procurers that they would be "transporting food for [military] cafeterias and bars, doing menial tasks, or working as waitresses and barmaids only, not selling your body," so the women accepted these offers.[60] Others were deceived by promises of nursing jobs or of work cleaning and cooking.

Ten of these forty-four women were rounded up by force, the second most common method of assembling future comfort women. According to a report on Taiwanese former comfort women, five women were assigned by government offices to serve as comfort women. Three women were coerced, under the pretext of becoming nurses, by their uncles or procurers or by the hospitals' chief nurses. There were also cases of women being coerced by stepfathers and procurers. In addition, there were two women who went to the front as nurses and worked as nurses for a period of time before being forced to become comfort women.[61]

There were three women who accepted the offer aware of the nature of comfort women's work, and one who was deceived by a broker and sold.[62] It is unclear how the remaining six women were rounded up.[63]

Nine of forty-four comfort women received advances of between 100 and 500 yen. If we interpret this as trafficking in people, then a total of ten women were sold. Three of those ten realized when they arrived at their destinations that they would be made to perform sexual services and thought they would refuse to do it. But not having the money to repay the cash advanced to them, they had no choice but to resign themselves to the situation. Four women had signed contracts for periods of one year, one year and a half, or one year and eight months. The woman with the year-and-eight-month contract finished her contract and was replaced by another Taiwanese woman, so she was able to return home. But two other women said they were not allowed to return home even though they had completed their contracts.[64]

One of the aforementioned women deceived by offers of work as a nurse came to Tokyo and gave the following testimony.[65] She worked as a nurse at a hospital for four years after graduating from public school (equivalent to Japanese elementary school, though attendance was not compulsory). She responded to the offer of a nursing job because future prospects at the hospital where she was working were not bright. Along with more than ten other women, she was sent to Timor. Though she thought she was going to work as a nurse, she was given an examination for sexually transmitted diseases and then raped by an officer before being put to work in a comfort station. She was seventeen years old at the time.

In the case of Taiwan as well, the fact that half of the women rounded up were minors is important. As in Korea, many women in Taiwan were led off under false pretenses. It is characteristic of the Taiwanese case that nine women acknowledged that they received cash advances. These women were not, however, told that they would be working as comfort women. Aside from these nine women, there were three who responded to offers knowing that they would work as comfort women. One did so in order to pay off loans; another did so rashly, without really thinking about it; and one did so in order to "buy furniture for when she got married."[66] Even these three women, had they had other options to make a living, would probably not have become comfort women.

These forty-four Taiwanese comfort women were sent to Hainan Island (thirteen women), the Dutch East Indies (ten), the Philippines (eight), Burma (six), Guangdong Province (five), Singapore (four), the Portuguese colony of Timor (two), and Okinawa (one) (these figures include some overlapping in cases where women were moved from one place to another).[67]

THE CASE OF CHINA

Methods of Rounding Up Comfort Women in Occupied Territories

What were conditions like in the occupied territories of China, Southeast Asia, and the Pacific? We still don't have much testimony from former comfort women in China, so here I will focus on the recollections of former soldiers. When rounding up comfort women from among the local population, the rear staff or adjutants of the army, division, brigade, or regiment would receive orders from the Expeditionary Forces and execute them with the manpower of the line of communications unit, the accounting section, or the military police. In the occupied territories, unlike in the colonies, the army gave the orders directly. Let's examine several examples.

On April 21, 1941, the 48th Division of the Taiwan Army occupied Foochow. The division didn't bring along its comfort women, so the division staff ordered the line of communications unit to set up a military comfort station.[68] The line of communications unit asked the chief of the military police in Foochow for his cooperation. They offered influential local people rewards and had them round up women.[69]

On May 25, 1944, after the invasion of Luoyang, a second lieutenant in the Accounting Section of the 3rd Tank Division was summoned by the rear staff and ordered to "refurbish a civilian house immediately and create a comfort station for the troops. Then come to Luoyang and gather up some women." Thinking to himself, "you've got to be kidding," he loaded two or three bags of salt onto a truck and went to Luoyang. There he went to two or three establishments and gathered a dozen or so women.[70] This same officer was in charge of rounding up comfort women in Hengyang as well during the summer of 1944. He bought fifteen Chinese women from brothel owners for several bags of salt.[71]

In the fall of 1944, Japanese troops triumphantly entered Baoqing in Hubei Province. Military Police Warrant Officer Yamada Sadamu, who was appointed chief of the military police unit in Baoqing, was asked by the rear staff of the 116th Division to round up comfort women in order to prevent rapes by military personnel. He ordered a Sergeant Major to gather a dozen or so women and turn them over to an adjutant.[72]

In June 1945, the 2nd Independent Mountain Artillery Regiment was massed in the area around Hongqiao in Hubei Province. Hirahara Kazuo, Commander of the 1st Battalion (after the war, he became a Major General in the Ground Self-Defense Force), ordered the establishment of a military comfort station after hearing the opinions of subordinates. The Accounting Section then gathered together six Chinese comfort women. Hirahara describes conditions at the time as follows.

> The largest problem with establishing comfort stations was that the army's paper money suffered a steep decline in value. So the comfort women could not make ends meet with the army money they received from soldiers' monthly salaries. Then we set up a system whereby the Accounting Section at the Battalion Headquarters provided comfort women with daily necessities in return for the army money they earned. I remember that the bulk of the daily necessities given to comfort women were food items or cloth commandeered in the occupied areas. Worried that among the soldiers sent out to requisition these items there were individuals who looted Chinese paper money and valuables to give to the comfort women they visited, I ordered that the goods doled out to comfort women by the Accounting Section be decidedly generous.[73]

It seems clear once again that the battalion commander gave the order to set up a comfort station, and the entire operation was run by the battalion's Accounting Section. It is also important to note that the army provided such daily necessities as food and clothing.

Ordering Village Notables to Gather Women

Next, let's look at the actual nature of the coercion employed. According to the recollections of Battalion Commander Hirahara, the former commander of the garrison stationed in Liangshitang requested that the head of the local organization for maintaining public order provide women. When Hirahara learned of this, he thought, "As a small garrison, we didn't have the ability to manage a comfort station on our own, so we hoped to have the cooperation of the Chinese side. But in some cases, this may have been

coerced."[74] This statement implies that while military units the size of battalions and larger were capable of managing comfort stations and rounding
up comfort women by themselves, smaller units did not have that capabil-
ity. As a result, these smaller units sometimes resorted to rounding up
women by force. The suggestion that there was a tendency at the lower
reaches of the army to use force merits our attention.

It was a common occurrence for garrisons to demand women for the
use of garrison commanders. Saying that it was for the safety of the village,
local notables often offered women. It was normal operating procedure to
request the cooperation of local notables when comfort stations were being
built. Since army orders could not be defied and in order to prevent the
spread of sexually transmitted diseases, many of the women rounded up
were not prostitutes; there were definitely cases of women being rounded
up by force and without their consent.

Another example also comes from the 2nd Independent Mountain
Artillery Regiment. According to the diary of a military physician attached
to the 2nd Battalion, in 1940 in a village near Dongshi in Hubei Province
on the banks of the Yangtze River, local women who were not prostitutes
were rounded up. He describes their first medical examination for sexually
transmitted diseases in the August 11 entry in his diary as follows.

Well, when it came time for her internal examination, she became
more and more embarrassed and wouldn't take off her pants. The
interpreter and head of the organization for maintaining order shouted
at her, and she finally took them off. When I had her lie down on
the bed and began conducting a pelvic exam, she frantically scratched
at my hand. When I looked up, she was crying. It seems that she
cried for a long time after leaving the room.

It was the same with the next young woman, and I got so upset
I wanted to cry as well. I think it was the first time I experienced
them being so embarrassed, but the purpose {of the examination}
being what it was, it was probably natural for them to feel humili-
ated. Did they come along crying the whole way, being told by the
village headman or the head of the organization for maintaining order
that it was for the good of the village?

There may be some among them who accepted the offer because they were told they could make money, but when China loses the war, they will really be pitiful {for having sacrificed themselves for naught}. It's not pleasant to conduct these examinations. This kind of work doesn't appeal to me, and the awareness that I am trampling on their humanity is never far from my mind.[75]

This excerpt indicates clearly what kind of women were being rounded up. This doctor recalls that "the battalion commander consulted with the village headman or the head of the organization for maintaining order, and asked them to round up comfort women locally," but that "it was not a coercive request at all. Everything was left up to their discretion."[76] To local residents, however, wasn't a request from the {Japanese} army tantamount to an order? We should consider these practices as the forced rounding up of women by the village headman or head of the organization for maintaining order, with the army pretending not to know. The women were then forced to work as comfort women.

Medical examinations of twenty-two women between the ages of fifteen and thirty-six concluded that four women were in good health, thirteen were in acceptable health, and five failed. Taking their appearances and attitudes into consideration as well, fifteen women were retained. Ten of those were assigned for soldiers' use, five would be used in the officers' club, and one was reserved for the exclusive use of the battalion commander. The operator who was charged with the task of managing these women was a Korean who had been brought along with the army as an interpreter. These Chinese comfort women were not popular with the soldiers because they did not understand Japanese, so they were replaced two months later with Korean comfort women whom the operator brought from Hankow. The doctor worried that when the army had withdrawn from the area, the (former comfort) women would be despised by the villagers, who would have forgotten the fact that they "had been sacrificed for the good of the village."[77] He wrote in his diary that, though they only worked (as comfort women) for a short time, he was worried about their futures. "This story is not something completely removed from me; it upsets me personally."[78]

There is also the case of a noncommissioned officer from the 13th Railway Regiment, who built a temporary special comfort station south of Yancheng in Henan Province in the summer of 1944. This noncommissioned officer was ordered to set up a comfort station because military discipline had degenerated, so he went to Yancheng where the front lines headquarters was located. There, he was given custody of twenty-five Chinese comfort women and their supervisors, a total of thirty people. He put them aboard two trucks, assigned them bodyguards so they wouldn't flee, and brought them to the special comfort station.

The building housing the comfort station was an estate rented from the village headman. The noncommissioned officer divided the building into six separate establishments and the rooms inside into many small rooms, and then readied the comfort station for business. When the doctor came to perform medical examinations, however, he discovered that "to our surprise . . . every single one of [the good-looking women] was crippled."[79] Since it was a request from the army, which essentially amounted to outright coercion, the head of the organization for maintaining order had sacrificed these women. The women were all around twenty years old. On the first day, soldiers thronged to the comfort station, and officers came by at night. On the second day, it was so busy that the women pleaded to be given some rest because their bodies couldn't stand having to work from 10 in the morning until late into the night.[80]

Impressment During "Subjugation" Operations

Another method of forcibly rounding up comfort women was direct gathering while soldiers were out on "subjugation" operations. Because there have been so few surveys asking former comfort women in China about their experiences, we don't know very much about these cases. But at present, we do have the following testimonies. Wan Aihua was born in Inner Mongolia in 1929. Her family was very poor, and she was sold at age four in Yu District in Shanxi Province. From the age of eleven she participated in resistance movements against the Japanese. In 1943, when arrested by the Japanese army for the third time (she was imprisoned for periods of twenty to twenty-six days), she was gang-raped.[81] This was an instance of gang rape during a fixed prison term.

According to a report on Taiwanese former comfort women, among the forty-eight women interviewed, there were two Chinese women who had lived in Guangdong Province and one who had lived on Hainan Island. These women had been rounded up in those areas, and, given "no reason whatsoever," they were forced to go with soldiers.[82] At present, very few testimonies by former comfort women in China have become available, but when surveys are made, it will likely become clear that many cases are similar to those in the Philippines, which we will examine next.

During the Asia Pacific War, the number of Chinese comfort women sent from China to Southeast Asia was not insignificant. For example, two of the three Chinese former comfort women currently living in Taiwan were sent to Burma. In that period, China was the next largest supply base for comfort women after Korea and Taiwan.

THE CASE OF SOUTHEAST ASIA

The Rounding Up of Comfort Women by the Military

One characteristic of the rounding up of comfort women in Southeast Asia, as in China, was the prominent role played by the military. In the early phases of the invasion of Southeast Asia, army line of communications units were in charge of rounding up comfort women. According to the testimony of a soldier attached to the line of communications unit of the 25th Army (in charge of operations in Malaysia), three line of communications officers stationed in Shingora (the spot where the army landed on the Malay Peninsula) were ordered to go to Bangkok, Thailand.[83] There they had resident Japanese businessmen round up twenty-three prostitutes. They returned to Malaysia with three Thai women who passed the medical examinations for sexually transmitted diseases and took charge of setting up military comfort stations in various regions.[84]

The navy itself was also connected with the rounding up of comfort women. The officers in charge of the comfort stations directly managed by the navy in the cities of Kendari, Amoito, and Baubau in the south of Sulawesi Island in Indonesia rounded up comfort women.[85] In twenty-three comfort stations supervised by the Civilian Affairs Branch, the rounding up of comfort women and negotiation of their employment contracts were conducted by civilian military personnel and members of civilian business groups; then the women were sent along to the various military comfort stations.[86]

Rounding Up Comfort Women in Singapore

There was an ad in the Chinese-language newspaper, *Shōnan Nippō*, "calling for hostesses" (March 5–8, 1942). The ad stated that several hundred "hostesses" aged seventeen to twenty-eight from all ethnic groups were being sought. The pay amounted to more than $150, and those engaged in the "shameful calling" were eligible to apply. Interested parties were told to come to the Raffles Hotel.[87] This was a hotel for officers run by the local line of communications unit. According to the recollections of Fusayama Takao, an officer in the Signal Corps of the Imperial Guard Division (who became a member of the Japan Academy after the war), a military comfort station was opened on February 27. The ad in the *Shōnan Nippō* was probably linked to this event. At any rate, when those in the Headquarters of the 25th Army in charge of the rear staff began recruiting women, many women who had previously had English soldiers as partners responded.[88] In Singapore, comfort women were openly recruited immediately after the occupation. Women having difficulty making ends meet, such as prostitutes, were the first to respond.

These women thought that having one partner per day would be all right, but they cried out in distress when soldiers formed lines and pressed in on them. When they had had intercourse with four or five soldiers, the soldier in charge of the comfort women tried to put a stop to it. But this caused rioting, so he reluctantly "tied the womens' arms and legs to their beds" and forced them to continue.[89] Such was the coercion that occurred.

The Coercion of Local Notables

As we saw in chapter 2, before the invasion of Southeast Asia, the army's Central Command had prepared a plan for the construction of comfort stations that would put an end to rapes and prevent the spread of sexually transmitted diseases. Village headmen were to be charged with the task of rounding up comfort women.

Instances in which local notables were ordered to round up women can be seen throughout Southeast Asia. In May 1942, as a result of an attempted rape committed by a soldier from a company stationed in Aritao in Nueva Vizcaya on the island of Luzon in the Philippines, an adjutant in the Bayombong Battalion ordered that comfort stations be set up for each company. Shimotsu Isamu, a first lieutenant attached to the Battalion Headquarters, traveled around accompanied by an interpreter, meeting with town managers and gathering women. He conducted interviews with the women who had been rounded up and checked on their backgrounds, finally accepting some fifty-odd young, healthy women.[90]

In June 1944, immediately after arriving in the Philippines, the second lieutenant who served as paymaster for the 126th Field Airfield Construction Unit (which had begun building an airfield near the Davao Penal Colony in the Lasang region on the island of Mindanao) visited local notables in Mindanao, taking with him cloth for making dresses. He asked for their aid in rounding up comfort women. One week later, six women were brought to him, and he opened a military comfort station.[91]

In Kuwarapira in Malaya, a company commander in the 11th Infantry Regiment summoned representatives of the chiefs of the local organizations for maintaining peace (who were ethnic Chinese) and ordered them to gather some women. At this time, there were massacres of ethnic Chinese people wherever the Japanese army went, so the representatives, terrified that they would be massacred if they refused, gathered up eighteen widows and other women and turned them over to the commander. The women cried and pleaded with the representatives to allow them to return to their homes.[92] This can only be called coercion.

Women Led Off by Fraudulent Means

There were huge numbers of women led off by fraudulent means. Francisca Napeza Austari, born in Laguna on the island of Luzon in the Philippines, was recruited this way. Sometime in December 1942, she was approached by a *Makapili* (a collaborator with the Japanese army) while washing clothes in a river. She was told, "If you work as a washing woman (for the Japanese army), your salary will be sent back to your family."[93] So she went along with four other women to the area where the Japanese army was stationed. Two of the four were only twelve years old, and they were told that they were too young to wash big, heavy clothes and were sent home. The remaining three were forced to become comfort women. At the time, Francisca Napeza Austari was eighteen years old.[94]

A soldier in the 1st Company of the 32nd Transport Regiment in Tarakan, on the island of Borneo in Indonesia, was told by a comfort woman named Lena in the comfort station there that she was promised that she would be made an office worker in a fisheries company. She was then brought from Menado, on the island of Sulawesi, to Galera and forced to become a comfort woman.[95]

Seizing Women by Force in the Philippines

In the Philippines, large numbers of former comfort women have gone public with their stories. One fact that has come to light through their testimonies is that an extremely large number of women were forcibly seized by the Japanese army. According to the "Written Complaints," almost all of the forty-six victims were forcibly seized by the Japanese army. The youngest among them was ten years old, the oldest was thirty, and a total of thirty-three were minors (in their teens). The following are typical cases gathered from the testimonies of the women I interviewed.[96]

Maria Rosa Luna Henson's father was a large landowner in Angeles on the island of Luzon. Her mother was his maid. In 1942, after the Japanese invasion, when Maria was gathering firewood in an evacuated village, she was raped by a Japanese soldier. She was fourteen years old at the time. The following year, she was riding in a cart pulled by a water buffalo with some members of a guerrilla group resisting the Japanese occupation when they were stopped at a Japanese army checkpoint in the city of Angeles. She was the only one in the group taken away. She was imprisoned in a hospital used as a barracks by the Japanese army. Then she was moved to a building that had once been a rice mill and forced to have intercourse with Japanese soldiers. Since she was subjected to examinations for sexually transmitted diseases once a week, it is probably safe to consider this set-up a military comfort station.

Rosita Pacardo Nacino was born in Iloilo on the island of Panay. In 1942, during the Japanese occupation, her mother died. The following year, her father died of starvation. She was working in a candy factory, but she quit in 1944 to go live with her grandmother in Estancia. Not far from her grandmother's house, she was taken captive by Japanese soldiers. There was a Japanese army barracks about twenty minutes from the house. Rosita Pacardo Nacino was taken to an old ice factory in Estancia, where she was raped by officers, noncommissioned officers, and soldiers, one after another. She was imprisoned in that factory for about one month, and it seems that there were about fifteen other women imprisoned there as well.[97]

These sorts of incidents are one reason for the outbreak of guerrilla activities against the Japanese army. In the Philippines, where the Japanese army regarded the Filipino population as enemies, incidents of the forcible seizure of women were particularly numerous.

Seizing Women by Force in Indonesia

The forcible seizure of women was not uncommon in Indonesia as well. According to Ōmura Tetsuo's research, which is based on Dutch military documents, in the first half of 1943 in the city of Pontianak on the island of Kalimantan, the commander of the naval detachment issued an "order banning the keeping of concubines" by Japanese residents, in addition to ordering the forced internment of local residents who had sexual relations with Japanese. Women rounded up by the Naval Special Police Corps were put to work in three comfort stations reserved for naval use and five or six comfort stations reserved for civilian use.[98]

In 1944, Japanese comfort women on the island of Anbon Pulau were sent to the rear because of the worsening war conditions. In August, comfort stations with local women were also closed. According to the recollections of an officer in the Naval Special Police Corps, however, military personnel continued to commit crimes, so military comfort stations were set up once more on the advice of the senior staff of the Headquarters for the 4th South Fleet (more accurately, this was probably the 25th Special Naval Base Headquarters). A list of women with experience as comfort women, prostitutes, women rumored to be prostitutes, and women who wanted to become comfort women was drawn up. There were negotiations with these women, but "a certain degree of coercion was inevitable."[99] Since it was considered unseemly for the Special Police Corps, who were in change of maintaining order, to take too prominent a role in rounding up comfort women, their role was limited to cooperation. An adjutant took charge of these tasks, and the Political Affairs Corps (the civilian police) rounded up the women. According to the account related to this officer by the civil administrator charged with carrying out these instructions, when the women whose names were on the list were assembled and put aboard a ship in Saparua, local residents rushed to the port and screamed, "Give back our daughters! Give back our daughters!"[100] The women rounded up were Eurasian (in this case, women of mixed Caucasian and Indonesian ancestry) and Indonesian.

Let's consider another case that overlaps somewhat with the previous one. According to the recollections of Sakabe Yasumasa, the paymaster officer attached to the 25th Special Naval Base Headquarters, after the Japanese comfort women on the island of Anbon were sent home, the staff of the Headquarters drew up a plan to open four new comfort stations with one hundred comfort women "procured locally."[101] The plan was to issue a proclamation declaring that "Japanese military personnel involved in rapes will be severely punished," to "encourage the divulging of secret information" by local residents, and, with the help of the local civilian police, to gather together women "who will become friendly with Japanese military personnel." Attractive women among that group who were not infected with sexually transmitted diseases would be chosen to work as comfort women. Sakabe describes how he "felt depressed listening to the voices of the young Indonesian women crying out over and over again at the club."[102]

All across Southeast Asia and the Pacific, there were numerous cases of the forcible seizure of local residents for use as comfort women. Furthermore, in the case of Indonesia, there were also women being taken overseas to other islands, Burma, or the Philippines. Indonesia ranked after Korea, Taiwan, and China as a source of comfort women.

Chapter Four

The Lives Comfort Women Were Forced to Lead

MANAGEMENT AND CONTROL IN PRACTICE

Army Supervision and Control

The supervision and control of military comfort stations was the responsibility of such authorities as the rear staffs, management sections of the armies' headquarters in the field, the line of communications officers in charge of comfort operations, the paymasters or adjutants of each regiment or division, or the military police. According to General Imamura Hitoshi's recollections of his years as commander of the 5th Division, for example, as soon as the Headquarters of the 22nd Army in Nanning was formed in the middle of February 1940, 150 comfort women in the charge of approximately 15 procurers arrived.[1] The Chief of the Management Section of the Headquarters of the 22nd Army thereupon told an assembled group of the commander of the 5th Division and the commanders of the various brigades that the Management Section would "make arrangements for the buildings," but that he wanted the imperial guard brigade stationed far away to handle the distribution of comfort women among the brigades.[2] In the 5th Division, an adjutant was ordered to research methods of administering military-managed comfort stations. After discussions with the Management Section, it was decided that a system granting each soldier one ticket {to enter the comfort station} per day would be implemented.[3]

At comfort stations directly managed by the military, the army oversaw every aspect of operations. The army strictly supervised and controlled the administration of military comfort stations managed by civilians as well. Those who gave the orders for this supervision and control and who should have borne responsibility for them were the commanders of the various armies in the field. We have already seen that this system was created and

Soldiers awaiting their turns at a military comfort station in China.
MURASE MORIYASU, WATASHI NO JŪGUN CHŪGOKU SENSEN
(MY WAR EXPERIENCE AT THE CHINA THEATER)
(OSAKA: JAPAN'S BULLETIN PUBLISHER'S CENTER, 1987)

managed with the approval and on the orders of the Army Central Command. Here, I would like to examine the concrete details of the army's supervision and control.

The Construction of Military Comfort Stations

The decision to set up a military comfort station was made by unit commanders, and adjutants ordered paymaster officers to take charge of establishing them. The first thing the army procured was a building to house the comfort station. The establishment of comfort stations was restricted to areas and buildings designated by the army, but when there were a large number of buildings available, those requisitioned for use as comfort stations were often hotels, restaurants, shops, large mansions, or similar buildings with a large number of rooms. There are also cases of schools and Buddhist temples being made into military comfort stations because of their many rooms. Another requirement for buildings eligible to be made into comfort stations was that they be conveniently located for soldiers and officers.

According to Colonel Nagasawa Kenichi, a military doctor attached to the line of communications unit headquarters in Hankow, the securing of buildings for military comfort stations was one of the duties of the line of

communications unit. In October 1938, a line of communications construction corps that arrived in Hankow immediately after the occupation
began was ordered to secure a location that could accommodate about three
hundred comfort women.[4] The corps made a search for suitable buildings
and secured an area named Sekkeiri, where sixty-eight two-story buildings
were clustered together.[5] This district was surrounded by a fence and conveniently located, so it became a military comfort station.[6]

The sketch on the preceding page by Murakami Sennosuke clearly con-
veys a sense of the Sekkeiri comfort station in Hankow.

Military comfort stations were usually set up in locations removed from
the soldiers' barracks, but there were also instances of them being built within
the barracks. For example, in June 1944, the 126th Field Airfield Construction Unit, which was building an airfield near the Davao Penal Colony on
the island of Mindanao, refurbished the innermost barracks in the camp,
turning the first floor into a PX and the second floor into a comfort station.[8]

When there was not an appropriate building nearby, a new one would
be built. In Okinawa, from 1944 on, numerous military comfort stations
were built for the large number of troops massed in preparation for the
impending American attacks. For example, the "Field Diary" of the 6th
Fort Construction Company, which was building a fort on Iejima, records
that for several days beginning May 24, the soldiers set to the task of constructing new buildings for a military comfort station.[9] And according to
the "Field Diary" of the 56th Airfield Battalion Shigenobu Group at the
northern airfield on the island, December 24 found the troops busy turning the military club into a military comfort station.[10]

Once a building was secured, the process of making it into a comfort
station began. Soldiers with carpentry and plastering skills refurbished the
interiors, dividing the space into small rooms and putting in bathrooms,
washrooms, and reception desks. Then each room was furnished with a
bed, blankets, and disinfectant liquid.

Sketch of a comfort station by Murakami Sennosuke,
from an exhibition published as
Yasen yobi byōin 'Aru eiseihei no shiki'
(THE PRIVATE MEMOIRS OF A HYGIENE CORPSMAN), 1992[7]

In the spring of 1945, an adjutant and a military doctor (a first lieu-tenant) in a unit under the command of the 23rd Brigade stationed at Qiongshan near Haikou on Hainan Island were charged with the task of setting up a temporary military comfort station. This doctor describes his decision to refurbish a barracks to house the fifty mobile comfort women referred to as the "special platoon."

> I called together all the people in each company with construction experience as carpenters or cabinetmakers. The barracks had one large common room, which we split up into fifty smaller rooms with antechambers. The rooms were divided into ones for officers' use, ones for noncommissioned officers' use, and ones for soldiers' use. Large wooden beds were brought in, bedding was prepared, and every detail was carefully arranged.[11]

The army did not merely prepare buildings; it even provided beds and bed-ding for military comfort stations.

The Appearance of the Rooms

There were many different kinds of rooms in military comfort stations. In the Sekkeiri comfort stations in Hankow, at first the rooms were separated from one another only by hanging woven rush mats. The bedding and tableware were requisitioned (looted) from the abandoned homes of Chi-nese civilians.[12] Later, operators put up wooden plank walls, laid down tatami, installed lattice doors, and acquired brightly colored bedding and furnishings from recently opened department stores in Hankow such as Daimaru and Takashimaya.[13]

Military comfort stations close to the front lines were completely dif-ferent. At a comfort station in the suburbs of Changsha, the rooms were about 5 square meters (about 6 square yards), each with a futon and one square meter of dirt floor.[14] According to the recollection of an orderly attached to an adjutant in the 110th Field Artillery Regiment, sometime around February 1941, the interiors of the rooms in the comfort station at Shijiazhuang in China could be described as follows.

> The rooms were divided into small individual rooms. When you opened the door, there was only a small space with a cramped dirt

floor. Since the comfort women lived in there, their possessions and furniture were all crowded into the space. A strange smell permeated the narrow rooms.[15]

These were the kinds of rooms comfort women were stuffed into–many so small that when a futon or bed and a tiny bit of furniture was added, the rooms were completely filled. There were cases of rooms being eight mats in size {by current standards, a mat is three feet by six feet (eighteen square feet)}, but usually they were between two or three mats and four and a half mats in size. Even closer to the front lines, the better comfort stations were set up in ruined civilian homes. There were also comfort stations where "a simple wooden fence was put up and inside a rush mat was laid down. It was just like a communal latrine."[16]

The Registration of Comfort Women

When comfort women arrived in Hankow, they had to bring the necessary documents and present themselves to the line of communications officer in charge of comfort operations. Then the following inquiries and registration procedures were conducted.

1. A noncommissioned officer examined the comfort woman's photograph, a copy of her family registry, her written pledge, her parental consent form, her permit from the police, her identification papers from local officials where she lived, and similar documents.

2. Then he filled out a prescribed personal examination form, recording her personal history, her guardians' addresses and occupations, the makeup of her family, the amount of cash advanced to her or her family. This information was later supplemented with reports of such events as her departure from the business or a hospitalization. Comments on her character, such as "she has a habit of drinking," were also added as time passed.

3. A copy of the personal examination form was sent to the military police.[17]

In short, not only was the army well aware of how comfort women had been brought there, it was managing the entire process. The situation in

Manila was the same. According to a district line of communications unit document entitled "Rules for Authorized Restaurants and Houses of Prostitution in Manila" (dated 1943), which was among the materials captured by the Allied Army and compiled in "Daily Amenities in the Japanese Armed Forces," comfort station operators had to submit a request for permission to open for business, a business plan, a written pledge, a list of the comfort women's birth dates, family registers, and cash advances in order to receive the necessary permission for the women to work as comfort women.[18]

Regulations for the Use of Comfort Stations

The army formulated minutely detailed regulations for the use of comfort stations. The "Regulations for the Use of the Soldiers' Club" for the 13th Independent Infantry Brigade Chūzan Garrison stationed in Zhongshan, Guangdong Province is a typical example of the regulations for garrisons stationed in small towns.[19] I have quoted the appropriate clauses from this document, which runs to twenty clauses. Here, the cafeteria reserved for the garrison is referred to as "Soldiers' Club No. 1," and the comfort station reserved for their use is called "Soldiers' Club No. 2."

CLAUSE NO. 3—The unit's adjutant is in charge of supervising, controlling, and advising the management of the soldiers' clubs to ensure smooth and proper management.

CLAUSE NO. 4—The medical officer (military doctor) attached to the unit is responsible for hygiene facilities in the soldiers' clubs and the implementation of hygiene services. In addition, he is in charge of all hygiene-related aspects of the health, food preparation, and schedules of families, working women, and employees of the soldiers' clubs.

CLAUSE NO. 5—The unit's paymaster is responsible for all matters relating to accounting for the soldiers' clubs.

CLAUSE NO. 18—Those visiting the clubs should be on their guard to prevent leaks of secret information [espionage prevention].

CLAUSE NO. 19—If those visiting the soldiers' clubs hear or see that something is amiss with the managers, prostitutes, facilities, and such, they should report it to the adjutant of the unit.[20]

Thus, even in cases where operators ran the military comfort stations, the army decided on or participated in deciding on everything from the rules for use, fees, hours of use, days on which each unit could use the facilities, and details of hygiene management to the accounting. Clauses 13 to 17 deal exclusively with the rules for using the military comfort station referred to as "Soldiers' Club No. 2."

CLAUSE NO. 13—Eating and drinking in Soldiers' Club No. 2 is forbidden.

CLAUSE NO. 14—Fees are to be paid in cash in advance.

CLAUSE NO. 15—As a rule, outings by prostitutes are forbidden.

CLAUSE NO. 16—The following are not allowed to use Soldiers' Club No. 2:

1. people who try to use it at times other than their appointed hours;

2. people who are not properly dressed;

3. people who are extremely drunk;

4. people who are likely to bother others;

5. people not mentioned in Clause No. 17, and those accompanying them.

CLAUSE NO. 17—The use of Soldiers' Club No. 2 is restricted to military personnel and civilian employees of the army. If accompanied by an officer, however, local people [civilians] are permitted to use Soldiers' Club No. 1.[21]

According to the schedule for the use of Soldiers' Club No. 2, enlisted men could use it from 9:30 A.M. to 3:30 P.M.; noncommissioned officers could use it from 4:00 P.M. to 8:00 P.M.; and officers could use it from 8:30 P.M. until morning.[22] Only officers could use it late at night, and only they could stay overnight. The fee for thirty minutes was 6 Chinese yen for enlisted men, 9 Chinese yen for noncommissioned officers, and 11 Chinese yen for officers.[23] The military comfort station was thus more accessible to noncommissioned officers than to enlisted men, and more accessible to officers than to non-commissioned officers. And the schedule was set up so that enlisted men, noncommissioned officers, and officers would never overlap at the comfort station. Besides this sort of arrangement, in many other places there were comfort stations reserved for the exclusive use of officers as well as comfort women reserved for the exclusive use of unit commanders.

The rules governing the use of comfort stations for personnel from the 2nd Independent Heavy Siege Artillery Battalion stationed in Changchow in 1938 specified that Chinese comfort women be paid 1 Japanese yen, Korean comfort women be paid 1 Japanese yen and 50 sen, and Japanese comfort women be paid 2 Japanese yen (noncommissioned officers and officers paid twice these amounts).[24]

Why Were the Rules for the Use of Comfort Stations So Strict?

The reason the rules for the use of comfort stations were so strict was because they were meant to serve contradictory functions; at the same time that comfort stations were set up as places for sexual comfort and self-indulgence, they were also supposed to help maintain military discipline. Additionally, while they were supposed to prevent the spread of sexually transmitted diseases, they were also supposed to keep a vigilant eye out to prevent espionage.

Accordingly, the army made operators submit detailed reports about who used the military comfort stations. For example, according to the "Regulations for Going Out on the Town and Soldiers' Clubs" (dated 1944) of the Tōyama Unit of the 13th Independent Infantry Brigade, the operator had to submit daily reports on the number of soldiers serviced, the amount of money earned, and the number of condoms used by each comfort woman.[25]

Thus, even in cases in which comfort stations were run by civilians, the actual managers were army personnel and the operators were subordinated to the army.

WHAT WERE COMFORT WOMEN'S DAILY LIVES LIKE?

Coerced Sexual Intercourse

Discussions {of the comfort women issue} in Japan have thus far prob-
lematized the coercion used when comfort women were rounded up, but
another and more important issue is the treatment and coercion they were
subjected to in the comfort stations. It goes without saying that forced sexual intercourse is what awaited the women rounded up by the methods
outlined in chapter 3. Before that, though, they were subjected to examinations for sexually transmitted diseases by military doctors. Kim Hak-sun,
who was taken to Peking by her foster father after she graduated from *kiseng*
{traditional Korean entertainer} school and then taken to a military comfort station on an army truck, described her first night there as follows.

An officer came into the room and led me into the room next door,
separated from the first by a cloth curtain . . . I struggled against him,
but he dragged me into the neighboring room by force. The officer
tried to undress me while he was hugging me. I resisted, but my
clothes were eventually all torn off. In the end, he took my virginity. That night I was violated twice by the officer.[26]

This took place in 1941, when she was seventeen years old. Thereafter she
was forced to have intercourse with soldiers every afternoon. After subjugation operations, the number of soldiers using the comfort station would
be especially high. She was forced to have intercourse with seven or eight
men in one day.[27]

The numbers of men comfort women were forced to have intercourse
with in comfort stations reserved for officers' use was not large. But in
comfort stations reserved for noncommissioned officers and enlisted men,
there were cases of comfort women forced to have intercourse with as
many as twenty or thirty men a day. According to Katsuki Kyūji, who
operated a military comfort station in Burma, there were times when comfort women were forced to have intercourse with sixty men in a single day.
After that, though, the women had to rest for about three days (according
to an interview with the author).[28] Even if such cases were exceptions, they

must have caused the women terrible agony. Even during the "innumer-able times when {her} genitals were swollen," Li Yong-suk could not re-fuse.[29] This was because the sex-starved soldiers were bloodthirsty, and if she refused, she would be brutally assaulted.

These conditions in the military comfort stations even seemed grotesque to some soldiers. An officer gives the following description of the condi-tions in a military comfort station in Nha-trang in Vietnam.

> It was a comfort station often talked about. The none-too-simple reality of it was that, rather than being stimulated, I felt I had been exposed to some grotesque world. Standing in line in broad daylight, doing it right under the nose of the people waiting for their turn, and the vivid image of men coming out one after another with their pants still half open. This ritual proceeded in conveyer-belt fashion in an atmosphere of a particular sort of tension, and rather than rais-ing my spirits, made me, who knew nothing of the forbidden fruit of the tree of knowledge, flinch.[30]

Even officers shrank back, trembling, from what they saw at military com-fort stations. It's only natural that comfort women were terrified of the sol-diers who lined up and crowded in on them. Yet it was impossible for them to refuse. Li Yong-suk describes how she "always had to curl up her body for fear that something she did would be cause for the manager to beat her."[31] Mun Pil-gi describes how "there were many [drunk] soldiers who," saying if she didn't do exactly what they said, "stuck their swords into the tatami and had intercourse standing up."[32] When the women wouldn't accept any more, soldiers demanding sex or operators who wanted to make large profits brutally assaulted them, coercing them into it.

Drunken Violence

There were considerable numbers of soldiers who got drunk and became violent at military comfort stations. Here I'd like to examine several inci-dents that became serious issues. One occurred in November 1941. A ser-geant entered a military comfort station without buying a ticket and beat a comfort woman who refused to have intercourse with him. In another incident, a soldier went to a military comfort station in Wuchang, and when a comfort woman refused to let him in because the comfort station was closed, he became angry, dragged her out into the street, and beat her. In February 1942, a corporal entered a comfort station with Chinese comfort women, drew his sword, and went on a rampage. Another sergeant drew his sword, hacked through the wooden fence around the comfort station, and screamed at the operator and comfort women. A reserve second lieutenant went to a military comfort station in the middle of the night. When he was refused entry, he caused a disturbance at the reception desk. (All of the above incidents from the "List of Illegal Activities Engaged in by Army Personnel and Civilian Army Employees," November 1941 and February 1942, issued by the Headquarters of the Military Police Stationed in Central China.)[33]

All this violence was committed under the influence of alcohol. These incidents happened to have been recorded because they were so egregious. But it was rare for soldiers' coercion inside individual rooms to become an issue. Even in those cases of violent behavior that came to light, the perpetrators were not severely punished. They were let off with only strong reprimands or house arrest.

Did Comfort Women Have Days Off?

As we saw in the previous section, according to the regulations for use, comfort women were forced to have intercourse from morning until late at night with enlisted men, noncommissioned officers, and officers, in that order. When officers stayed overnight, the comfort women were completely restricted twenty-four hours a day.

Comfort women were not given any special days off, or, when they were, they were given approximately one or two days off per month. In the "Regulations for Internal Affairs While Stationed in Changchow" (March 1938)[34] of the 2nd Independent Heavy Artillery Siege Battalion and the "Internal Regulations" (December 1944)[35] of the Yama 3475 Unit in Okinawa, comfort women were only given one day off per month. In the regulations for garrison units on Masbate Island in the Philippines, each unit was allotted one day between Sunday and Friday for using the comfort station. Comfort women were only allowed to rest during the afternoon on Saturday (on Saturday mornings they were subjected to examinations for sexually transmitted diseases, and from 5:00 P.M. to 7:30 P.M. they were forced to have intercourse with noncommissioned officers; after that officers were allowed to use the comfort station).[36]

Remuneration of Comfort Women

Soldiers using military comfort stations usually paid a fee. Therefore, to soldiers, going to a military comfort station was not much different from purchasing the services of a prostitute at a civilian brothel in Japan or the colonies. Yet the plight of comfort women was far worse than the worst conditions endured by prostitutes.

The money paid by soldiers did not only go to the comfort women. The army set the percentage of the fees that would go to the women. According to the "Regulations for the Management of Comfort Facilities and Inns" (1943) issued by the Malay Army Administrative Inspector, comfort women's percentage was as follows: 1) those who received cash advances of over 1,500 yen received 40 percent or more of the fees; 2) those who received cash advances of less than 1,500 yen received 50 percent or more of the fees; and 3) those who received no cash advances received 60 percent or more of the fees.[37] As these regulations were intended to protect comfort women, the rates were even regarded as good percentages. The rules stipulated that 3 in every 100 yen the women received was to be put toward savings, and over two thirds of the money comfort women received was applied to the repayment of their cash advances. In addition, the rules specified that if comfort women became pregnant or fell ill while working, they would bear 50 percent of the costs of medical treatment. For other illnesses, the women had to bear 100 percent of these costs.

This was the best-case scenario for comfort women. In many cases, the costs of clothing, cosmetics, and other daily necessities were illegally added to their debts, and almost all of their share (40 or 60 percent) was garnished to pay off those debts. Even in cases where comfort women had no debts, on the pretext of forced savings or contributions to the national defense, not a few comfort women received no pay whatsoever.

According to the women's testimonies, out of nineteen Korean comfort women, seven were paid money by operators, but after they settled their accounts they had nothing left. Five of those women were never paid, while four put their pay in the charge of the operator. Only three of the nineteen received cash. According to their testimonies, the vast majority of comfort women received no pay. Among Filipina comfort women, there was only one who said she received one peso.[38] Thus, looking at the suit filed by Filipina women, we see that there were many cases of imprisonment and gang rape that did not take the form of comfort stations where fees were paid. And there were many instances of soldiers not paying.

On the other hand, in the case of Taiwanese women, forty-four out of forty-eight received their pay in cash. There were four women who didn't receive payment this way. According to this survey, eight of the forty-eight women sent money back to their families, while nine saved their money in bank or postal savings accounts.[39]

It has come to light that the original record of the military postal savings account of one Korean former comfort woman, Mun Ok-chu (Japanese name: Fumihara Yoshiko/Gyokushu), is on record in the Kumamoto Savings Office Center. She left a military comfort station in 1941, but in 1942 she signed up again to earn money and help her mother.[40] Between March 1943 and September 1945, she saved 26,145 yen, which earned 197 yen in interest during that period.[41] That amounts to monthly savings of 843 yen. She says that in addition to this sum, she sent 5,000 yen back to her parents in the countryside. She was able to save these amounts because she didn't receive a cash advance and because soldiers heading for the front gave her extra money. Mun Ok-chu, however, is still unable to withdraw this money.

According to the memoirs of a soldier who fought in Burma, comfort women could occasionally be seen wandering around in the hills and fields, following the army escape from attacks by the Allied Forces. A paymaster recorded the following description.

> They followed along behind my unit as we went along the road leading out of Kalow and heading across the mountains. At some point, the four or five women ended up falling behind again. We immediately understood that they were women who had come to sell their bodies to Japanese soldiers. They were not just Korean women; there were Japanese women among them too. . . . They carried large pieces

of luggage on their backs. The heavy burden they carried in knap-
sacks, in bundles wrapped in cloth, and in trunks hefted on their backs
was military currency from the Imperial Army in Burma. They
wouldn't let anyone carry these things for them and insisted on carrying them themselves. They practically crawled over the ground,
backs bent over under the weight.[42]

Not only did those who saved their money take huge losses when their
old yen were converted to new yen and inflation soared after the war, but
those born in the colonies, like Mun Ok-chu, were unable to withdraw
their money after the war. Also, those women who were forced to accept
military currency for their pay lost everything because after the defeat, military currency was worthless.

Under Strict Surveillance

It was very difficult for comfort women to flee from military comfort stations. This was because the army and operators kept them under surveillance. It was no simple matter to leave. Operators were not likely to make
the foolish mistake of losing the comfort women who were their key source
of income. Also, to the army, comfort women were very important "materiel," and they were "prohibited from going out except in specially designated areas."[43]

Sentries were stationed in the areas around comfort stations. For example, in Xihe, where the 1st Battalion of the 3rd Field Artillery Regiment
was stationed, there was a miniature Japan Town and a comfort station in
one corner of the fort, and sentries were posted at the entrances.[44]

At the military comfort station in the city of Iloilo on the island of Panay
in the Philippines, there was a rule that operators were to "strictly control"
the outings of comfort women. The times and places of the comfort
women's walks were also controlled. They were only allowed out for walks
for two hours between 8:00 A.M. and 10:00 A.M., and they were only allowed
to walk around in an area about the size of one city block with a park in
the center.[45]

It goes without saying that when comfort women were taken to occupied territories outside their own countries, it was especially difficult for

them to flee. Ha Sun-nyo, who once fled from a comfort station in Shanghai, gives the following description of her experience.

> It was winter, about a year after I came to Shanghai. In the midst of the falling snow, I fled from the comfort station. Just as I reached the end of the ricksha's route, night fell. Not knowing where someone who'd fled should go and not understanding the language, I just curled up and tried to sleep. But I kept waking up, afraid that any moment someone would find me and take me back to the comfort station. Finally, the sun rose without me getting much sleep. No matter how hard I thought, I couldn't think of a place where I could go. With no other options, I quietly crept back into the kitchen of the comfort station. When I boiled some rice and set it down on a low table, the manager came in and told me not to eat. When I sat down and ate anyway, he beat me severely, calling me the bitch who took off.[46]

Comfort women in foreign countries couldn't speak the local language and stood out because their customs and habits were different. Also, in war zones in China or areas with a lot of guerrilla activity such as the Philippines, there was the danger that Korean comfort women would be mistaken for enemies and killed. Furthermore, even if they did manage to hide themselves among the local population, they had no way to get home because in order to travel through Japanese occupied territory, one needed the permission of the Japanese army.

What about local women in occupied areas who were made into comfort women in their own countries? Let's examine the case of Filipina comfort women as a typical example of the situation local women faced.

Maria Rosa Luna Henson was imprisoned in the center of the city of Angeles on the island of Luzon for approximately nine months between April 1943 and January 1944. During this time, she became pregnant and suffered a miscarriage. She was guarded, so escaping was difficult. The thing that finally allowed her to escape was a guerrilla attack on the comfort station.[47]

In 1944, Rosita Pacardo Nacino was imprisoned in an old ice factory in Estancia on the island of Panay. A typical day for her entailed getting up between 7:00 and 8:00 in the morning, lying in the sun for a few minutes, washing her face, and then making breakfast for the soldiers and her guards.

After the soldiers were done eating, she would wash the dishes and then eat her own breakfast. It would be 3:00 by the time she had cleaned the rice, finished cleaning and doing the laundry, and prepared lunch. From that time on, she would be forced to have intercourse with soldiers. After dinner, beginning around 8:00 P.M., she would have to have intercourse with more soldiers. She says that hygiene controls were effective and the soldiers wore condoms. Because she was always guarded and the windows were too small, she wasn't able to escape.[48]

Amonita Balajadia was kidnapped by soldiers from a garrison in Santiago in Isabela, then imprisoned and gang-raped. When she resisted, she was beaten until liquid dripped from her left ear, leaving her hearing permanently impaired. In the room where she was kept, there was a simple bed, a desk, and a typewriter. An officer slept in the bed, and she was forced to sleep on the floor. About a week later, while the officer was sleeping, she slipped out of the room, made her way through a barbed wire barrier, and crawled back to her mother's house.[49] This is a clear example of a woman imprisoned as a comfort woman and reserved for the exclusive use of an officer.

Economic and Psychic Shackles

For comfort women born in the colonies, one reason they couldn't flee was that they were made into indentured slaves by the cash advances extended to them. The army directed operators to make comfort women work off their loans. But it didn't intercede when operators engaged in practices that compounded comfort women's loans, such as charging them interest, adding to their debts the amount of income lost when they were ill and couldn't work, and lending them money to pay illegally inflated prices for clothing and cosmetics. For example, Colonel Nagasawa Ken'ichi, a military doctor, relates the following account of a comfort woman with debts who was never given any cash.

> Accordingly, she took out loans from the operator or the bookkeeper to buy daily necessities. These sorts of loans were not recorded in the ledger, so to get the money back, the operator would, for example, record that she had received only eight guests when she had received ten. He would force her to repay the loan at high interest rates by forfeiting the fees from the two additional customers. The line of

communications unit's supervisory eye didn't extend to this level, so in reality, these practices were overlooked.[50]

Under these conditions of increasing indebtedness, comfort women's spirits were shackled and their activities constrained. In the cases of comfort women who had contracts for a certain length of time, they were supposed to be able to return home when their contract period had expired and they had paid back their loans, but there were many who had to give up their hopes of going home because they had no means of transport. For example, in June 1943, the Headquarters of the 15th Army in Burma approved the return home of women who had finished paying off their debts. Some of them were able to return, but the Korean comfort women of the 114th Regiment were not allowed to, purportedly because of the military situation. The comfort women who wanted to return home because they had fulfilled their contracts ended up being "persuaded to remain."[51]

The Habitual Use of Drugs to Escape from Torment

Many comfort women came to rely on drugs to escape the physical pain and mental anguish of their daily lives in military comfort stations.

One Hygiene Sergeant heard the following story from a Korean comfort woman who came to the front lines in Hengyang from northern China following the army in 1944.

> I was deceived by an agent from the Korean Peninsula. I thought that comfort for the army meant comforting the troops by dancing and singing, and that would be all right. And the agent told me the same thing. When we crossed the border into China, [he] ordered me to "Take customers." Without understanding what "taking customers" meant, I went to a customer's house. With no warning, they raped me. I became desperate. One after another, so many of them. And then the soldiers came one after another, and I had to {have intercourse with them}. When it is busy, I just lie down on my back, eating rice balls with my legs spread apart, and the soldiers come and mount me and leave, mount me and leave. Finally, I am beyond pain. From the waist down I get numb and lose all feeling. It's a struggle just getting up each day. When the feeling [in my lower body] returns

little by little, my legs cramp up and my abdomen gets cramped as well. There's a heavy, dull pain that lasts all day. I know that if I rested for two or three days, it would get better. But customers come one after another, so I can't rest. When people talk about a living hell, this is exactly what they mean.[52]

Because of her pain, this comfort woman ended up using drugs regularly. When she was transferred to central China, the influence of the Chinese New Life Movement, which aimed at the eradication of drugs, made it impossible for her to get drugs. So she went to the medical office and asked for morphine injections. With the justification that she was "doing her part for the army," they gave her the injections.[53]

In November 1941, a Hygiene Sergeant was arrested when he tried to give morphine from army supplies to a comfort woman who had asked for it. He received a punishment of thirty days' imprisonment (also cited above, "List of Illegal Activities Engaged in by Army Personnel and Civilian Army Employees"). Also, a Hygiene Sergeant arrested in December had given a miserable comfort woman the tens of doses of morphine she'd asked for over a period of more than five months.[54]

The Transmission of Sexually Transmitted Diseases to Comfort Women

Despite regular examinations for sexually transmitted diseases, comfort women's risk of contracting a disease was high. Almost all comfort women who had no previous experience with prostitution were not infected with sexually transmitted diseases at the outset {of their ordeals}. They were infected with diseases by soldiers at military comfort stations. According to their testimonies, seven of nineteen comfort women became infected with sexually transmitted diseases.

According to the medical examinations conducted on comfort women in Nanking, Wuhu, Jintan, Zhenjiang, Chao Xian, and Lishui by the 15th Division in February 1943, 2.5 percent of the Japanese comfort women failed, 4.6 percent of the Korean comfort women failed, and 11 percent of the Chinese women failed.[55]

Even if they passed, it didn't mean they didn't have a sexually transmitted disease. This is because if they had a mild case of a disease, they were forced to work anyway. A military doctor whose specialty was obstetrics states that there were almost no uninfected comfort women in China during the Asia Pacific War, so those with mild cases were forced to keep working while they were being treated, and "it was a matter of requiring the soldiers to use condoms."[56] The examinations for sexually transmitted diseases conducted on comfort women who passed through Qiongshan on Hainan Island were "mere formalities-everyone passed" because the two attending physicians were not gynecologists.[57] In April 1943, when Hara Tōru, an officer-in-training from the Army Hygiene Department, conducted examinations for sexually transmitted diseases in Huaiyin, he passed all but one of nine comfort women. But on his "List of Examination Results," he noted that "even with those who passed, preventative measures should always be taken" and urged soldiers to keep this in mind.[58]

Soldiers also underwent examinations for sexually transmitted diseases, but these were only conducted once a month. And, as mentioned above, officers and noncommissioned officers who contracted sexually transmitted diseases often concealed their condition. Thus, thanks to military comfort stations, sexually transmitted diseases spread among soldiers and comfort women. For comfort women, contracting a disease from soldiers was a terrifying thing. And there were many soldiers who, reasoning that since they didn't know when they were going to die, getting a sexually transmitted disease was no big deal, would set upon comfort women without using condoms. Mun Pil-gi "tried threatening soldiers," telling them, "if they didn't use a condom, I would report them to an officer; or persuading them that it would be bad for us both if we got a sexually transmitted disease, so I want you to use a condom."[59] Mun Ok-chu remarked in regard to soldiers who didn't use condoms that, "I would kick at those soldiers' groins and refuse [to have intercourse], and then if they didn't listen to what I said, I would report them to the military police."[60] Comfort women were exposed on a daily basis to the threat that they would be infected with a sexually transmitted disease.

Death from Illness, Suicide, and Coerced Double Suicide

Daily life in military comfort stations cost many comfort women their lives. An Army Secret Service soldier reports that during the Henan Operation in 1941, he "once cremated the body of a Korean comfort woman along the bank of the Yellow River after she died of purpura."[61] In the spring of 1944, a private who'd been dispatched to Hebei Province witnessed the death of a comfort woman there. He wrote the following poem about the episode.

> Seeing coolies
> carrying a coffin on their backs
> I asked them about it.
> They told me
> a comfort woman had died suddenly.[62]

According to Li Yong-suk, a friend who was brought to Guangdong Province as a comfort woman together with Li died of an illness there one year later.[63] In the military comfort station in Shanghai where Ha Sun-nyo was kept, there was a comfort woman born in Pyongyang who died of opium poisoning.[64] Mun Ok-chu testified that on the way from Mandalay to Akyab (Sittwe) an older comfort woman caught pneumonia and died.[65]

Many comfort women were driven to despair by their lives in military comfort stations and plotted to kill themselves. In a military comfort station in Shanghai, Kim Dok-chin (a fictitious name) heard that "many Chinese women captured by the Japanese army and made into comfort women flee and commit suicide."[66] When she was in pain, she thought of killing herself many times, but she couldn't.[67] Li Yong-nyo, who was kept in a comfort station in Yangoon, Burma, reports that there was a comfort woman at the station who committed suicide by drinking cheap liquor and taking opium. When her body was placed upon a pile of kindling and burned, the army gathered together all the comfort women and forced them to watch.[68]

Even comfort women who managed to survive and return home had often attempted suicide while they were confined in military comfort stations. Mun Ok-chu went to Burma willingly, but once she realized how grim her life would be there, she got drunk and threw herself out a third-story window, sustaining serious injuries.[69] Li Duk-nam (a fictitious name), who was held in a military comfort station in Kutaradja (Banda Atjeh), Indonesia, tried to kill herself by taking medicine, but her mother's face appeared to her, and she couldn't let herself die.[70]

There were also many cases of soldiers in despair who forced comfort women to commit double suicide with them. According to a report by Lieutenant General Uchiyama Eitarō, commander of the 13th Division, in March 1942, a soldier (who already had a wife in Niigata) wanted in the future to live with a Korean comfort woman from the military comfort station in Ichang. He requested that the woman leave the comfort station and be transferred to a restaurant, but his request was denied. Thereupon, he tried to force her to commit suicide with him and shot her with a revolver. He inflicted serious injuries on the comfort woman and killed himself.[71] Song Shin-do was stabbed in the side of the chest by a miserable soldier who tried to force her to commit double suicide.[72] To comfort women, the soldiers who tried to force them into double suicides were probably just as terrifying as those who drew their swords and became violent.

In the conditions described above, the women in military comfort stations were forced, day in and day out, to serve as sexual servants for the soldiers of the Japanese army. The army, while pressing large number of these women into service, never drew up military laws for their protection. Even in Japan's domestic prostitution system, which was in reality a system of sexual slavery, there was a ban on employing women under the age of eighteen, and the prostitutes' freedoms of movement, of communication, and of assembly, and their right to quit their jobs, were recognized. Comfort women did not even have this measure of protective legislation. Military comfort women were nothing less than sexual slaves for the Japanese military.

Chapter Five

Violations of International Law and War Crime Trials

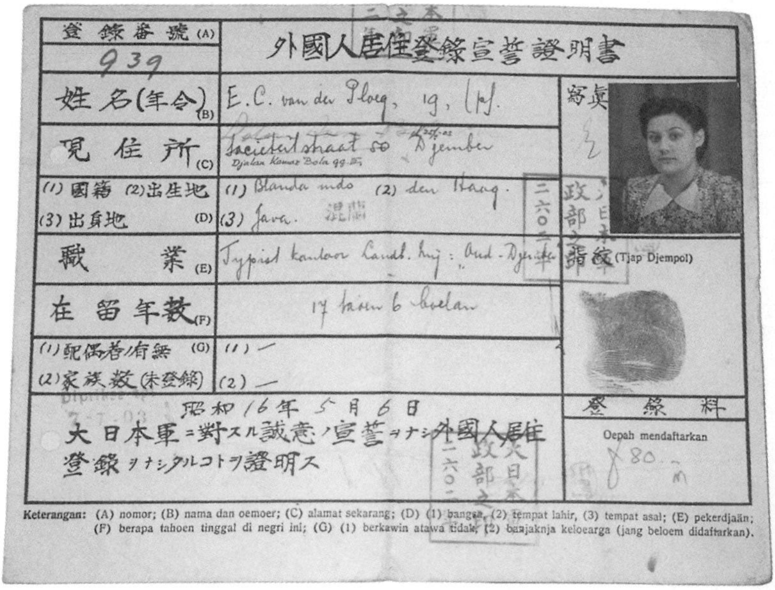

登錄番號 (A) 939

外國人居住登錄宣誓證明書

姓名(年令) (B) E.C. van der Ploeg, 19, (P).

現住所 (C) Societeitstraat 50 Djember
Djalan Kamar Bola 99

(1) 國籍 (2) 出生地 (3) 出身地 (D) (1) Blanda indo (2) den Haag. (3) Java. 混蘭

職業 (E) Typist kantoor Landb. Mij.: "Oud-Djember"

在留年數 (F) 17 taoen 6 boelan

(1) 配偶者ノ有無 (G) (1) —
(2) 家族數(未登錄) (2) —

寫眞

指紋 (Tjap Djempol)

登錄料

Oepah mendaftarkan

ƒ 80.—

昭和16年5月6日

大日本軍ニ對スル誠意ノ宣誓ヲナシ外國人居住登錄ヲナシタルコトヲ證明ス

Keterangan: (A) nomor; (B) nama dan oemoer; (C) alamat sekarang; (D) (1) bangsa, (2) tempat lahir, (3) tempat asal; (E) pekerdjaän; (F) berapa tahoen tinggal di negri ini; (G) (1) berkawin atawa tidak, (2) banjaknja keloearga (jang beloem didaftarkan).

REASONS WHY WOMEN FROM THE COLONIES AND OCCUPIED AREAS WERE FORCED TO SERVE AS COMFORT WOMEN

Ethnicity and the Oppression of Comfort Women

As is clear from the documents examined thus far, when we consider the numbers of military comfort women broken down by ethnicity, the proportion of Koreans is high as is the number of Chinese, including Taiwanese. After these two groups come Southeast Asian and Pacific islander women, with Indonesians making up most of this group. While we can say that the number of Japanese comfort women was never small, the percentage of women from colonized and occupied areas was extremely high. What does this mean?

In contrast to the "local rounding up" of women in occupied areas in China and Southeast Asia, Korean and Taiwanese women were rounded up in Korea, Taiwan, and Japan and purposely transported by ship, train, and truck to the battlefields. That this could be accomplished in the absence of government and military policies is unthinkable. Kim Il-myon considers the high percentage of Korean women among the comfort women as one aspect of a "fundamental policy to frustrate and strangle the desire of the Korean people for national independence" because in making young, unmarried women into "army prostitutes," they aimed at the "ethnic annihilation" (*minzoku shōmetsu*) of the Korean people.[1] While I can't agree with the argument that Japan followed a policy of "ethnic annihilation" aimed at eradicating Korean people, it is true that Japan pursued a policy of "expunging the ethnicity" (*minzoku massatsu*) of Koreans by such measures as depriving them of their own names and forcing them to adopt Japanese names, imposing Japanese as the language of instruction in schools,

Foreigner's Residence Registration Card issued by the Japanese army to Ellie C. van der Ploeg. (The date is incorrectly entered as Shōwa 16 [1941]. It should have been Shōwa 17 [1942]).
COURTESY OF NISHINO RUMIKO

and forcing Koreans to take an oath as imperial subjects. The question of whether comfort women policy was one aspect of a larger project to wipe out Korean ethnicity demands further analysis. At any rate, ethnic discrimination was at the root of the act of making women from the colonies into comfort women,which amounted to their enslavement. But it is fairly certain that no thought was given to how this might humiliate the people concerned as an ethnic group. One reason that the preponderance of colonized women among the ranks of the comfort women cannot be overlooked is the problems arising from international law.

In this chapter, I will examine the international law of the time as it relates to the rounding up of comfort women and consider the comfort women issue from that perspective. It goes without saying that racial and ethnic discrimination was behind the rounding up of women in the occupied territories. I will investigate the similarities and differences in those expressions of discrimination in relation to international law. I will also consider the case of Dutch women forced to serve as comfort women, as this issue was pursued in the postwar courts trying Class B and C war crimes.

Documents Indicating the Government's Intentions

The document "Matters Concerning the Handling of Women Sailing to China" (February 23, 1938), which I quoted from in chapter 3, is crucial in revealing the {government's} reasons for making women from the colonies into comfort women and in demonstrating the extent to which the government was aware of international law. I will quote the relevant sections again here. As mentioned above (p. 100), this notice was issued by the Home Ministry's Chief of the Police Bureau and sent to the governor of each prefecture and metropolitan district. It sets out instructions relating to the travel to China of women intending to work in the "shameful calling" (prostitution) serving Japanese military personnel.

> If the recruitment of these women [who intend to work as prostitutes] and the regulation of {recruiting} agents is improper, it will not only compromise the authority of the empire and damage the honor of the Imperial Army, it will exert a baleful influence on citizens on the home front, especially on the families of soldiers who are stationed overseas. Also, we cannot be assured that it is not contrary to the spirit of inter-

national treaties relating to the traffic in women and girls. You are hereby notified of your orders to handle these matters from now on in accordance with the following instructions.[2]

The notice goes on to stipulate regulations that gave tacit approval of the transport to northern and central China of women who were prostitutes, over the age of twenty-one, and free of sexually transmitted diseases. The points that should be noted here are the observation that "it will exert a baleful influence on the citizens on the home front, especially the families of soldiers who are stationed overseas" and the warning that it may be "contrary to the spirit of international treaties relating to the traffic in women and girls."[3]

The former notes that if Japanese women who were not prostitutes were sent from Japan to China as comfort women, it would exert a grave influence on citizens, and especially on families whose sons were stationed overseas. Also, if the sisters, wives, or female acquaintances of soldiers stationed overseas came to the battlefields as comfort women, it would probably destroy soldiers' sense of trust in the state and the army. The Home Ministry grasped, in its own way, the fact that rounding up comfort women entailed these kinds of serious problems. Therefore, the rounding up of comfort women from Japan was extremely limited.

Conversely, the Japanese government considered it unnecessary to take these issues into consideration when the women concerned were not Japanese, or when they were rounded up outside Japan. If the women were Korean or Taiwanese, making them into comfort women was considered acceptable. This is evident from the fact that this notice was not sent to {Government-Generals of} Korea or Taiwan.

Ethnic discrimination is clearly at work here. This discrimination is linked to the loopholes the Japanese government had already created for itself by 1925.

International Treaties Forbidding Traffic in Women and Children

What was the Home Ministry's Chief of the Police Bureau referring to when he mentioned "international treaties relating to the traffic in women and girls"? At the time, there were four international treaties banning such traffic:

A. The International Agreement for the Suppression of White Slave Traffic (1904)

B. The International Convention for the Suppression of White Slave Traffic (1910)

C. The International Convention for the Suppression of Traffic in Women and Children (1921)

D. The International Convention for the Suppression of Traffic in Adult Women and Girls (1933)

In 1925, Japan was a signatory to three of these treaties, A, B, and C (D was never ratified). To explore what sorts of things were prohibited, let's take up the example of treaty B.

> ARTICLE 1. Whoever, in order to gratify the passions of another person, has procured, enticed, or led away, even with her consent, a woman or girl under age, for immoral purposes, shall be punished, notwithstanding that the various acts constituting the offence may have been committed in different countries.
>
> ARTICLE 2. Whoever, in order to satisfy the passions of another person, has, by fraud or by means of violence, threats, abuse of authority, or any method of compulsion, produced, enticed, or led away a woman or girl over age, for immoral purposes, shall also be punished, notwithstanding the fact that the various acts constituting the offence may have been committed in different countries.[4]

In short, in the case of underaged women, regardless of whether their consent had been given, forcing them to engage in prostitution was completely forbidden. And in the case of adult women, if fraudulent or coercive means were involved, the offenders must be prosecuted. The definition of "underaged" in these treaties varies. In treaty B, it is under twenty years old; in treaty C, it is under twenty-one years old. At first, when signing the treaty, the Japanese government attached a proviso that defined minors as those under age eighteen. In 1927, however, Japan removed this proviso. Therefore, at the time when military comfort stations were beginning to be built, even in Japan, people were defined as minors until they reached the age of twenty-one.

The Chief of the Police Bureau's instruction to limit women going to China to prostitutes over the age of twenty-one was natural in light of these international laws. Then the authorities exploited an ingenious loophole they had created-they had placed the colonies and such territories beyond the jurisdiction of those laws.

Loopholes in International Law

There was a provision in these international treaties stipulating that it was permissible not to apply the laws in colonies. In the 1910 treaty, a provision stipulated that when the treaty's laws were applicable in colonial territories, a notice in writing to that effect should be submitted (Article 11). In the 1921 treaty, signatories were allowed to declare that colonial territories were excluded from the treaty's provisions (Article 14). The Japanese government, using these articles, did not apply the laws of the treaties to territories such as Korea and Taiwan. That is to say, it expressly treated the colonies differently.

Thus the government and the military considered the rounding up of women in Korea and Taiwan exempt from the restrictions imposed by international law and turned Korea and Taiwan into supply depots for military comfort women. Korean women became the primary targets of efforts to round up comfort women. Reasons for this include the fact that Korea's population was many times that of Taiwan and the assumption that, since China was consistently the main battlefield, it was better to make Korean women serve as comfort women than Taiwanese women, who were compatriots of the Chinese.

Judging that there were no legal restrictions on these activities according to wartime international law, the Japanese government treated the rounding up of women in the occupied territories the same way. Thus it was that women with no experience as prostitutes and underaged girls in Korea, Taiwan, China, Southeast Asia, and the Pacific region were gathered in large numbers.

Can it be said that the Japanese government and military were not violating international law?

WHAT WAS PROHIBITED BY INTERNATIONAL LAW?

Treaties Outlawing the Traffic in Women and Children

The military comfort women system violated a host of international laws. Here I will examine what was prohibited by the international laws of the time and what sorts of activities violated those laws. On this matter, I will quote from the latest report from the International Commission of Jurists (the ICJ, a powerful nongovernmental organization), "Comfort Women: An Unfinished Ordeal,"[5] and from the work of the international legal scholar Abe Kōki, "Legal Responsibility and the Military 'Comfort Woman' Issue."[6]

First, let's investigate the four treaties mentioned above relating to the ban on traffic in women and children. This set of treaties came into being in the midst of an international trend toward the protection of women's rights. Though there were still many limitations on the protections guaranteeing the rights of women and children and those safeguards were still insufficient, in Japan, where the sale and imprisonment of people for the purpose of prostitution had gone unchallenged, these treaties were enough to cause a panic among procurers and brothel owners at the time. The proviso appended by Japan when it signed the treaties was linked to this state of panic.

One problematic issue was the regulation about the age at which minors become adults. Even though the 1921 treaty set that age at twenty-one, Japan appended a proviso defining the age of majority as eighteen because the domestic prostitution system condoned the prostitution of women eighteen and older. The Japanese government did this out of consideration for the operators of domestic prostitution businesses. However, in the Privy Council's investigation report on whether Japan should sign the treaty or not, Tomii Masaaki, chairman of the investigation committee, severely criticized the proviso, concluding that "this is an issue that reflects on the dignity of the empire, and we officials find it regrettable and unbearable."[7] Consequently, the government removed the proviso in 1927.

Another important issue, needless to say, was the fact that these treaties were not applicable in such special territories as colonies. In Japan's case, these comprised Korea, Taiwan, the Kwantung Leasehold Territories, Sakhalin, and the South Seas islands under mandate. There was an investigative committee report prepared for the Privy Council to the effect that when the exemption claimed for these territories was no longer necessary in the future, it was earnestly desired that it be relinquished. But there was no harsh criticism of this practice.[8]

So were people really completely free under international law to drag women off in colonial territories? Abe makes the following observations on this question. Many Korean comfort women, excluding those transported out of Korea by train, were transported on Japanese ships. Though the act of kidnapping actually occurred in colonial territory, since Japanese ships "can, under international law, be considered equivalent to Japanese territory itself," the treaties were in force.[9] Transport from Taiwan was, of course, unimaginable except by ship (even if, for the sake of argument, we assume the women were transported by air, airplanes were also considered equivalent to Japan itself).

In addition, Abe observes that in cases where the order to round up comfort women was issued by the Army Central Command, "it is not impossible to interpret the act [of solicitation] as having actually taken place on Japanese territory as well."[10] The Army Central Command was aware that such activities were taking place, and its sanction of these activities was a necessary condition for their being carried out. Assuming this was the case, from March 4, 1938, when the Adjutant of the Ministry of War issued the document "Matters Concerning the Recruitment of Women Employed in Military Comfort Stations,"[11] these regulations were probably applied to activities in the colonies as well.

This interpretation is more strict than that of the ICJ. The ICJ maintains that the regulations in Article 14 of the 1921 treaty that exempted colonies and such territories also incorporated such customs as paying bride prices and dowries that could not be abolished in one fell swoop (there was no such custom in Korea).[12] Since it was not the intention of the treaty to facilitate the rounding up of women for the purpose of prostitution, "Japan cannot invoke that provision to escape its liability for the treatment given by it to the Korean women under the Convention."[13] The ICJ also points out that many former comfort women testified that when they were transported from Korea by ship, the ships made a stop on the Japanese mainland.[14] In any case, the interpretation that this treaty did not apply to women dispatched from Korea and Taiwan is untenable.

The Convention Concerning Forced or Compulsory Labor

The ICJ takes the position that considering the coerced activities of comfort women as "labor" must be done cautiously, so it doesn't touch on the Convention Concerning Forced or Compulsory Labor (International Labor Organization Treaty No. 29, signed in 1930). Abe, however, considers "labor" precisely as "all kinds of labor or service," and points out that since comfort women provided exactly that, the coercion they were subjected to violated this convention.[15]

In October 1932, Japan ratified the convention. According to its terms, forced labor is defined as all labor or service "which is exacted from any person under the menace of any penalty." Signatories were pledged to abolish completely all forms of forced labor, excluding such special types as compulsory military service and penal servitude. Exceptions had to be in accordance with guarantees set out in this convention. Even types of labor or service recognized as exceptions were subject to regulations requiring, for example, that only "adult able-bodied males who are of an apparent age of not less than eighteen and not more than forty-five years may be called upon for forced or compulsory labor" (Article 11), while women could not be drafted into labor service at all. In addition, the duration of the labor service and working hours had to be limited; there had to be guaranteed pay; workers had to be compensated for injuries and sicknesses incurred while working; and measures to protect workers' health were mandated. Clearly, the military comfort women system was a forced labor system that drafted women into service and did not provide them with "suitable wages, remuneration for injuries sustained while working, or health care." Thus it must be considered a violation of the treaty.[16] According to Abe, the failure to punish those responsible for these activities was also a violation of international law.[17]

The Prohibition of Slavery

The Slavery Convention was concluded in 1926. Japan never ratified this treaty, so it can be argued that Japan was not bound by it. The ICJ, however, maintains that at the beginning of the twentieth century, "it was generally accepted that customary international law prohibited the practice of slavery and that all nations were under a duty to prohibit the slave trade."[18] In addition, the Covenant of the League of Nations demanded that member countries actively work to free people held in slavery, prohibit the taking of slaves, and ban forced labor (Article 22, Paragraph 5), and this is commonly regarded as a statement of customary international law. As Abe has also noted, if we take the fundamental provisions of this convention as "representative of international customary law, it is possible to consider all nations, including countries that were not signatories, as already bound by this treaty at that time."[19] That is, to restrain or take individuals into custody and dispose of them, virtually considering them possessions, to take them as slaves, and to transport them overseas were all prohibited.

Abe further suggests an interpretation that includes "debt slavery" in international customary law's ban on slavery.[20] Ustinia Dolgopol of the University of Southern Australia at Flinders, who drafted the final report of the ICJ, declared in answer to a question of mine that, at the time, all of the so-called "civilized countries," of which Japan was one, bore a responsibility to ban all forms of slavery, including debt slavery.[21] Assuming this was the case, even those instances in which people were sold for lump sum cash advances must be called violations of international law.

The Regulations of the Hague Convention

The Convention on Laws and Customs of Land Warfare was concluded in 1907. Japan ratified the treaty in November 1911. Article 46 of the appendix "Regulations Concerning the Laws and Customs of Land Warfare" required that signatories respect "family honor and rights, the lives of persons, and private property" in occupied territories. The ICJ noted that this treaty had a clause that stipulated that if all countries involved in a conflict were not signatories to the treaty, then none were bound by it, so the treaty's provisions did not apply directly. But the ICJ went on to declare that Article 46 reflected international customary law.[22] Thus, the ICJ pointed out, if "the concept of family honor" included "the right of women in a family not to be subjected to the humiliating practice of rape," then "respect for the lives of persons" not only refers to their lives but also extends to "their dignity as human beings."[23]

Abe also considers these provisions as a document that codified international customary law, and regardless of the stipulation that all countries must be signatories for the treaty to be binding, Japan was bound by them. He declares that Japan had pledged to protect women from rape and forced prostitution during wartime.[24] These international customary laws protected people living in occupied territories, so we can't apply them to women in colonies, but activities that violated those laws were, literally, war crimes.

Crimes Against Humanity

The concept of crimes against humanity had already been articulated in the peace treaty with Germany after World War I. This concept was first put into practice in the Charter of the Nuremberg International Military Tribunal established after World War II. Then it was taken up in the Charter of the International Military Tribunal for the Far East. In Article 5-C, "crimes against humanity" are defined as "murders, extermination, enslavement, deportation, and other inhumane acts committed against any civilian population, before or during the war" as well as "persecutions on political or racial grounds." This definition includes not only the usual war crimes but also inhumane acts, so it is not limited to crimes committed during wartime or in war zones. At the International Military Tribunal for the Far East, however, not even one person was tried for crimes against humanity. This was not because Japan had not committed these types of crimes; it was because the American and European prosecutors and judges did not attempt to confront the issue of the large-scale crimes Japan had committed against other Asian peoples, and had no intention of pursuing the matter.

In Article 11 of the San Francisco Peace Treaty concluded in 1951, Japan "accepted the judgements of the International Military Tribunal for the Far East and of other Allied war crimes courts both within and outside of Japan." That is, Japan was subject to this definition of crimes against humanity.[25] Various fundamental principles of international law acknowledged by the charters and rulings of the Nuremberg International Military Tribunal and the International Military Tribunal for the Far East were unanimously affirmed in the first full session of the first United Nations General Assembly.[26] This seems to indicate that it was just and legal to interrogate acts committed before 1945.

Responsibility for Acts Committed by the Nation

Let's return once more, finally, to the treaties banning the trafficking in women and children.

Of the four treaties, Japan did not ratify the 1933 treaty (D) in which it was established as a crime for adult women, for example, to be rounded up and put to work as prostitutes, even with their consent. The treaty demonstrated that an international consensus had been established on these issues. It was so uncontroversial that the Japanese government even responded to the effect that it had no objections to the content. The larger reason that Japan did not ratify the treaty is said to be that it didn't accord with domestic law. It can be argued that Japan was not bound by this treaty but the government was well aware of the international trend.

This set of treaties was concluded in order to tighten controls on civilian operators who forced women to engage in prostitution. Yet it was the state that became the agent violating these treaties. Furthermore, the fact that these violations were committed in order to provide services exclusively for military personnel (soldiers and civilian employees of the military) is inexcusable. The fact that the military and the government continued to actively dispatch comfort women was itself shameful behavior.

DUTCH COMFORT WOMEN: THE CIRCUMSTANCES SURROUNDING THE CASE OF THE SEMARANG COMFORT STATIONS

Comfort Stations and War Crimes

After the war, the comfort women issue was raised as a war crime. In the case of comfort stations in Semarang on the island of Java, those involved were tried for war crimes.

Many young Dutch women were forced to become comfort women in the former Dutch East Indies (Indonesia). After the war, these acts were prosecuted as Class B and C war crimes. Previously, the facts of this case were not well known, but the *Asahi Shimbun* came into possession of court documents and published them in detail on August 30, 1992 (an initial brief report was published on July 21). In addition, the Dutch government, rather than making the documents public directly, published a report entitled "Report of a Study of Dutch Government Documents on the Forced Prostitution of Dutch Women in the Dutch East Indies During the Japanese Occupation" (hereafter "Dutch Government Report").[27] In what follows, I will trace the development of this case, based on the documents contained in "Court Documents Concerning the Case of the Semarang Comfort Stations" (hereafter "Court Documents")[28] and the "Dutch Government Report," and inquire into its significance.

In January 1944, in the district capital of Semarang in the central region of the island of Java, the Japanese army planned to establish new military comfort stations. According to testimony given at the trials of those in charge of rounding up the comfort women, there were already military comfort stations in Semarang at the time. "Sexually transmitted diseases," however, "were spreading amongst the occupation army," and "the behavior of the occupation army toward the local inhabitants was already provoking the inhabitants' antagonism."[29] In this case as well, the spread of sexually transmitted diseases and crimes by soldiers became motives for building new military comfort stations.

The cause of the problems was the Officer Candidate Corps of the Southern Army. The Officer Candidate Corps was attached directly to the Southern Army, but at that time the corps' commanding officer was concurrently serving as the commander of the Semarang Occupation Army. As such, he was under the authority of the 16th Army Headquarters in Batavia. The camps where residents of European descent were interned were under the jurisdiction of the Java Military Administrator. That post was held concurrently by the Chief of Staff of the 16th Army (Major General Kokubu Shinshichirō). In November 1943, the "Official Regulations for the Treatment of Military Internees" were drafted. According to these regulations, military internment camps were to be formally set up, and their administration was transferred from military administrators to army commanders (the military internment camp on Java was formally opened in March 1944). In order to force the women in the internment camps to become comfort women, permission had to be granted by the Headquarters of the 16th Army. At the trials, however, the culpability of the army administrators and the civil administrators who still managed the camps at the time was not made clear.

The commander of the Officer Candidate Corps who was called on by the administrator of the district of Semarang to take charge of setting up comfort stations requested permission from the 16th Army Headquarters (commanded by Lieutenant General Harada Kumakichi) to use women in the internment camps as comfort women. According to the testimony of the Officer Candidate Corps commander, the officer who was to become commander of the army's interment camps on Java told him that "it would be wise to have the women who consented (to become comfort women) write notes to that effect, so there won't be problems afterward."[30] In addition, according to the testimony of the major in the line of communication branch who submitted the proposal for setting up the comfort stations and received the proper authorization, the army Headquarters told him emphatically to "take special care that only freely consenting people were employed at the comfort station."[31]

The Development of the Incident, Part II

The Officer Candidate Corps, however, ignored these orders. In the latter half of February, the officers in charge, along with police and comfort station operators, forcefully gathered together young women from the internment camps.

When European leaders at the Sumawono, Bangkong, and Lampersari camps realized the purpose for which the women were being rounded up, they "put up so much opposition that the Japanese abandoned their attempts."[32] Consequently, the young women eventually assembled {and forced to become comfort women} were taken from the following four internment camps.

- Halmahera Internment Camp: eleven women were rounded up and taken away, but three were {subsequently} sent home due to illness. Several days later, a sixteen-year-old girl was sent home because she was too young.[33] (The court's ruling counts eight women who were rounded up.)

- Ambarawa Numbers 6 and 9 Internment Camps (referred to in the court's ruling as Numbers 4 and 6): the women resisted fiercely, but about eighteen women were rounded up and taken off against their will.[34] (The court's ruling counts seventeen women).

- Gedangan Internment Camp: because of "fierce resistance," forced rounding up was abandoned, and tens of "consenting" women rumored to have been prostitutes were assembled. Several of these women were soon sent back to the camp.[35]

About thirty-five women were rounded up. (The ruling handed down by a military court in Batavia shortly after the war confirms that twenty-five women taken from the Halmahera and Ambarawa Numbers 4 and 6 camps were rounded up and forced to engage in prostitution). From March 1 onward, these women were kept at four comfort stations: the Officers' Club, the Semarang Club, the Hinomaru Club, and the Seiun Club. Among these four, the Officers' Club was reserved for the exclusive use of the officers of the Southern Army's Officer Candidate Corps.

The Experiences of Jeanne O'Herne

What awaited the women rounded up and taken off to comfort stations?

Jeanne O'Herne was born into a wealth family living on its sugar plantation near Semarang. Her parents were Dutch, and she was the third of five children.[36] She was studying at a Franciscan college to become a nun when the Japanese army invaded, and she was forcibly interned in one of the Ambarawa camps.[37] She was twenty-one years old at the time. She described the internment camp as a horrible place, overrun with filth, rats, and sewage, where heavy labor, starvation, violence, and disease were rampant.[38]

One day in February 1944, Japanese army officers came and ordered that all "single girls from seventeen and up were to line up." With a sense of foreboding, she went, trying to make herself as inconspicuous as possible and avoiding attracting the officers' attention. The officers looked the girls up and down and laughed among themselves.[39] According to her memories, sixteen girls were separated out and ordered to collect their belongings and board a truck.[40] Beginning with the girls' mothers, the women in the camp tried to resist, but they were pushed aside.[41] When they reached Semarang, seven girls were taken off the truck and put alone in separate rooms[42] (according to the "Court Documents," approximately thirty-five women were brought to a hotel in the city, where seven women were first selected for the Officers' Club and the remaining women were divided among the other three comfort stations). On the night the club opened, many officers came.[43] The young women were assembled in the dining hall, cowering and shaking in terror. One by one, they were dragged from the room crying and struggling.[44] When her own turn came, Jeanne O'Herne resisted fiercely, but "my fighting, kicking, crying and protesting made no difference." The angry officer drew his sword, held it against her, stripped her clothes off, and stroked her with the sword.[45]

> He played with me like a cat with a helpless mouse. This game went on for a while, then he started to undress himself. And I realized that he had no intention of killing me. . . . He threw himself on top of me, pinning me down under his heavy body. I tried to fight him off, I kicked him, I scratched him, but he was too strong. The tears were streaming down my face as he raped me. It seemed as if he would never stop. . . .
>
> My whole body was shaking when he eventually left the room. I gathered what was left of my clothing and ran off to the bathroom. I wanted to wash all the dirt, the shame and hurt off my body. . . .
>
> In the bathroom I found some of the other girls. We were all in shock and crying, not knowing what to do, trying to help each other. We washed ourselves as if it could wash away all that happened to us.[46]

After washing, she hid in a back room but was soon discovered. That night, she was raped by several other officers.[47] The next day, she faced more of the same from evening onward.[48]

According to O'Herne's recollection, the seven women were able to support each other on account of their Christian faith. She always wore a cross around her waist, so she was nicknamed the "Girl of the Cross" by the Japanese people around her. She continued to resist each time she was raped, kicking, punching, and pushing away her attackers.[49] She was also raped by the military doctor who made regular visits to inspect the comfort women for sexually transmitted diseases.[50] She says it was her faith in God that barely managed to sustain her in these desperate circumstances.[51]

The Experiences of Ellie C. van der Ploeg

Ellie C. van der Ploeg was born in January 1923 in Holland. When the Japanese army invaded in 1942, she was living in Jember in eastern Java with her parents, brother, and sister. At the time, she was nineteen years old. Her father was Dutch, and her mother was Indonesian. Together they ran several grocery stores.[52]

In May 1942, they were registered by the Japanese army and forced to live in group housing in Jember. The picture of the "Foreigner's Residence Registration Card" found on the title page of this chapter is a product of that time. Later, they were transferred to the Halmahera Internment Camp in Semarang. In February 1944, several Japanese people came to the internment camp, called together all the women aged fifteen to thirty-five, and had the women parade in front of them. Saying "this one . . . this one," the Japanese picked out one woman after another. Then they ordered them to gather up their belongings and get on a bus. She remembers fifteen women being selected. It seems that the Dutch leaders of the internment camp, unable to disobey orders, did not resist.

The women were told that they would be working in tobacco factories or as secretaries, office workers, nurses, or nannies, but these were all lies. Tens of women were rounded up and distributed among four houses, which were all comfort stations. The house where Ellie van der Ploeg was kept was a large one-story mansion requisitioned from a Dutch person. The mansion was remodeled: in the main wing, there was a place where the operator, called "Papa-san," sold tickets, living quarters, a lounge, a dining hall, bathrooms, and numerous bedrooms. In the back were six rooms used by the servants and another bathroom. She was shoved into one of these back rooms.

She was told by a Japanese woman there to give the Japanese soldiers a good time, but what that meant, she didn't really understand. According to her recollection, the comfort station opened for business on February 26. On that first night, the women resisted fiercely, so a new rule was imposed: if they didn't work, they wouldn't be given any food. The Japanese men who came bought tickets at the front desk, chose the women they liked from pictures, came into the rooms, and showed their tickets. There were three kinds: one-hour, two-hour, and all-night tickets. The women never handled any money. The comfort station opened in the evening, and the women were forced to have intercourse with two or three customers every night. In the bathrooms, there were bidets with red water (manganic acid had been added to the water). After they had been forced to have intercourse with an officer or civilian military employee, they always washed themselves. She tried to remain in the bathroom as long as possible, because it was the only time she could escape being forced to have intercourse with the comfort station's customers. She was examined for sexually transmitted diseases once a week, but she eventually contracted gonorrhea.

The women had one day off per week, though which day was not fixed. It was decided at the discretion of officers, civilian military employees, or "Papa-san," the operator. The Japanese men who made up the usual clientele at the comfort station wore military swords and uniforms with insignia and were of high rank. Sunday, however, was "soldiers' day." The women were taken to a separate building where they were forced to have intercourse with soldiers. Since the numbers of soldiers were so much greater, Sunday was the most terrifying day.

The women thought about trying to escape if they had an opportunity, but they couldn't. There were always two guards armed with swords outside the comfort station. The women were always told that "if you escape, you'll be caught by the military police." And they were threatened: "If you escape, there's no telling what will happen to your family in the internment camp." One friend who did manage to escape was caught and brought back. Women of European descent were easily found because of their facial features and hair color. In addition, Indonesian people who tried to help people of European descent were punished by the Japanese army, so escapees were generally not given refuge.

Testimony at the Trial

When O'Herne and van der Ploeg gave their testimony, almost fifty years had passed since the events took place. Except for a few contradictions in their testimony, it accords to a remarkable extent with the testimony given at the trial immediately following Japan's defeat. This probably reflects how wretched and intense the women's experiences were. The main points, summarized in the court's ruling, are as follows.

The women lined up for selection in the internment camps were from seventeen or eighteen to about twenty-eight years of age (according to various testimonies). "{I} refused to enter the bedroom, but I was beaten and shoved in. It was no use" (according to a woman taken from Ambarawa Internment Camp Number 4 to the Semarang Club).

The seven women (by other accounts, nine women) gathered in a main room were taken off to individual rooms, where "after a long struggle, {my} virginity was stolen" (according to a woman taken from Ambarawa Internment Camp Number 6 to the Officers' Club).

"After a struggle lasting about half an hour," another woman was raped. Thereafter, she was forced to have intercourse with three to four men every day (according to another woman taken from the same internment camp to the Seiun Club).

The women were threatened that if they didn't stop refusing, they would be transferred to comfort stations where conditions were even worse (according to a woman taken from the same internment camp to the Officers' Club).

"After a struggle in which {she} kicked, punched and pushed," another woman was overcome. Thereafter, every night she was forced to have intercourse with three men, or spend the entire night with one man (according to a woman taken from the Halmahera Internment Camp to the Hinomaru Club).

Another woman was raped by officers, and from that time on was forced to have intercourse with seven or eight men every day (according to another woman taken from the Halmahera Internment Camp to the Hinomaru Club).

The official opening day of these comfort stations was March 1, but there were cases of crimes committed several days before that date.

According to the "Court Documents," there were two women who escaped and were captured by the police and returned to the comfort stations. Another woman planned to commit suicide, while another pretended to be mentally ill and was committed to a mental hospital. One woman became pregnant and was hospitalized for an abortion procedure. That many of the victims resisted fiercely but were overcome by violence and raped is virtually beyond question.

The Closing of the Comfort Stations

At the end of April 1944, these four comfort stations were closed as a result of the efforts of one of the Dutch leaders interned in Ambarawa Internment Camp Number 9, whose own daughter had been taken away. He managed to meet with Colonel Odashima Tadashi, in charge of prisoners of war and internment camps as a staff officer in the Ministry of War's Prisoner of War Affairs Department and the administrator of the Prisoner of War Information Office. In this meeting the Dutch leader protested the forced rounding up of women and the forced prostitution. Since this colonel had come to Java to inspect conditions, he promptly made reports to the Ministry of War, the South Army Headquarters, the 7th Area Army Headquarters (established in March 1944), and the 16th Army Headquarters recommending the closure of the comfort stations. The 16th Army Headquarters immediately ordered the comfort stations closed. The officers involved, however, were not punished. These comfort stations operated for a total of about two months.

According to Jeanne O'Herne, as a result of the order to close the comfort station, the women were transferred to the Kramat Internment Camp. In order to conceal the fact that the army had engaged in forced prostitution, this camp was completely isolated from the other internment camps. But precisely because the women were kept quarantined, the rumors of what had taken place spread and the camp became known as the "camp of prostitutes."[53] Ellie van der Ploeg was taken away from the comfort station without any explanation after about three months there. She was taken to the place where the comfort women had first been gathered together, and then transferred to the Kota Paris Internment Camp in Buitenzorg (Bogor).[54]

The Ruling of the Ad Hoc Military Court

After Japan's defeat, the case of the Semarang comfort stations was brought before a Dutch military court in Batavia. There were thirteen defendants, and the following verdicts were handed down against them on March 24, 1948 (and against the corps commander on August 29, 1951).

RANK/ STATUS	SENTENCE SOUGHT	SENTENCE IMPOSED	CRIMES	NOTES
Army— Lt. General	death penalty	12 years penal servitude	2, 3, 4	Officer Candidate; Corps Commander
Army— Colonel	death penalty	15 years penal serv.	1, 2, 3	attached to Officer Candidate Corps
Army— Major	death penalty	death penalty	1, 2, 3	primary officer in charge
Army— Major General	10 years penal serv.	10 years penal serv.	1, 2	adjutant
Army doctor— Major	10 years penal serv.	7 years penal serv.	4	attached to Officer Candidate Corps
Army doctor— Captain	20 years penal serv.	16 years penal serv.	3, 4	attached to Officer Candidate Corps
Army— Captain	2 years penal serv.	2 years penal serv.	4	attached to Officer Candidate Corps
Army— Sergeant Major	not guilty	not guilty		
Army— Civil Administrator	5 years penal serv.	not guilty		
Civilian Mil. Employee (operator)	death penalty	20 years penal serv.	2	operator of Semarang Club
Civilian Mil. Employee (operator)	20 years penal serv.	15 years penal serv.	2	operator of Hinomaru Club
Civilian Mil. Employee (operator)	5 years penal serv.	10 years penal serv	2	operator of Seiun Club
Civilian Mil. Employee (operator)	5 years penal serv.	7 years penal serv.	2	operator of Officers' Club

NOTES: Ranks reflect those held at the time of defeat. Crimes: 1) rounding up women and girls for the purpose of forced prostitution; 2) forcing girls and women to engage in prostitution; 3) rape; 4) mistreating internment camp inmates.[55]

Seven officers and four comfort station operators (civilian military employees) were found guilty. Three of the officers were convicted of rounding up women for the purpose of forced prostitution. Four officers and all of the comfort station operators were convicted of coerced prostitution. Four officers, including the commander of the Southern Army's Officer Candidate Corps, were convicted of rape. The fact that the women were raped at the comfort stations was acknowledged. In addition, three officers were convicted of mistreating internment camp inmates. The major who was in charge of setting up the comfort stations was given the death penalty (execution by firing squad). An army civil administrator and a non-commissioned officer were acquitted. The colonel who was considered to have played a central role in the planning of the comfort stations returned to Japan, but upon learning that he was being pursued by the Dutch, he committed suicide in January 1947.

Instances of Coerced Prostitution Acknowledged in the "Dutch Government Report"

According to the "Dutch Government Report," the cases that came to light during the war crimes trials were not the only cases of comfort stations set up by the Japanese army.

At the Muntilan Internment Camp in late January 1944, the Japanese army gathered together young women for the military comfort station in Magelang. When they tried to take the women out of the camp, the internment camp leaders resisted, and a riot broke out. But the internees were unable to prevent the army from taking the women away.[56] Three days later, a soldier came to the camp and told the internees that if "volunteers" were provided, the women who had been taken away would be allowed to return. As a result, several "volunteers" rumored to be prostitutes were taken away (thereupon, two women, including a fourteen-year-old girl, and two "volunteers" were sent back to the camp).[57] In all, thirteen women were taken to Magelang, where they were "examined very roughly, raped, and forced to work as prostitutes."[58]

In the middle of April 1944, the police and military police from Semarang procured women of European descent who were not in internment camps and Indonesian women. About twenty of these women were sent to

Surabaja. Two months later, ten Indonesian women and seven women of European descent were sent to Flores Island, where they were "forced to work as prostitutes."[59]

Many examples of these sorts of incidents are taken up in the "Dutch Government Report." Excluding the cases of those women acknowledged to have acted more or less "voluntarily," the report's compilers conducted an extremely rigorous investigation. From that investigation, researchers concluded that among the two to three hundred women of European descent who worked in military comfort stations, at least sixty-five were "forced into prostitution."[60]

But can women who "volunteered" to go in place of girls who had been taken away really be said to have been recruited of their own free will? In addition, the following example is brought up in the "Dutch Government Report." In October 1943, eleven women interned in the Padang Internment Camp on the island of Sumatra went to a military comfort station in Fort de Kock (Bukittinggi) in response to the Japanese army's "persuasion." The women say they went because they thought living at the comfort station would be better than returning to the internment camp.[61] As in the camps on Java, the living conditions in those on Sumatra were horrible. According to the opinion of the Allied armies that liberated the camps, the internees were not only reduced to skin and bones, "they were apathetic and had given up on everything; they had no energy and nothing moved them."[62] It's doubtful whether people can be said to be capable of making choices of their own free will under these sorts of conditions. Thus we should consider the approximate figure of sixty-five to be the absolute minimum number {of women forced to engage in prostitution}.

According to Tanaka Toshiyuki's research, Australian army nurses taken prisoner by the Japanese army were also coerced into becoming comfort women on Sumatra.[63] It is possible that future investigations will turn up more cases of women of European descent being forced to become comfort women.

What Does the Semarang Case Tell Us?

One of the critical facts made clear during the trials was that Japanese army headquarters were well aware of international laws that defined the forcible rounding up of women for the purpose of prostitution as a war crime. This is amply demonstrated by the warnings issued when the comfort stations were set up and by the fact that the stations were shut down when the circumstances of the case came to light.

Another important point is the fact that the order not to force women into prostitution was issued in regard to women of European descent, but the same order was not given in regard to Asian women except for Japanese women. Aware that coerced prostitution was a crime, the Japanese military limited its attempts to prevent it to those instances involving women of European descent. This was because {the military} feared that these cases would become an international problem after the war. Asian women other than Japanese women were not given this kind of consideration (both the trials conducted by the Dutch and the "Dutch Government Report" were only concerned with women of European descent; neither substantively addressed the experiences of Indonesian women).

Thus, as a matter of course for Asian women and even for some women of European descent, there was no punishment for those responsible even after the facts of the cases came to light. Here the fundamental outlines of the Japanese army's comfort women policy are clearly visible.

The Significance of the Dutch War Crimes Trials

At any rate, the Ad Hoc Military Court held by the Dutch played a critical role in shaping new international laws. The law applied in the case of the Semarang comfort stations was the "Order of the Secretary-General Concerning the Provisions of the Concept of War Crimes." This order was issued on June 1, 1946;[64] it defined as war crimes violations of wartime regulations and customary law, and gave thirty-nine examples. (Such examples as "rape," "the abduction of women and girls for the purpose of enforced prostitution and forcing women and girls to engage in prostitution," and "the ill-treatment of interned civilians or prisoners" are listed in the document.)[65]

The examples of crimes were adopted wholesale from a list of examples of war crimes selected by the United Nations War Crimes Commission in 1944. This was an expanded version of a list of thirty-two war crimes drawn up by a fifteen-member commission (which included two Japanese) investigating war crimes in preparation for the 1919 Paris peace conference. Already included in the list compiled by that commission were "rape," "the kidnapping of women and girls for the purpose of coerced prostitution," and "the internment of average civilians under inhumane conditions."[66] It is true that this list was not binding on the nations involved. After the war, however, Japan accepted the judgments of the International Military Tribunal for the Far East (the Tokyo Trials) and the definitions of Classes B and C War Crimes in Clause 11 of the 1951 San Francisco Peace Treaty, so Japan probably also accepted the ruling in the Semarang comfort stations case. This means that Japan had accepted the view that not only rape but also the rounding up of girls and women for the purpose of coerced prostitution, and forcing them to engage in prostitution, were war crimes.

In 1956, Japan paid the Dutch government $10 million in order to resolve certain private claims by Dutch civilian internees. Since there were approximately 110,000 internees, however, that figure amounts to only $91 per person (about ¥32,727 at the time).

Chapter Six

Conditions After the Defeat

COMFORT STATIONS FOR THE USE OF THE ALLIED FORCES IMMEDIATELY AFTER THE DEFEAT

Fear of the Allied Forces

On August 15, 1945, Japan accepted the Potsdam Declaration and surrendered. One of the greatest concerns of Japanese civilians immediately after the surrender was whether the Allied soldiers who occupied Japan would commit rapes on a massive scale.

Behind the spread of confusion and fears of this nature was the vivid memory of the countless rapes committed by Japanese troops in every occupied area of Asia and the Pacific islands. Wartime propaganda circulated by the Japanese government also had a profound influence. The director of a factory in Nihonbashi Ward wrote that "[the government] told us that the American and English soldiers are wild animals, and that if we are defeated, there's no telling what kinds of humiliations will be visited upon citizens, particularly women and girls. All 100 million citizens believe this" (entry for August 20 in a police intelligence report).[1] Thus the administrative machinery {of the state} further exacerbated citizens' anxieties.

In Kanagawa Prefecture, for example, even as early as August 15, female employees of the prefectural government were given three months' pay and were fired, having been advised to evacuate the area. On account of this action, people in Kanagawa Prefecture were thrown into "extreme confusion as a circulating notice ordered the forced evacuation of women and girls."[2] In Tokyo as well, there were many families who evacuated their daughters. The Metropolitan Police Board intelligence report from August 20 cited above records that the greatest worry of Tokyo residents was "the fear of the violent rape of women and girls."[3]

But the foremost issue, the report continues, was that "[to prevent this], there are many who demand the establishment of complete and large-scale comfort and pleasure facilities (and especially those with prostitutes)."[4] Shortly thereafter (on October 2), we see indications of the same sort of

---

Former comfort women from North and South Korea
at an international hearing in Tokyo, December 1992.

ITŌ TAKASHI © 1992

thinking in a report from the governor of Mie Prefecture. Speculation and rumors about the "violence of American troops" were rampant, and demands that "complete comfort facilities for the occupying army be actively expanded by this office" were being insistently voiced. The report notes that particularly "among women and girls, (many) make this demand."[5] In short, by offering up the bodies of some women, people contrived to guarantee the safety of others.

The Orders to Set Up Comfort Stations for the Use of the Allied Forces

The emergence of voices among the citizenry, and particularly among women, calling for the provision of sacrificial victims to the Allied soldiers is a tragic spectacle. But, more than anything else, the government's anti-Allied forces policies provided the basis for this sort of thinking.

The Allied forces moved in to occupy Japan on August 28. Preceding that, on August 18, the Japanese government ordered on its own initiative the construction of comfort stations for the use of the Allied troops. Fear spread among the people, and when the clamor became great enough, the Japanese government set to work at once. It was only due to the fact that Japan already had a military comfort station system that action was taken so quickly.

The August 18 order was issued by Hashimoto Masami, bureau chief of the Home Ministry's Police Protection Bureau, and addressed to the governor of each prefecture and the Chief of the Metropolitan Police. It was a notice entitled "Concerning the Establishment of Comfort Facilities in Areas Under Foreign Occupation." This notice specified "in regard to comfort facilities for foreign occupying forces," that police chiefs would designate certain special areas and that Japanese would not be permitted to use the facilities. It also ordered police chiefs to be actively involved by giving guidance on the establishment of "sexual comfort facilities," "eating and drinking facilities," and "recreation centers," and that "{authorities} strive for the speedy completion of the facilities." The notice specified that in the rounding up of "the women necessary for the operation {of the facilities}," "geisha, licensed and unlicensed prostitutes, waitresses, serving women, and women imprisoned for repeatedly engaging in illegal prostitution" would be the first enlisted.[6]

In short, the primary comfort facilities referred to in this notice were "sexual comfort facilities" reserved for the use of Allied troops. In order to carry out this plan, the government attempted to mobilize even the women imprisoned as a result of the government's own efforts to crack down on illegal prostitution.

In response to this notice, comfort stations for the Allied forces were established throughout the country. In Tokyo, eight professional organizations (including the Tokyo Restaurant Association, the Federation of Tokyo Assignation House Operators' Associations, and the Tokyo House of Assignation [Brothel] Association), "upon receiving internal orders from the Bureau" and acting in "the greater spirit of preserving the national polity," formed the Recreation and Amusement Association (RAA). On August 28, in the plaza in front of the Imperial Palace, they held a ceremony announcing the founding of the association. Then on September 3, the RAA placed an ad in the *Mainichi Shimbun*, recruiting "special female workers."[7]

The first comfort station, Komachien, was set up in the Tokyo-Yokohama area. It was opened as early as August 27. "The women were petrified" of the U.S. soldiers pouring in "and began weeping. There were even some who clung to the posts {holding up the roof} and wouldn't move."[8] The RAA planned to round up 5,000 comfort women, but by the beginning of the occupation they had actually managed to gather together only 1,360.[9] In addition, special facilities for the exclusive use of high-ranking officers were set up.

According to an intelligence report from the governor of Aichi Prefecture, five local notables in the city of Nagoya rounded up 211 dancers, 219 waitresses, and 250 guides in order to set up the "International First-Class Enjoyment Nagoya Club," a comfort facility for the use of the Allied soldiers.[10]

U.S. forces arrived in Hokkaidō to begin their occupation on October 4. The district government immediately began advocating the setting up of comfort facilities. A document complied on October 30 by the Public Peace Section of the District Police Department gives the following account of these efforts.

The Public Peace Section, newly created on September 18, has concentrated since October 5 on the establishment of special comfort facilities for the occupying Allied forces in Sapporo and four other cities. In accordance with their plan to make use of existing houses of assignation and small restaurants and to fill them with sufficient comfort women, houses of assignation have voluntarily closed and remodeled as restaurants. As a result of efforts to recruit comfort women, the existing population of no more than 450 women has been increased to more than 770 women. Relying on the urgent steps taken in regard to comfort, there have been virtually no incidents involving women so far, and everything continues to be managed smoothly.[11]

Immediately following the occupation by the U.S. forces, the construction of "special comfort facilities" proceeded under the direction of the district government. Houses of assignation that managed prostitution operations were formally termed "restaurants," and comfort women were gathered together, bringing their number to more than 770.

The Active Intervention of Right-Wing Activists

Comfort facilities were set up with the guidance and aid of prefectural and metropolitan governments and the police. When looking at examples of who actually set up comfort facilities, we should note, in addition to those directly involved in the prostitution business, rightists who actively intervened as financiers. An intelligence report entitled "The Activities of the Defunct National Essence League" from the Special Secret Service Section in the Osaka Prefectural Police relates the following account.

In regard to the now defunct National Essence League, Sasagawa Ryōzō, the younger brother of president Sasagawa Ryōichi, has become the league's leader. Along with former secretary Okada Tasaburō and Matsuoka Sanji as managers, they opened a comfort station for Allied troops, the American Club, in Kuroemon-chō in Minami Ward of Osaka in what is left of the old restaurant Mikasaya. It opened on the 18th.[12]

The Sasagawa group, under the name of the Association for the Promotion of Shipping, opened up comfort stations for the Allied forces in Osaka immediately after the defeat.

According to an intelligence report from the governor of Iwate Prefecture dated September 26, Hishitani Toshio, head of the Iwate branch of the Greater Japan Sincerity Association, intended to run for office in the general elections expected to be held, so he "involved himself with the people establishing comfort facilities for accommodating the Allied forces currently occupying the area. He has taken command and is very active in making plans to relocate them to the licensed area of Ueda."[13]

The police, rightists, and those in the prostitution business collaborated in establishing comfort facilities to serve the Allied troops.

Rapes Committed by Allied Troops

Rapes committed by Allied troops were not as numerous as those committed by the Japanese army, but there were a considerable number of them, so {people's} fears were not groundless. The first instances of rape in Kanagawa Prefecture occurred on August 30; there were three rapes that day. The Section Chief of the Home Ministry's Public Peace Section wrote a memo, "Matters Concerning Materials on Countermeasures Against Illegal Activities Committed by U.S. Soldiers," dated September 4. The memo describes instances of rape committed in Kanagawa and Chiba as cases in which "soldiers communicated their requests for sex through gestures. When their requests were refused, they pulled out their revolvers and raped the women."[14]

According to documents from the Central Liaison Office, the number of incidents involving rape reached forty-four (thirty of which were attempted rapes) by the end of September.[15] In cases of rape, many victims don't report the incident, so the actual number of victims was probably much larger.

The fact that in order to prevent rapes, the first idea considered was a comfort station system that sacrificed some women {to save others}, and the attitudes that promptly transformed that idea into reality must be regarded as problematic. In the report of the Public Peace Section of the Hokkaidō Police Department cited above, those involved sang their own praises, noting the smoothness with which the setting up of comfort facilities and gathering of comfort women proceeded and the fact that "there have been hardly any incidents involving women thus far." But how, then, should we deal with the fact that though it opened comfort stations, the

Japanese military was not able to prevent the occurrence of large numbers of rapes?

The idea that rapes could be prevented by the provision of sexual comfort facilities had not changed at all after the war.

The Closing of the Comfort Stations

Under these sorts of conditions, there are examples of instances in which key officers of the Allied forces themselves requested that women (be provided). In September 1945, Yosano Hikaru, chief of Tokyo's Public Health Section, was called to General Headquarters. There the Surgeon General of the Army discussed the "problem of women" with Yosano. Then responsibility for the comfort facilities for the Allied troops were divided between Yosano and Colonel C. F. Sams, Chief of the Public Health and Welfare Department.[16] In addition, according to the recollections of Komatsu Yasuhiro, the paymaster of the navy's military attaché office in Moji, the commanding officer of the U.S. forces in the Kanmon area had a "discussion about whether {he} could build a comfort station for the use of the U.S. forces." And the "P houses" (comfort stations) used by noncommissioned Japanese navy officers remaining in Moji were converted {for the use of the American troops}. The Japanese navy decided to "give severance pay to women who didn't want to have intercourse with American servicemen and let them go" before opening the comfort station to American troops, so only those who were willing would have intercourse with Americans.[17]

But on March 25, 1946, the U.S. 8th Army Headquarters issued an order forbidding American officers and soldiers to engage "licensed, unlicensed, or illicit prostitutes" or to enter "establishments where prostitution is conducted."[18] The reasoning behind this order was, first, that sexually transmitted diseases had been spreading among Allied troops. This was not unrelated to the issuance of a memo on January 21 by the Supreme Commander for the Allied Powers entitled "Abolition of Licensed Prostitution in Japan." Upon receiving the March order, the Chief of the Metropolitan Police Board's Public Peace Section sent out notices on March 26 to all police chiefs ordering them to cooperate with the U.S. military.[19] Thus the comfort stations for the use of Allied troops disappeared.

These comfort stations were promoted by the Japanese government and opened with the help of brothel operators, and then disappeared (by American decree). That many residents in the areas occupied by Allied forces had demanded the establishment of these facilities and that they were set up in major cities throughout the country within a very brief period of time are very serious issues. In addition, the Allied forces accepted these facilities, though only for a short time. (It is common knowledge that in reality, even after the ban on engaging prostitutes, facilities for prostitution did not disappear from areas where the occupation forces were stationed.) In the end, both the Japanese people and the Allied forces transitioned {into the postwar period} with only a faint awareness that the wartime military comfort women system was a violation of human rights.

ARE COMFORT WOMEN AN INEVITABLE FIXTURE ACCOMPANYING ARMIES? THE CASES OF VARIOUS COUNTRIES

The Cases of the English and American Armies

Here, I will investigate whether Japan was the only nation that created something resembling the military comfort women system during World War II. It is a fact that American soldiers committed rapes during the occupation period. It is also true that the establishment of comfort facilities was proposed by the American military. One often hears the argument that, "It's something the Allied forces did too, only to a lesser extent. In wartime, it's inevitable. The Japanese military wasn't the only one that did bad things." But are these assertions valid? After first pointing out the flawed nature of the logic proclaiming that "since others do bad things too, Japan's bad behavior can be allowed," I'd like to examine these arguments.

In fact, it is gradually becoming clear that in areas surrounding the armies of all countries, facilities resembling the Japanese military's comfort stations were built in similar numbers. Tanaka Toshiyuki surveyed European and American scholarship and collated the facts.[20] Drawing on this research, I will summarize the information about the British and U.S. forces.

The following are examples that have been uncovered.

- (North Africa: Tripoli) British army commanders permitted brothels to remain open but compelled women working as prostitutes to undergo military physicals. Some of Tripoli's brothels were even brought under direct control, with a Royal Army Service Corps noncommissioned officer placed in charge. Each of the army's different ranks and racial groups had its own brothel: one for colored soldiers, others for white men in the ordinary ranks, still another for NCOs and warrant officers, and the most exclusive brothels reserved for British officers. One soldier described Britain's militarized prostitution system in Tripoli in the early 1940s as follows: "a pavement in Tripoli held a long queue of men, four deep, standing in orderly patience to pay their money and break the monotony of desert celibacy. The queue was four deep because there were only four women in the brothel. . . ." Who were these four women? We are told nothing, only that they were Italians. They were probably products of Mussolini's earlier imperialist ambitions in North Africa.[21]

- (India: Delhi) British army commanders stationed in India ran official brothels at the start of the war. Later, when orders from London shut down the brothels, prostitutes were moved elsewhere; officers claimed that v.d. rates soared as a consequence of the military's loss of direct control of the women. As in Tripoli, Delhi's military brothels were differentiated so as to match the British army's own class and race stratifications: "The officers' brothel was in Thompson Road. . . . Most of the women there were white, some of them the wives of absent officers keen on a little money."[22]

- (North Africa) It was said that the late George Patton, who always understood the needs of his troops, would have been quite willing to experiment with the idea but finally gave it up when he was made to realize that the ruckus kicked up by the outraged wives and mothers of America would probably result in a congressional uproar that would slow down the war by several months.[23]

- (China: Kunming) In 1942, Brigadier General Claire Chennault, commander of the U.S. China Air Task Force, the ninety-aircraft volunteer corps of American fighters known as the Flying Tigers that flew combat missions on behalf of the Chinese military, brought over twelve Indian prostitutes by plane and employed them to service his flight and ground crews, over half of whom were infected with sexually transmitted diseases. Treating these infections resulted in the occasional grounding of as many as half his aircraft, and prompted Chennault to address this problem by opening a brothel for his men. But when Joseph Stilwell, commander of the India, Burma, and China regional forces, learned of this, he became enraged and forced the brothel to close.[24]

From the examples above, we know that both the U.S. and British militaries had comfort facilities exclusively for their own use, or at least experimented with them. Most were quickly shut down for fear of opposition on the home front. We can discern a tendency in armies themselves to create facilities like comfort stations in the absence of the voices of social movements, public opinion, or legislatures to defend women's human rights. In this, Japan can't be said to be unique.

Other important issues are whether women were forcibly rounded up and coerced into prostitution, whether minors were forced into prostitution, and whether orders to close the facilities were given when the situation came to light. The answers to these questions will probably be made clear by future research. First and foremost, however, is whether the top echelons of the militaries planned and promoted {the establishment of these facilities}. Herein lies the crucial difference between the British and U.S. militaries on the one hand, and the Japanese military on the other. In regard to the strictness of military discipline as well, we have the following testimony {as to critical differences between the forces}. The translator who accompanied Kawabe Torashirō, the Vice Chief of Staff sent to Manila as a military envoy immediately after the defeat, made the following observation: "Their [the U.S. military's] military discipline is extremely strict. . . . The French government offered to provide comfort facilities, but the U.S. army declined. We should {follow the example of} the Americans in this case and do the same."[25] It is indeed true that, in the last phase of the war as imminent victory approached, the U.S. military's policy of apparent abstinence broke down. It is a fact that after the landing at Normandy, the French provided a number of brothels for the exclusive use of the U.S. military (which the Headquarters of the U.S. army ordered closed three days later). It was also true that heretofore the use of existing brothels had not been forbidden.[26] It has already been noted that after the occupation of Japan, the U.S. military accepted the RAA, which had been set up by the Japanese government, and made use of those facilities until they were closed due to the spread of sexually transmitted diseases among American troops. The Allied forces' ability to enforce strict military discipline was probably related to the system of holidays they had in place. In the case of the U.S. military, when troops took part in large-scale combat, they were given leave afterward and could take a holiday in Australia, Hawaii, or on the West Coast of the United States. Troops were able to get together with their families, friends, and lovers, or "enjoy" themselves.

The Case of the Soviet Military

It is not known whether the Soviet military had brothels reserved for its own use, but it is definitely true that the Soviet military committed large numbers of rapes. There is copious evidence that after the USSR's entry into the war against Japan, Soviet troops raped Japanese women in northeast China. It is said that at that time, some Japanese requested that comfort facilities be set up to prevent further rapes.

According to oral histories collected by Ōhara Makiko from women in a settler group near the Sino-Soviet border, on one occasion, when the women were staying in a refugee shelter, Soviet soldiers came in and separated them out. One woman said she witnessed the young women, including some fourteen- and fifteen-year-old girls, being led away. The women who were taken were raped and then returned to the shelter.[27] According to the recollections of the president of the Mukden Residents Association, at noon one day, three Soviet soldiers broke into the house of a sake brewer's family at noontime. After they gang-raped the twenty-one-year-old wife, they bludgeoned her genitals with sake bottles and killed her.[28]

In the midst of these conditions, Japanese built comfort stations for the use of Soviet troops. According to the recollections of an employee of the South Manchuria Railway's Fushun coal mine, invading Soviet troops robbed {him} of such valuables as his watch and pen, and then at night pounded on the doors of the company housing demanding liquor and menacing {residents} with shouts of "Send out the women!"[29] Then in mid-August, the authorities in charge of the coal mine established a dance hall and other comfort facilities, and "gathered together prostitutes from the city and women like that from among the refugees who had fled from other regions . . . and outfitted comfort facilities for Soviet troops."[30] These facilities are said to have later been reserved for the use of Chinese Nationalist troops. According to Hayashi Iku's oral history, in an entry in the end of September, a certain settler group, on the orders of its vice president, presented fifteen young women between the ages of fifteen and twenty-one to Soviet troops for "the troops' comfort."[31] Thus Japanese people provided young women as sacrificial offerings to Soviet troops as well.

The Case of the German Army

It appears that each branch of the German military, such as the Reichswehr and the SS, had its own comfort stations. To cite research that takes the problematic perspective of boasting about the Reichswehr's hygiene management, the Reichswehr set up large numbers of brothels (comfort stations) for the exclusive use of the troops in the territories it occupied. By 1942, the number of these facilities had reached five hundred.[32] The commanding officer of the occupying army was in charge of equipping, supervising, and provisioning these facilities. Provisions were treated as military supplies and transported on supply trains in the occupied territories.[33] The primary impetus for setting up these comfort stations was the apparent spread of sexually transmitted diseases {among the troops}. Large numbers of soldiers in the German army had contracted sexually transmitted diseases during World War I, so the military strove to practice exhaustive hygiene management. Examinations for sexually transmitted diseases were conducted twice a week.[34] In France and Holland, German military personnel used existing brothels. Many of the women who were drafted in the eastern occupied territories were forced to choose between doing forced labor and working in a brothel reserved for soldiers.[35]

Preventing the spread of sexually transmitted diseases was of paramount concern to the German Reichswehr.

The Constitution of the Japanese Military

The commonalities and differences among the various national armies in regard to comfort stations and comfort women are inextricably intertwined with the structure and character of the armies. Let's return to the case of the Japanese military. Why was such a large-scale system of comfort stations considered indispensable? This was related to problems the Japanese military had maintaining military discipline. Yoshida Yutaka has analyzed the particular difficulties of the Japanese military as follows.

From the time of the Taishō democracy movement onward, the soldiers of the Japanese military became aware of their rights and matured intellectually and culturally. The military's central command realized that it was impossible to demand from soldiers the same kind of absolute obedience to military discipline that had been required in the past, and in 1921 the army's set of internal regulations was revised. It attempted to implement discipline based on the soldiers' "self-consciousness."[36]

From the end of the Taishō period (1912–1926) through the beginning of the Shōwa period (1926–1989), however, the Laborer-Farmer Party movement flourished, the activities of the Communist Party of Japan came to the fore, and anti-imperialist people's liberation movements in China became more active. The Japanese military did an about-face, making the supervision of soldiers more rigorous and trying to inculcate a consciousness appropriate to the Imperial Military.[37] In short, the Japanese military did not produce new doctrines or organizational principles in order to get soldiers to internalize the virtues of loyalty and sincerity, in response to soldiers' self-consciousness. Rather, unable to recognize soldiers' human rights, it once again aimed at maintaining military discipline through strict supervision.[38]

When Japan plunged into all-out war in China in 1937, the scale on which people were mobilized expanded drastically, and officers could no longer adequately control the men under their command. There were soldiers who hated military life, were perpetually critical, were not respectful toward officers, and were in general resistant to the army's internal discipline. Military crimes, especially insubordination, were increasing.[39] The dissatisfaction of soldiers oppressed in the barracks was exploding onto the inhabitants of the occupied territories. Some military authorities came to believe that illegal acts committed against the inhabitants of occupied territories were merely boorish and should be overlooked, and that under these conditions, punishing the acts severely would be counterproductive.[40]

This attitude gave rise to the vicious cycle of overlooking rapes committed in the occupied territories and then expanding sexual comfort facilities because the frequency of rapes was hindering military governance. In fact, since the outbreak of full-scale hostilities in China in 1937, an attitude privately acknowledging rape as a "wartime benefit" permeated all ranks of the Japanese military.

> A commonality found in the statements made before the military tribunals by young soldiers [who committed rapes and were being prosecuted] include having rape . . . suggested to them at events such as send-off parties in their hometowns by men who had served in the war and returned home and who told them that 'there are some good things in the war zone in China'; and then {the departing soldiers} were seized with the desire {to rape}. . . . This is how {we} learned how poor the concept of military discipline was among all types of reserve soldiers who had served on the front lines in China and returned.[41]

In this context, the Japanese military considered the establishment of military comfort stations essential to maintaining military discipline and to motivating soldiers (especially noncommissioned officers and veterans) to follow orders unconditionally. In such a situation, it was inevitable that the following sort of views would arise among the soldiers.

> Because hot-blooded youths were oppressed by the inhumane world known as the army and believed that life should be short but sweet, it was inevitable that they occasionally sought an outlet for their sexual desires there.[42]
>
> In order to be able to work efficiently on the battlefield, it is necessary to preserve at all times a combination of robust physical condition and a fierce spirit. The expending of sexual desire harmonizes the body and spirit, and is a lubricator for war. The fact that military authorities considered comfort stations to be necessities was natural for those in charge of the war.[43]

Here we see the theory of the necessity of the comfort women system clearly expressed. This theory does not recognize the reality of the violation of {comfort women's} human rights and became an enabling condition that facilitated those violations.

Of course, not all officers and enlisted men visited military comfort stations. There were probably officers who valued women's dignity, restrained their sexual desires, and never went to military comfort stations, or who scorned going. There were many who didn't go out of fear of contracting a sexually transmitted disease. Surely it cannot be denied, however, that the majority of officers and enlisted men considered military comfort stations a necessary evil.

COMFORT WOMEN'S POSTWAR EXPERIENCES

Abandonment

After Japan's surrender, the vast majority of Japanese military personnel and civilians living abroad returned to Japan aboard evacuation ships within two years. By 1950, even most of the detainees in Siberia had returned to Japan. At the end of 1956, 2,689 people convicted of crimes were released and returned home.

In the case of comfort women, the navy issued a repatriation order in September 1944, and Japanese comfort women were sent back to the Japanese mainland.[44] It appears, however, that the army did not return comfort women from other countries to their homes, except in a few special cases.

We can gather from the following documents that a considerable number of comfort women were sent home after Japan's defeat. On September 7, 1945, the commander of the Allied forces in French Indochina issued his first order, which included a clause specifying that "all Japanese brothel operators and comfort corps must be evacuated along with Japanese military personnel."[45] According to a report of the U.S. military government in Okinawa, the U.S. military determined that Korean comfort women dispersed throughout the Okinawan islands were "a constant source of trouble in some districts." The Americans gathered together 40 Korean women from Okinawa and 110 from other islands (a total of 150 women), and sent them home to Korea in November 1945.[46]

There were many comfort women, however, who were left out of these kinds of plans and were unable to return home to their own countries. In 1988, Yun Jong-ok, the person who turned the spotlight on the comfort women issue, visited a former comfort woman living in Hat Yai in Thailand.[47] Pe Pong-gi, who was forcibly brought to Okinawa's Tokashikijima, entered a civilian relocation camp in Ishikawa in Okinawa after the Japanese military's surrender, but she was not given an opportunity to return to her hometown. When she left the relocation center, she said, she was beaten down by the thought that "she had been deceived and brought there by the Japanese military and then abandoned in a strange country."[48] She never returned to Korea and passed away in October 1991. In 1992, a list of the names of twenty-six Korean former comfort women who remained behind in the Wuhan area was submitted to the Korean embassy by a representative of the former comfort women.[49]

The above examples are drawn from the experiences of Korean women, but it is possible that cases of Chinese and Taiwanese women who stayed behind in Southeast Asia and the Pacific islands, as well as cases of Indonesian and other women who were taken away from their countries and never returned, will eventually be confirmed.

Suffering the Aftereffects of Disease and Injury

After the war, former comfort women suffered the aftereffects of diseases, injuries, and psychological trauma, as well as social discrimination on account of having been made comfort women. Things that stand out in the case histories of these women are physical afflictions such as sexually transmitted diseases, uterine diseases, hysterectomies, and sterility; and mental illnesses such as nervous diseases, depression, and speech impediments.

According to Korean women's testimony, among nineteen Korean former comfort women, two suffered chronic problems from sexually transmitted diseases. There was even a case in which a family was destroyed when the oldest son born to a former comfort woman began to exhibit symptoms of syphilis.[50] Many women were afflicted with uterine diseases, and some even had hysterectomies. There were also some whose bodies ached on rainy days because they had been beaten repeatedly in the comfort stations. Six of the nineteen women got married, but five of them were second wives. All six were later divorced. Eight were unable to marry formally, and cohabitated with their partners or lived as concubines. The remaining five women neither married nor cohabitated with a partner. I Yeong-suk was unable to have children because of the abuse she had suffered as a comfort woman, so her partner's feelings changed, and they had to break up.[51] There were also women who suffered from their experiences but with the support of their families were able to live happily after the war. But the former comfort women who came forward with their stories had unhappy lives after the war.

According to a report on Taiwanese former comfort women, in the case of the forty-eight former comfort women living in Taiwan, it seems that none were afflicted with sexually transmitted diseases that lasted into the postwar period. Thirty-one of the women got married, but twelve were later divorced. Ten cohabitated with their partners.[52] There were only four couples in which the husband knew that the wife had been a comfort woman who were living "peaceful lives." Many of the women didn't think they wanted their husbands to know about their pasts.[53] Twenty-six of the women were unable to have children because of {the abuse they suffered as comfort women}, and many of them adopted children.[54] Ten women suffered from uterine diseases.

In the case of Filipina women, many were forced to be comfort women for periods lasting from a few days to a several months, with the longest period lasting more than two years. Thus while many Filipina women suffered injuries from violence, the number with bodily injuries resulting specifically from sexual servitude is not as large as the number of Korean and Taiwanese women with those types of injuries. One woman was diagnosed with gonorrhea when she went to a doctor in 1950; another woman had to have stitches in her vagina when she was liberated; another woman had a hysterectomy; and another woman was rendered unable to have children.[55]

Needless to say, the damage done to these women was not minor. There was a woman who'd been kicked so hard her arm broke and it healed crooked; there were also women who had injuries from being stabbed in the shoulder. Though not a physical injury, one testimony described how when one woman confided to the man she lived with about her experiences as a comfort woman, he stopped coming home. Tomasa Salinog remained single out of fear of male sexual violence.

Post-Traumatic Stress Disorder (PTSD)

Former comfort women also suffered severe PTSD (mental trauma). Kikumaru, a Japanese former comfort woman, committed suicide by gas asphyxiation in her apartment in Ichikawa city in Chiba Prefecture on April 26,

1972. She was forty-seven years old. Hirota Kazuko, who has taken Kiku-maru as a subject of research, argues that the Japanese military "took advantage of the vulnerability of {women's} poverty and cajoled {them}, saying it was for the country's sake and telling them that they would be civilian military employees, and then making them into comfort women." She describes how "no matter how great the cause, when you sell your body, your spirit can never go back to the way it was. Taking this fact as my object of inquiry, I felt its truth any number of times."[56]

In the case of Korean women, many former comfort women shared such suffering as being unable "to sleep without the door being open, even in wintertime, when {I} get depressed."[57] Another example of PTSD {that haunts former comfort women} is evident in the case of Choi Myong-sun (a fictitious name). She became neurotic after her thirtieth birthday, and she began to experience symptoms of dementia. She described how at the time she "would suddenly despise her husband, break out in goose flesh, and go out of her mind, yelling at him to 'Get out!!' "[58]

Among Taiwanese women, a sense of private self-loathing persists even now. This sense includes such sentiments as, "My heart aches with shame," "I want to keep my distance from groups of people, and I don't even want to get near my sons, daughters, or other family members," and "I don't want to go out."[59] One woman reported that on account of her PTSD, she couldn't face ordinary everyday life. She was continually leaving the house and getting lost, and "thought 'I want to kill myself' so many times."[60] In Taiwan, a state of affairs in which the women blame themselves persists, even though the Japanese state is to blame.

Looking at the cases of Filipina women, there are experiences like that of Amonita Balajadia, who escaped a military comfort station after being imprisoned there for one week. She fled back to her home, but for months afterward she was mentally unstable because of the shock and bodily injuries she had sustained, and spent day after day just staring blankly into space.[61] According to the stories Maria Rosa Luna Henson's mother told her, for about a year and a half after she {Maria} was liberated, she was "like a baby." She had to go back and relearn everything, beginning with practicing how to walk.[62] She also said that, despised by everyone around her, she lived hidden in the house and came to distrust people. Even now, when she remembers life in the comfort station or has dreams about it, "I end up wandering around in a daze for several days, talking to myself, and {it} destroys my health."[63]

The damage done to Dutch former comfort woman Jeanne O'Herne was also extremely profound. She describes one aspect of her suffering as follows.

> Even after almost fifty years, I still experience this feeling of total fear going through my body and through all my limbs, burning me up. It comes to me at the oddest moments in which I wake up with nightmares and even feel it when just lying in bed at night. But worst of all, I felt this fear every time my husband made love to me. I have never been able to enjoy intercourse as a consequence of what the Japanese did to me.[64]

Living with Social Discrimination

Social discrimination also oppressed these women. Hwang Kum-ju confided that, "I get sick of thinking about how I can live out my life and then die without being despised by other people and without suffering from illness as well."[65] Park Sun-e recalled that "I couldn't lead a dignified life, and when I think of how I ruined my child's whole life, I am mortified, but there's no help for it."[66] The discrimination from their families as well as the pressure these women exerted on themselves was profound. Kim Hak-sun married but was told by her husband that "she was a filthy woman, who'd had sex with soldiers."[67] Mun Ok-chu's aunt would scream at her, saying, "Who would have thought that a daughter like you would come from a *yangban* family?"[68]

In Taiwan, conditions are such that not even one woman feels it would be all right to step forward and tell her story. Reasons given for this {reluctance to come forward} include the belief that it would cause trouble for their families, and that if the truth were known, they would be "beaten to death" by family members. The sense that "if {the truth} were known, it would be all over {for them}" is extremely strong.[69]

Filipina former comfort woman Gertrude Balisalisa returned to her home after being liberated from a comfort station in May 1945. But her husband treated her "like I {had} a contagious disease," and her parents and relatives "looked down on her as if she was something filthy."[70] Rosita Pacardo Nacino was stabbed by Japanese soldiers in the left side of her chest. In 1944, after she was set free from Japanese soldiers' barracks, she walked around searching for her family. While she was looking for them, she was hauled off to USAFFE guerrillas' headquarters and raped (this account and what follows are from interviews conducted by the author). She was attacked because she was thought to be attached to the Japanese military. After the war, she went to Marakanian Palace and to the Justice Ministry, reporting that she wanted to sue the guerrillas, but no one would hear her case, telling her that "she was crazy."[71]

The Suffering Never Ends

In the midst of all this oppression, abandoning efforts to conceal the past and coming forward itself became a certain sort of liberation from mental restraints. Kim Dok-chin (a fictitious name) described how she went to the Korean Council to testify, and "since I said what I wanted to say, it seems that half of my bitter feelings dissolved."[72] Mun Pil-gi related how, "when I finally spewed out all the things I had kept locked up inside me all that time, I felt a great weight had been lifted off my chest."[73]

In Taiwan as well, there are victims who feel that they "cannot consent to" their own pasts and want to "restore public righteousness" and to "clear away their discontent."[74]

When Japanese people deny the Japanese state's responsibility in the comfort women issue, however, as in instances like former Minister of Justice Nagano's statements, these women's dignity is violated and it causes them pain. Li Sun-ok (a fictitious name) made the following comments on this point.

> Society still despises me. Despite the fact that it will be humiliating if I receive compensation, if I can't receive compensation, it will be so mortifying that there will be no holding me back. When I think of the past, my heart races, and my insides get tied in knots.[75]

Until the Japanese government unambiguously acknowledges its responsibility, apologizes, pays compensation, and restores the honor of the victims, their suffering will not end.

Conclusion

DISCRIMINATORY ATTITUDES TOWARD WOMEN

Finally, I would like to raise the issue of discrimination against women, which hasn't been treated in its own right thus far, and look at the problems of Japanese society that supported the military comfort women system.

I have read many accounts of soldiers' war experiences and have had my fill of descriptions of comfort women. The thing that bothers me most about them is the attitude that considers women only as things or sex objects that pervades former soldiers' thinking and affirmed {the existence of} comfort stations as a necessary evil. An officer in the 11th Army Signal Corps gives the following description.

> During the battle, which lasted about fifty days, I did not see any women at all. I knew that as a result of (being without access to women), men's mental condition ends up declining, and that's when I realized once again the necessity of special comfort stations. This desire is the same as hunger or the need to urinate, and soldiers merely thought of comfort stations as practically the same as latrines.[1]

Women who were forced to become comfort women were regarded only as tools for the management of the sexual desires of military personnel. Their human rights were considered trivial, and even their basic dignity as human beings was ignored.

Many soldiers were caught up in the myth that a man who hadn't known a woman wasn't a man. In the military, a culture that promoted going to military comfort stations was dominant. A naval officer in Waingapu in Indonesia records the following experience.

> Asking, "Is the man who doesn't know comfort stations just a man ignorant of our beloved Sunda Isles, or is he a man who doesn't have

the courage to be a naval officer?" the company commander himself ordered an immediate full-scale attack on a nearby comfort station.[2]

On the orders of the company commander, the officers headed off en masse. As for examples of those who went on their own, one officer who went to a military comfort station near Vinhyen in Vietnam records that his motive {for going} was "for one last look {at women} before being killed in battle."[3] A soldier who went to a military comfort station in Kwangtung Province passed through the entrance the day after seeing the bodies of heavily wounded troops, telling himself, "this 'self' of mine, who doesn't know when it will die—I'm a human being too. And I want to see a woman's body once before I die!"[4]

The logic of male privilege that declared that a man who hadn't had sex was not a man and that life was futile supported the licensed prostitution system at home and in the colonies, as well as the military comfort station system in war zones.

CHARACTERISTICS OF JAPANESE SOCIETY

So where did the discriminatory attitudes toward women held by the Japanese military and Japanese men come from? They came from modern Japan itself, where culture sanctioned male sexual self-indulgence—that is, the fulfillment of male sexual desire regardless of the dignity and human rights of women. These attitudes were not restricted simply to capitalists and men of high social standing, but spread among the masses as well after World War I.

Let's trace this history for a moment. In the civil code promulgated in 1898, the rights of the household head were established. The household head was invested with power, including control of all household assets and the power of {granting or withholding} legal recognition of marriages and adoptions. In matters of succession to the family headship, the succession of the oldest son was made the rule. Wives were defined as legally incompetent, and the practice of husbands keeping concubines was legalized. It became possible for husbands to recognize legally, without the consent of their wives, children born through unions with other women. Not only did this become the legal foundation for despising women, but it also sanctioned husbands' sexual self-indulgence.

Furthermore, in the criminal code that came into force in 1908, adultery was made a crime. In cases where a wife committed adultery, the woman and her partner would be punished upon her husband's report of the crime. But in cases where a husband committed adultery, he was not punished unless his partner was someone else's wife. If his partner was not someone's wife, the husband's sexual self-indulgence was sanctioned by law as well as in practice.

The double standard that allowed sexual self-indulgence for men and demanded chastity of women gave rise to a sexual division of labor that secured that standard. The rule that men could not have sexual relations with married women, along with the legal recognition of concubines, made the state's legal perpetuation of the public prostitution system inherited from the early modern period inevitable. Thus, from men's perspective, women were constrained to assume one of the following roles: wives, who were for having children; prostitutes, who were for having fun; and concubines, who fell somewhere between wives and prostitutes.

THE HISTORY OF THE LICENSED
PROSTITUTION SYSTEM, PART I

At the beginning of the early modern period (which is usually dated from around 1600 to 1868), the Tokugawa shogunate attempted to gather prostitutes who had been living scattered around the urban centers of Edo {later Tokyo}, Kyoto, and Osaka and settle them in one place, segregated from the rest of the city, in order to control them. This policy aimed at maintaining public order and enforcing the discipline of samurai society. By sanctioning sexual self-indulgence in a specific space set aside for that purpose, it enabled a temporary feeling of release from the strict social status system. This policy was intended to allow the shogunate to contain anything out of the ordinary that heralded the breakdown of the status system and to glean, through the licensed quarter system, information about possible dangers to the political system.[5]

The licensed prostitution system persisted after the Meiji Restoration {in 1868} but became a topic of debate by chance in 1872 (Meiji 5) as a result of the *Maria Luz* incident. A Chinese passenger on a Peruvian vessel named the *Maria Luz* anchored in Yokohama Bay jumped ship and fled. When he was captured and questioned, he reported that he had been tricked and forced aboard the ship bound for Peru. When it became clear that this was a case of trade in coolie laborers, an inquiry into the matter was launched by the Yokohama prefectural government. The lawyer representing the Chinese man who refused to return to the ship insisted that since the contract contravened "virtuous morals," it was not binding.[6] The lawyer representing the ship's captain, who was demanding the man's return, argued that since there were "even more restrictive, truly terrible contracts, namely, coerced prostitution contracts" in Japan, the contract was binding.[7]

Japan ruled against the ship's captain, but at Peru's request the Russian emperor acted as international arbitrator of the dispute. It was in this context that the licensed prostitution system was raised as a problem. The suspicion was that the system was in fact a form of traffic in people. In Official Order Number 295 that year, the Japanese government hastily confirmed the ban on traffic in people, released prostitutes from their contracts, and settled the issue of their debts, which had not been raised in the court case. Upon the issuance of this order, the Justice Ministry issued its own order, Number 22. This order on the one hand affirmed that prostitutes "differ from horses and cattle that have lost their bodily rights" and acknowledged that {the prostitution system} amounted to slavery.[8] On the other hand, since "it made no sense to demand that horses and cattle repay their debts," the Justice Ministry order rendered the debts incurred by prostitutes upon signing their contracts invalid and forbade attempts to recover them.[9]

The Japanese government, however, did not thereby intend to abolish the licensed prostitution system. Brothels changed their names to "houses of assignation," and their operators switched to a routine of renting out rooms with prostitutes who worked of their own free will. Prostitutes, however, were not free to refuse customers, to take time off for recuperation, to come and go as they pleased, or to communicate and meet with whomever they pleased. The ransoms that restrained these women persisted, in practice, in the form of loans given in advance {often to a parent or a third party, which prostitutes then worked to repay}.

With the rise of movements to abolish prostitution, laws to regulate it were finally passed in 1900 (Meiji 33) and prostitutes' freedom to quit was established. However, following from the fact that the prostitution business was legally recognized, even though contracts based on the principle of prostitutes' working to pay off loans advanced to them were not binding as labor contracts, they were treated as binding loan contracts as a rule, so quitting was in reality very difficult. Women had to submit notification of their intention to quit to the police in person, and the police who had jurisdiction would often call local assignation house operators. In order to guarantee the claims of the brothel proprietors {on prostitutes for repayment of loans}, police would try to hand prostitutes back over to proprietors.

THE HISTORY OF THE LICENSED PROSTITUTION SYSTEM, PART II

The licensed prostitution system was in reality a system of sexual slavery that amounted to traffic in people, the sale of sex, and restraints on freedom. Japan transplanted this system to Taiwan and Korea, the Kwantung leased territories, and various mandated territories in the South Seas. In 1881 (Meiji 14), Japan introduced the licensed prostitution system into Korea with the enactment of "Regulations Concerning Houses of Assignation and the Prostitution Business" in Pusan, the first treaty port opened. After the "Amalgamation {Annexation} of Korea" in 1910, the licensed prostitution system was established in region after region. In 1916, the "Laws Regulating Houses of Assignation and Prostitutes" consolidated the system on a national scale.[10] In the beginning, Japanese women were brought to Korea to serve as prostitutes, but soon Korean women were being made into prostitutes.

In both Japan and Korea, prostitutes had to live in designated areas, and their freedom to leave those areas was restricted. In 1933 (Shōwa 8), Home Ministry Order Number 15 lifted the restrictions on prostitutes leaving the licensed quarters, but the police made great efforts to minimize prostitutes' trips outside and to prevent them from fleeing. For example, the Chief of Police for Aichi prefecture instructed the chiefs of local police stations to "make (prostitutes) report where they are going and what the purposes of their trips are" whenever they left the licensed quarters, to "make great efforts to see that they are given plenty of opportunities for self-cultivation and recreation in order to minimize trips outside of the licensed quarters and escapes," and, "since it's not inconceivable that people attempting to agitate {among} prostitutes will appear, to warn prostitutes often about these people to prevent prostitutes from falling in with such bad company."[11]

There were differences between the regulations protecting prostitutes in Japan and those in Korea. It was illegal to employ women under age eighteen as prostitutes in Japan, while in Korea the minimum age was seventeen. Furthermore, in Japan, prostitutes' freedoms of communication, of association, of access to reading material, of ownership of personal property, and of consumption were mandated. But in Korea, only the freedoms to enter into contracts and to communicate and meet with whomever they pleased were mandated. The freedom to quit was theoretically established by law, but since quitting was difficult even in Japan, it was extremely difficult in Korea where women were even more restricted. "To Korean prostitutes who were isolated by language and literacy as well, the freedom to quit was nothing more than a set of words; in reality, their situation was as if there were no such legal freedom."[12] In the colonies, the character of the sexual slavery system grew even more severe.

There was also the important issue of the people's supportive attitude toward the licensed prostitution system. Many Japanese people could not imagine themselves in the position of women who had become prostitutes. The fact that participants in movements to abolish prostitution were limited to certain activists involved in the women's liberation movement and Christian or Buddhist activists (aside from the cases of a few prefectures that outlawed licensed prostitution) attests to {this failure to sympathize with the plight of prostitutes}.

There were houses of assignation near the Regimental Headquarters of army units stationed in the major cities of each prefecture. On their days off, soldiers would go to these brothels just like any other customers. According to Shigematsu Masashi's research, in 1909 (Meiji 42) when the 61st Infantry Regiment was called up to serve in Imafuku, a southern suburb of the city of Wakayama, whether to build houses of assignation became an issue for political debate.[13] In elections for the city government that took place the following year, many candidates who supported the building of brothels were elected. Their success was due to the fact that, economically speaking, among voters belonging to classes "below the middle classes," many supported building brothels.[14] A letter to the editor of a local newspaper illustrates this point clearly, arguing that "those of the middle class and above can enjoy themselves with geisha (even without brothels) and can even do it easily every night. But lower-class laborers can't even enjoy themselves {with geisha} once in ten years. Out of sympathy with them, I support the building of brothels."[15] At the same time that the Taishō democracy movement was expanding throughout the country, there was a movement to bring prostitution within the reach of those "below the middle classes." (In this case, however, the movement to build brothels failed.)

In a society so thoroughly pervaded by the licensed prostitution system, the idea of establishing comfort stations for the exclusive use of the military in war zones and occupied territories was, in a sense, natural. And for that reason, the violations of comfort women's human rights became invisible.

To what extent the attitudes that condoned the system of sexual slavery called the military comfort women system have been overcome today remains an important question. The licensed prostitution system has disappeared, and the civil and penal codes have been revised. But in reality the licensed prostitution system lives on, transformed into the bath house business and {so-called} "businesses that may affect public morals." When we consider such things as Japanese travelers' sex tours to foreign countries and the "Japayuki" phenomenon {women brought to Japan to work as prostitutes}, we can conclude that the essence {of those attitudes} has not changed much. Ways of thinking about sex cannot be said to have undergone significant changes either. As can be seen in the nudity flooding television, magazines, and comic books, and in lewd descriptions of sex, precisely because the rules about sex have disappeared, sexual desire has been laid bare. In this sort of context, statements such as "[Compared to the U.S. military, the Japanese military] couldn't keep soldiers supplied with weapons and food, but they did supply prostitutes. They understood the essential nature of human beings!!" can still be heard.[16] In regard to tolerating sexual violence against women, attitudes in the culture concerning sex have scarcely changed from prewar times through the postwar period.

MULTIPLE VIOLATIONS OF HUMAN RIGHTS

What is the essence of the military comfort women issue? Based on the investigations concluded thus far, we can at least specify the following points.

First, the army restrained women continuously, and soldiers raped them without considering their behavior as rape. This amounted to organized violence against women and constituted a grave violation of these women's human rights. Even in cases when the comfort women system took forms that could be considered variations of licensed prostitution, even the freedoms to quit, communicate, and associate recognized in the licensed prostitution system were not secured for military comfort women. They were placed in a position of having absolutely no rights. (Furthermore, we should not overestimate the rights of prostitutes recognized in the licensed prostitution system. On this point, I can't agree with the view that divides comfort women into two types, the "prostitute type" and the "sex-slave type.") Because in many cases the military comfort stations did pay the women, very few officers or enlisted men recognized this grave violation of human rights. With the sense that going to a comfort woman was the same as going to a licensed prostitute in Japan, soldiers went to comfort stations and harmed these women without realizing it.

Second, the military comfort women system constituted racial and ethnic discrimination. Though there were exceptions, as a rule, Japanese comfort women were adult prostitutes, while the vast majority of comfort women from other Asian countries (the colonies or occupied territories) were minors or were adults who had not been prostitutes. In this context, we can't overlook the fact that among Japanese men, sexual contempt for the women of other Asian countries was widespread. As we have already seen, the Research Team of the Army Department of the Imperial Headquarters' assertion that "[in war zones in China] the activity of Korean women surpasses the others. This should be taken into account in future battles," and the statement by a high-ranking Ministry of War official that the reason there were so many rapes committed in combat zones in the Philippines was because "the women are more appealing to Japanese" were probably typical. Also, the fact that Dutch women held in internment camps were forced to become comfort women, something that would never have happened to Japanese women, proves that discrimination was clearly at work.

Third, the military comfort women system constituted economic class discrimination. Setting aside the case of Dutch women, {we can say that} many of the women rounded up as comfort women, regardless of whether they were Japanese, from the colonies, or from occupied territories, were economically impoverished women without sufficient education. Even

Japanese women who had previously been prostitutes and then became comfort women on account of economic distress were sold by their parents when they were still minors or sank into that world of suffering in order to save their parents. In the case of women from the colonies or occupied territories who were tricked or coerced into becoming comfort women, the Japanese military took advantage of their poverty and forced them to provide "sexual comfort."

Fourth, the military comfort women system was in violation of international law and constitutes a war crime. In the cases of Korean, Taiwanese, Chinese, Southeast Asian, and Pacific island women, we have already seen that there were many instances of rounding up minors, placing people into debt servitude, duping them, rounding them up forcibly, and forcing them to serve in comfort stations against their wills.

The military comfort women issue is an instance of multiple violations of human rights of the sort mentioned above. And the gravity of the issue lies in the fact that it was by no means a contingent occurrence but rather a government policy promoted by the state itself.

TOWARD A SETTLEMENT

What can be done to lay these multiple and grave violations of human rights to rest? In my introduction, I brought up the settlement proposal put forward in 1990 by Korean women's organizations. Later, the Center for Research and Documentation on Japan's War Responsibility published "A Proposal for Reparations to the Victims of the 'Military Comfort Woman' System" (May 1994). Also, the ICJ made recommendations for a settlement in its final report, and the Japan Bar Association made public their "Proposal Regarding the 'Military Comfort Woman Issue'" (January 1995). Among the recommendations in these documents of steps the Japanese government should take, the following are what I consider to be the minimum.

1. All official documents in government possession relating to military comfort women must be made public, and a true accounting of events must be arrived at through interviews with all witnesses in victimized countries.

2. Acknowledgment of and apologies for all violations of international law and war crimes committed by the Japanese government must be made.

3. Acknowledgment of responsibility for not having punished those responsible for these acts must be made.

4. Rehabilitation of the victims must be conducted.

5. Victims' dignity must be restored and individual compensation paid.

6. What mistakes were made must be clarified, and educational programs about history and human rights must be instituted so that these mistakes will never be repeated. Monuments must be erected to mourn the victims. A research center to establish the historical facts must be set up. Memorial museums that preserve this history must be founded. Steps to prevent the repetition of these mistakes, through the above means or aid given to such efforts, must be taken.

The essence of the military comfort women issue must be acknowledged and the aforementioned steps taken in good faith. If this is done, I believe that Japanese culture and Japanese attitudes toward human rights and other ethnic groups will be revolutionized and that Japan will also secure international trust.

Epilogue

Three years have already passed since I first began investigating the military comfort women issue in December 1991. The experiences I have had in these past three years—giving reports at the International Public Hearings, participating in the founding of the Center for Research and Documentation on Japan's War Responsibility, cooperating in the investigations of the ICJ, surveying documents in Korea and Taiwan, participating in two joint research groups with the Korean Council for the Women Drafted for Military Sexual Slavery by Japan, giving a paper at the 1994 annual meeting of the U.S. Association of Asian Studies—have been priceless to me. Aided by the investigations and research, both in Japan and abroad, that have made such striking progress in those years, I managed to put this book together.

However, until the women who were formerly comfort women came forward, the fact that there are still people today who continue to suffer on account of having been forced to become comfort women was unclear to me, and I couldn't really fully imagine it. Nakano Shigeharu had already remarked in April 1947, while criticizing the writings of Nakayama Tadanao (cited in the body of this text), "Isn't now the time when we have to rethink entirely our conceptions about those people who have so long been referred to as the 'girl army' [here meaning military comfort women]?"[1] But what was necessary was to rethink "in its entirety" everything from the information dug up at the time the war began to conditions in the postwar period. In the course of my research, I felt keenly that the victims' suffering continues even today and that the issue is not something that happened fifty years ago but a contemporary problem. The recent instances of ethnic cleansing and mass rape that occurred in the former Yugoslavia are very similar to the issues surrounding comfort women during the Fifteen-Year War (1931–1945). And this forced me to realize that it is possible, even today, for this to happen again in some different form. If we were placed in this sort of situation, how on earth would we behave? A firm settlement of the comfort women issue and steps to prevent any recurrence are first and foremost contemporary issues.

By writing this book, I finally got the feeling that I was able to form a complete picture of the military comfort women issue in my own way. There are still many things I don't understand, but it is my hope that this book will be useful for comprehending the issue. And nothing will make me happier than if this book becomes a departure point for future research and contributes to a fundamental settlement.

Of course, it may turn out that this book has only gone halfway toward a complete explication of the issue. In it, I have left a more intensive analysis of the participation of the Governments-General of Korea and Taiwan as a topic for future research.

In order to present a complete picture in the future, it is essential that, at the very least, the following conditions change. First, the Japanese government did conduct a survey of government documents beginning in the spring of 1992, but since August 1993 the survey has, in practice, been abandoned. There are still important documents that have not been made public. Next, victims in China, Southeast Asia, and the Pacific islands, with the exception of the Philippines, have not, for the most part, come forward. And most of the governments in that region have not demanded that the truth be made clear.

In order for the aforementioned tasks to be accomplished, I would like to demand once again that the Japanese government make public all related documents. I also hope that investigations and research in all of the victimized countries will make progress.

In putting together this book I was aided by numerous people. Former comfort women graciously granted me lengthy interviews. And on those occasions, I was also aided by Yun Jong-ok, Nelia Sancho, Arimitsu Ken, and Usuki Keiko, as well as by members of the Korean Council for the Women Drafted for Military Sexual Slavery by Japan, the Association for the Bereaved Families of Korean Victims of the Pacific War, the TFFCW (Task Force on Filipino Victims of Military Sexual Slavery by Japan; it has recently changed its name, but still goes by its old acronym), the Association for Clarifying Japan's War Responsibility, the Filipina Former "Military Comfort Women" Aid Association, the Association to Support the

Suits Filed by "Comfort Women" in Japan, and attorneys Aitani Kunio and Takagi Ken'ichi. I would like to express my sincere appreciation to them as well as to apologize for being unable, for lack of space, to make full use of the materials generated in interviews. I was also given invaluable testimony by many people, first among them being Katsuki Kyūji. Yoshida Yutaka, Endō Tatsuhiko, and many others contributed crucial documents and information. The Asahi Newspaper Company sponsored the publication of "Court Documents Relating to the Semarang Comfort Station Incident."

This book is also indebted to the many volunteers who participated in the Center for Research and Documentation on Japan's War Responsibility survey of personal accounts and unit histories of the war. I also learned many things from the contributions of Kawata Fumiko, Kim Pu-ja, Nishino Rumiko, Hayakawa Noriyo, Hayashi Hirofumi, Fujii Tadatoshi, Yang Ching-ja, and Yun Myong-suk at each meeting of the Center's "Military Comfort Women" Research Group. I received great encouragement from Arai Shin'ichi and many others at the Center. I would like to express here my deep appreciation to all these people.

I would also like to thank both Ōyama Misako and Inoue Kazuo for kindly seeing this book through to completion. Mr. Inoue in particular gave me invaluable advice during the copyediting of the initial draft. It was due to the efforts of these two that I somehow managed to get the book together. I would like to offer them my thanks again here.

Yoshimi Yoshiaki
March 1995

Notes

Translator's Introduction

1. Estimates of the number of women enslaved in comfort stations vary from several thousand to as many as two hundred thousand. See Yoshimi's discussion of this issue on pages 91–94.

2. I place the terms "comfort women" and "comfort station" in quotation marks on first use to emphasize the fact that these terms themselves played a role in concealing and normalizing the violence used against these women. See note 1 in "Author's Introduction to the English Edition," below. Many survivors explicitly reject the term "comfort woman." Here I generally use "survivor" and "victim" interchangeably to refer to women who were forced to serve as comfort women. I've retained the use of "comfort women" to describe wartime practices and attitudes that perpetuate wartime views of the women.

3. Of course, this "debt" could never truly be repaid, as any compensation could never be commensurate with the suffering and losses these women have endured.

4. Hanguk Chŏngsindae Munje Daech'aek Hyŏbŭihoe (hereafter Korean Council), an umbrella group uniting women's, Buddhist, Christian, and civic groups, organized in November 1990 to aid Korean women who were victimized by the Japanese military and to pursue redress for Japanese war crimes against them.

5. See Norma Field, "War and Apology: Japan, Asia, the Fiftieth, and After," *positions* 5(1)(1997): 1–49, for a discussion of the language of Japanese apologies and its implications.

6. Yamada Akira, "Ima towareru sensō sekinin, sengo hoshō" [Current inquiries into war responsibility and postwar compensation] in Kyōkasho ni shinjitsu to jiyū wo renryakukai, ed., *Ima naze sensō sekinin wo mondai ni suru no ka* [Why problematize war responsibility now?] (Tokyo: Kyōiku shiryō shuppankai, 1998), 12.

7. I have translated *jiyūshugi* here as "free" because more literal translations, such as "liberal" or "libertarian," seem open to greater misinterpretation. Whereas "liberal" might seem to connote left-wing and "libertarian" an emphasis on individual rights, I chose "free" to communicate the insistence on national autonomy

in the writing of history that characterizes Society members' views. They call for a national history free from the intrusion of non-Japanese views and experiences, and free from the responsibility to confront the darker chapters of Japanese history.

8. See Fujime Yuki, Suzuki Yūko, and Kanō Mikiyo, "Joseishi to 'ianfu' mondai" [Women's history and the "comfort women" issue], *Impaction* 107(1998): 102–129, for a discussion of how various feminist historians first learned of the existence of comfort women and their reactions.

9. See Hyun Sook Kim, "History and Memory: The 'Comfort Women' Controversy," *positions* 5(1)(1997): 73–106, on textbook treatments of the war. See also Ian Baruma, *Wages of Guilt: Memories of War in Germany and Japan* (London: Vintage, 1995).

10. See, for example, Kim, "History and Memory."

11. See, for example, Kobayashi Yoshinori and Takeuchi Yoshikazu, *Kyōkasho ga oshiekanenai jigyaku* [The masochism that textbooks are perfectly capable of teaching] (Tokyo: Center for Research Into False Charges of War Crimes Against Japan, 1997), 24–25. Within two months of its publication on August 1, the book had already gone into its fourth printing.

12. Soh Kyon-shik, "Haha wo hazukashimeru na" [Don't humiliate/assault my mother!] in Komori Yōichi and Takahasji Testuya, eds., *Nashyonaru hisutorii wo koete* [Overcoming national history], (Tokyo: Tokyo daigaku shuppankai, 1998), 37.

13. Kobayashi and Takeuchi, *Kyōkasho ga oshiekanenai jigyaku*, 24–30.

14. Ueno Chizuko, "Kioku no seijigaku: kokumin, kojin, watashi" [The politics of memory: Japanese citizen, individual, me], *Impaction* 103(1997): 154–172.

15. For a summary of Yoshimi's rebuttal of Ueno, see Yoshimi, "'Jūgun ianfu' mondai to rekishizō: Ueno Chizukoshi ni kotaeru" [The "military comfort women" issue and images of history: a response to Ueno Chizuko] in *Nashyonarizumu to "ianfu" mondai* [Nationalism and the "comfort women" issue] (Tokyo: Center for Research and Documentation on Japan's War Responsibility, 1998).

16. Kobayashi and Takeuchi, *Kyōkasho ga oshiekanenai jigyaku*, 184.

17. This logic is echoed in Fujioka Nobukatsu, "Why Middle-School Students Should Not Be Taught About 'Military Comfort Women,'" in Japanese Society for History Textbook Reform, "The Restoration of a National History: Why Was the Japanese Society for History Textbook Reform Established and What Are Its Goals?" 1. See note 18.

18. Information on the Society is partially derived from "The Restoration of a National History: Why Was the Japanese Society for History Textbook Reform

Established and What Are Its Goals?" an English-language publication of the Society that was mailed, unsolicited, to the translator in Japan in February 1999. It is not clear how the Society selected recipients for this publication, but numerous other foreign researchers also received it.

19. Fujioka, "Why Middle-School Students Should Not Be Taught About 'Military Comfort Women,'" 11.

20. Namikawa Eita, "The Iniquities of History Education in Japan During the Postwar Period" in Society for History Textbook Reform, "The Restoration of a National History," 15.

21. Yi Tŭngnam (pseudonym), testimony in Keith Howard, ed., *True Stories of Korean Comfort Women* (London: Cassell, 1995) (Translation from the Korean, *Kangjero kkŭllyŏgan Chosŏnin kunwianbudŭl*, The Korean Council for Women Drafted for Military Sexual Slavery by Japan, 1993), 141.

22. Ibid., 176.

23. A 1998 International Labor Organization report on the "sex sector" in Malaysia, Indonesia, Thailand, and the Philippines estimates that prostitution accounts for between 2 and 14 percent of the GDP of these countries. See Lin Lean Lim, ed., "The Sex Sector: the Economic and Social Bases of Prostitution in Southeast Asia" (Geneva: International Labor Office, 1998).

24. Japan's sex industry amounts to one percent of its GNP, the same percentage as is spent on Japan's defense budget.

25. "Trafficking in Women and Prostitution in the Asia Pacific," The Coalition Against Trafficking in Women-Asia Pacific web site, http://www.uri.edu/artsci/hughes/catw/apmap.html. Information on the site compiled from Donna M. Hughes et al., *The Factbook on Global Sexual Exploitation* (Coalition Against Trafficking in Women, 1999).

26. Gay McDougall, Special Rapporteur to the UN Commission on Human Rights' Sub-Commission on Prevention of Discrimination and Protection of Minorities, "Contemporary Forms of Slavery: Systematic Rape, Sexual Slavery and Slavery-like Practices During Armed Conflict," paper submitted June 22, 1998.

Author's Introduction to the English Edition

1. Hereafter, quotations around the term "military comfort women" have been omitted in the interests of readability. See the introduction to the book ("The Emergence of the Issue") for a discussion of the controversy surrounding the use of this term.

2. All Japanese names are given in Japanese order, with the family name first followed by the personal name.

3. Text in [ ] are notes added to quoted materials by the author. Text in { } are translations of Japanese terms, clarifications, or supplementary information added by the translator.

4. All dollar equivalents are given in U.S. dollars and calculated based on an exchange rate of $1 = ¥120.

The Emergence of the Issue

1. Kim Hak-sun, interview on *Nyūsu 21*, NHK, 28 Nov. 1991.

2. *Dai 118 kai kokkai sangiin yosan iinkai kaigiroku* [118th Diet House of Councillors Committee on the Budget minutes] 19(6 June 1990): 6.

3. Yun Jong-ok, et al., *Chōsenjin josei ga mita "ianfu mondai"* [The "comfort woman" issue from the perspective of Korean women] (Tokyo: San'ichi shobō, 1992), 255.

4. *Asahi Shimbun*, 11 January 1992, page 1, lead article.

5. Yoshimi Yoshiaki, ed., *Jūgun ianfu shiryōshū* [Collected documents relating to military "comfort women"] (Tokyo: Ōtsuki shoten, 1992). Hereafter, *shiryōshū*.

6. Kōno Yōhei, "Kōno Yōhei naikaku kanbōchōkan danwa" [On the issue of wartime "comfort women"] (official statement of Chief Cabinet Secretary Kōno Yōhei), 4 August 1993.

7. *Asahi Shimbun*, 7 May 1994, page 1, lead article.

8. Kokusai kōchōkai jikkō iinkai [Executive Committee for International Public Hearings], ed., *Sekai ni towareru nihon no sengo shori* [War victimization and Japan: International Public Hearing Report], vol. 1 (Osaka: Toho Shuppan Inc., 1993), 79.

1. The Course and Conditions of the Establishment of the Military Comfort Station System

1. "Shōwa jūsannenjū ni okeru zairyū hōjin no tokushu fujo no jōkyō oyobi sono torishimari narabi ni sokai tōkyoku shishō torishimari jōkyō" [In regard to the current state of regulations on private prostitution in the concession and the regulation of special prostitutes reserved for Japanese citizens in Shanghai during 1938], cited in Yoshimi, *shiryōshū*, 184.

2. Ibid.

3. Ibid., 92.

4. Ibid.

5. Ibid., 100–101.

6. Inaba Masao, ed., *Okamura Yasuji taishō shiryō: senjō kaisōhen* (Tokyo: Hara Shobō, 1970), 302.

7. Okabe Naosaburō, *Okabe Naosaburō taishō no nikki* (Tokyo: Fuyō shobō, 1982), 23 (entry for March 14, 1932).

8. Hara Teruyuki, *Shiberia shuppei: kakumei to kanshō* (Tokyo: Chikuma shobō, 1989), 420–423.

9. Sanbō honbu [General Staff Office], ed., *Taishō 7 nen naishi 11 nen shiberia* (Siberia) *shuppei shi*, vol. 4 (Tokyo: Sanbō honbu, 1933), chart no. 2–2.

10. Kempei shireibu, ed., *Sacharin haken kempei shi* (Tokyo: Kempei shireibu, date of publication unknown), 167.

11. Ibid., 125–126.

12. Konsei dai 14 ryodan shireibu [14th Mixed Brigade Headquarters], "Eisei gyōmu jumpō," report from the middle of March 1933. Kokuritsu kōbunsho kan [Japanese National Archives], 11.

13. Ibid., report from the end of March, 9–10.

14. Ibid., report from the beginning of May, 9.

15. Ibid., report from the middle of July, 4.

16. Nakayama Tadanao, "Manmō no tabi (3)," *Tōyō* (Nov. 1933): 143.

17. Kantōgun sanbōbu senden sankō [Kwangtung Army General Staff Headquarters], "Kanminzoku no tokushitsu" (July 1933), in Rikugunshō, ed., *Manshū jihen rikugun eiseishi*, vol. 8 (Tokyo: Rikugunshō, 1938), 196.

18. Nankin senshi henshū iinkai [History of the Battle of Nanking Editorial Collective], ed., *Nankin senshi shiryōshū* (Tokyo: Kaikōsha, 1989), 211.

19. Ibid., 280.

20. Ibid., 411.

21. Dai 3 shidan eiseitai kaikoroku henshū iinkai [The 3rd Division Medical Corps Memoir Editorial Collective], ed., *Dai 3 shidan eiseitai kaikoroku* (Tabara, Aichi: Dai 3 shidan eiseitai kaikoroku kankōkai, 1979), 102.

22. Yoshimi, *shiryōshū*, 195.

23. Ibid., 196.

24. Ibid., 200.

25. Ibid., 202.

26. Ibid.

27. Tanaka Tsuneo, ed., *Tsuioku no shisen*, vol. 2 (Yokohama: Ōrupuraikingu, 1989), 100–102.

28. Asō Tetsuo, *Shanhai yori shanhai e* (Fukuoka: Sekifūsha, 1993), 42.

29. Yoshimi, *shiryōshū*, 184–185.

30. Ibid., 188.

31. Ibid., 260.

32. Ibid., 266.

33. Ibid., 263.

34. Ibid., 267.

35. Ibid., 191.

36. Ibid.

37. Ibid.

38. Ibid., 210.

39. Hokushi keimubu, "Hōjin shokugyōbetsu jinkō tōkeihyō," (July 1, 1939), Gaimushō gaikō shiryōkan [Ministry of Foreign Affairs Archives].

40. Yoshimi, *shiryōshū*, 215.

41. Ibid., 215–216.

42. Kinbara Setsuzō, "Rikugunshō gyōmu nisshi tekiroku," entry for 15 April 1939. Bōeichō bōei kenkyūjo toshokan [Defense Agency's Defense Research Institute Library].

43. See Shimada Toshihiko, *Kantōgun* (Tokyo: Chūō kōronsha, 1965), 176; and Senda Kakō, *Jūgun ianfu: Keiko*, vol. 1 (Tokyo: Kōbunsha, 1981), 103–104.

44. Yoshimi, *shiryōshū*, 105–106.

45. Ibid., 166–167.

46. Sakurada Takeshi and Shikanai Nobutaka, *Ima akasu sengo hishi*, vol. 1 (Tokyo: Sankei shuppan, 1983), 40–41.

47. Yoshimi, *shiryōshū*, 102–103.

48. Ibid., 179–180.

49. Ibid., 121–122.

50. Ibid., 131–137.

51. Inaba Masao, ed., *Okamura Yasuji taishō shiryō: senjo kaisō hen*, 302–303.

52. Ibid., 300–301.

53. Yoshimi, *shiryōshū*, 228–232.

54. Ibid., 237.

55. Ibid.

56. Kinbara Setsuzō, "Rikugunshō gyōmu nisshi tekiroku," entry for 14 February 1940.

57. Ibid.

58. Yoshimi, *shiryōshū*, 235.

59. Ibid., 235–236.

60. Ibid., 232.

61. Asō Tetsuo, *Shanhai yori shanhai e*, 229.

62. Rikujō jieitai eisei gakkō, ed., *Daitōa sensō rikugun eiseishi*, vol. 1 (Tokyo: Rikujō jieitai eisei gakkō [Ground Self-Defense Force Medical School], 1971), 605–607.

63. Kitashina hōmen gun shireibu, "Kyōsantō no waga guntai ni taisuru shisōteki gakai kōsaku no shinsō to kore ga bōatsu hōsaku" [The Communist Party's truth about the ideological campaign to undermine our troops and the means to stop it] (5 April 1939), Kokuritsu kōbun shōkan [Japanese National Archives].

64. Morikawa butai (Dokuritsu san hōhei daisan rentai), "Morikawa butai tokushu ian gyōmu ni kansuru kitei," dated November 14, 1939, in *Jinchū nisshi* (Nov. 1939). Dokuritsu san hōhei dai 3 rentai.

65. Asō Tetsuo, *Shanhai yori shanhai e*, 229.

66. Inaba Masao, ed., *Okamura Yasuji taishō shiryō: senjō kaisōhen*, 304.

67. Kameo Susumu, *Ma no shittangawa* (Tokyo: Ōshisha, 1980), 80.

68. Koromo dai 3040 butai kinen jigyō jikkō iinkai, ed., *Kōdo: hokushi haken koromo dai 3040 butai no sokuseki* (Tokyo: Koromo dai 3040 butai kinen jigyō jikkō iinkai, 1977), 210–211.

69. Yoshimi, *shiryōshū*, 354.

2. Expansion Into Southeast Asia and the Pacific

1. Kinbara Setsuzō, "Rikugunshō gyōmu nisshi tekiroku," entry for 26 July 1941. Bōeichō bōei kenkyūjo toshokan.

2. Ibid., entry for 12 February 1942.

3. Ibid., entry for 2 May 1942.

4. Ibid., entry for 9 May 1942.

5. Ibid., entry for 12 August 1942.

6. Yoshimi, *shiryōshū*, 145.

7. Ibid., 146.

8. Ibid., 459.

9. See Kumamoto hōsō, "Hōdō Tokushū: Hyōhaku no hate," broadcast March 16, 1992; Nishino Rumiko, *Jūgun ianfu to 15 nen sensō* (Tokyo: Akashi shoten, 1993), 82.

10. Yoshimi, *shiryōshū*, 143.

11. Rikuamitsu dai 1398, "Tokō tetsuzuki ni kansuru ken," entry dated 18 November 1942, *Rikuamitsu dainikki* 55 (1942). Bōeichō bōei kenkyūjo toshokan.

12. Yoshimi, *shiryōshū*, 171–172.

13. Kinbara Setsuzō, "Rikugunshō gyōmu nisshi tekiroku," entry for 22 December 1942.

14. Ibid., entry for 11 April 1943.

15. Ibid., entry for 30 July 1942.

16. Ibid., entry for 31 October 1942.

17. Ibid., entry for 3 September 1942.

18. Hayashi Hirofumi, "Rikugun no ianjo kanri no ichisokumen," *Sensō sekinin kenkyū* 1(Sept. 1993): 16–17.

19. Kinbara Setsuzō, "Rikugunshō gyōmu nisshi tekiroku," entry for 4 February 1943.

20. Shigemura Minoru, "Tokuyōin to iu na no butai," *Tokushū bungei shunjū* 1(Feb. 1955): 225.

21. Matsuura Takanori, ed., *Owarinaki kaigun* (Tokyo: Bunka hōsō kaihatsu sentā shuppanbu, 1978), 98.

22. Yoshimi, *shiryōshū*, 365–375.

23. Marai gunseikan, "Ian shisetsu oyobi ryokan eigyō junshu kisoku," *Gunsei kiteishū* 3(11 Nov. 1943). Marai (Malay) gunseikanbu. Bōeicho bōei kenkyūjo toshokan.

24. Nagamine Hideo, *Zuihitsu: Senjō*. (Chigasaki, Kanagawa: privately published, 1987), 94.

25. Mandaree chūtonchi shireibu, "Chūtonchi ianjo kitei," dated 26 May 1943. UK Imperial War Museum.

26. Nihon no sensō sekinin shiryō sentā, "Kokuritu kokkai toshokan shozō no sensō taikenki, butaishi chōsa ni tsuite," *Sensō sekinin kenkyū* 3(March 1994): 58.

27. Kakazu Katsuko, "Okinawaken no ianjo mappu sakusei o tōshite," *Dai 5 kai zenkoku joseishi kenkyū kōryū no tsudoi hōkokushū* (Tokyo: Zenkoku joseishi kenkyū kōryū jikkō iinkai, 1994), 25–31.

28. Senda Kakō, *Jūgun ianfu* (Tokyo: San'ichi shobō, 1978), 167.

29. Kim Il-myon, *Tennō no guntai to chōsenjin ianfu* (Tokyo: San'ichi shobō, 1976), 79.

30. Hata Ikuhiko, *Shōwashi no nazo o ou*, vol. 2 (Tokyo: Bungei shunjū, 1993), 328.

31. Kankoku teishintai mondai taisaku kyōgikai and Teishintai kenkyūkai, eds., *Shōgen: kyōsei renkō sareta chōsenjin gunianfutachi* (Tokyo: Akashi shoten, 1993).

32. Zaidan hōjin Taihokushi fujo kyūen shakaifukuri kikin kai, eds., *Taiwan chiku ianfu hōmon chōsa kobetsu bunseki hōkokusho* (Taipei: Taipei Women's Rescue Foundation, 1993).

33. Nagasawa Hide, ed., *Senjika chōsenjin chūgokujin rengōgun furyo kyōsei renkō shiryōshū*, vol. 3 (Tokyo: Ryokuin shobō, 1993), 16.

34. Ibid., 30.

35. Ogino Fujio, "Toyamaken ni okeru 'rōmu ianfu' ni tsuite." *Sensō sekinin kenkyū* 6(Dec. 1994): 65.

36. "Firipin (Filipine) 'jūgun ianfu' hoshō seikyū jiken sojō," Part I, April 1993; Part II, September 1993, Defense Counsel for Former Filipino "Comfort Women's" Compensation Trial.

37. Yoshimi, *shiryōshū*, 565–580.

38. Daihon'ei rikugunbu kenkyūhan, "Shina jihen ni okeru gunki fūki no kenchi yori kansatsuseru seibyō ni tsuite," dated October 1940. Bōeichō bōei kenkyūjo toshokan.

39. Yoshimi, *shiryōshū*, 276–277.

40. Kinbara Setsuzō, "Rikugunshō gyōmu nisshi tekiroku," entry for 7 January 1943.

3. How Were the Women Rounded Up?

1. Kankoku teishintai mondai taisaku kyōgikai and Teishintai kenkyūkai, eds., *Shōgen*, 7.

2. Yoshimi, *shiryōshū*, 103.

3. Senda Kakō, *Jūgun ianfu: Keiko* (Tokyo: Kōbunsha, 1981), 117.

4. Ibid., 55.

5. Tamai Noriko, *Hinomaru o koshi ni maite* (Tokyo: Gendaishi shuppankai, 1984), 80.

6. Ibid., 81.

7. Ibid., 84.

8. Hirota Kazuko, *Shōgen kiroku: jūgun ianfu, kangofu* (Tokyo: Shinjinbutsu ōraisha, 1994), 19.

9. Ibid., 24.

10. Ibid., 24.

11. Yoshimi, *shiryōshū*, 111.

12. Senda Kakō, *Jūgun ianfu: Keiko*, 59.

13. Yamaguchi Hikozō, *Rakujitu no fu* (Higashimatsuyama, Saitama: Matsuyama shobō, 1987), 47–48.

14. Isozaki Takako, *Sei aru kagiri ruson e* (Tokyo: Kōdansha, 1984), 48.

15. Kawata Fumiko, *Akagawara no ie* (Tokyo: Chikuma shobō, 1987), 95–111.

16. Kankoku teishintai mondai taisaku kyōgikai and Teishintai kenkyūkai, eds., *Shōgen*, 72.

17. Ibid., 72.

18. Ibid., 73.

19. Ibid., 74.

20. Ibid., 117–118.

21. Ibid., 118.

22. Ibid., 119.

23. Ibid.

24. Kang Je-on, *Nihon ni yoru chōsen shihai no 40 nen* (Tokyo: Asahi shimbunsha, 1992), 128.

25. Ibid., 133.

26. Yoshimi, *shiryōshū*, 441.

27. Kankoku teishintai mondai taisaku kyōgikai and Teishintai kenkyūkai, eds., *Shōgen*, 253–254.

28. Ibid., 254.

29. Ibid., 255.

30. Ibid., 256.

31. Ibid.

32. Ibid., 257.

33. Ibid., 159.

34. Ibid., 160.

35. Ibid., 161.

36. Ibid., 162.

37. Ibid., 166.

38. Ibid., 162.

39. Yoshimi, *shiryōshū*, 458.

40. Ibid., 458–459.

41. Naimu daijin seigi, "Chōsen sōtokufu bunai rinji shokuin setchiseichū kaisei no ken," 27 June 1944, *Kōbun ruishū* 68(25). Kokuritsu kōbunsho kan.

42. Kankoku teishintai mondai taisaku kyōgikai and Teishintai kenkyūkai, eds., *Shōgen*, 242.

43. From an interview conducted by the author in Tokyo on 21 June 1993.

44. Yoshimi, *shiryōshū*, 441.

45. Chōsengun rinji heitan shireibu jinsen shibu, "Dai 20 shidan tenzoku jinba yusō gyōmu shōhō," entry for January 1938, *Mitsu dainikki* 11(1938). Bōeichō bōei kenkyūjo toshokan.

46. *Mainichi Shinpō*, 27 October and 1 November 1944.

47. Yoshimi, *shiryōshū*, 97.

48. Yun Myong-suk, "Nitchū sensōki ni okeru chōsenjin guntai ianfu no keisei," *Chōsenshi kenkyūkai ronbunshū* 32(Oct. 1994): 105–106.

49. Ibid., 106.

50. Ibid., 108.

51. Ibid.

52. Yoshimi, *shiryōshū*, 116.

53. Ibid., 118.

54. Taihokushi fujo kyūen shakaifukuri kikin kai, eds., *Taiwan chiku ianfu hōmon chōsa kobetsu bunseki hōkokusho*, 6.

55. Ibid., 17.

56. Ibid., 6.

57. Ibid., 7. There was an additional woman, but her age is unknown.

58. Ibid., 8.

59. Ibid., 15.

60. Ibid., 13.

61. Ibid., 15–16.

62. Ibid., 14, 16.

63. Ibid., 15.

64. Ibid., 17.

65. Executive Committee for International Public Hearings, ed., "War Victimization and Japan: International Public Hearing Report," vol. 1, English edition (Osaka: Toho Shuppan Inc., 1993), 79–80.

66. Taihokushi fujo kyūen shakaifukuri kikin kai, eds., *Taiwan chiku ianfu hōmon chōsa kobetsu bunseki hōkokusho*, 16.

67. Ibid., 20.

68. Suzuki Takushirō, *Kempei kashikan* (Tokyo: Shinjinbutsu ōraisha, 1974), 50–51.

69. Ibid., 51.

70. Shinkyō rikugun keiri gakkō dai 5 ki sei kinen bunshū henshū iinkai jimukyoku, ed., *Tsuioku*, vol. 1 (Tokyo: Shinkyō rikugun keiri gakkō dai 5 ki sei kinen bunshū henshū iinkai jimukyoku, 1985), 146.

71. Ibid., 147.

72. Yamada Sadamu, *Kempei nikki* (Tokyo: Surugadai shobō, 1985), 273–276.

73. Hirahara Kazuo, *Sanpō no shikō sakusen* (Tokyo: Privately published, 1991), 384–385.

74. Ibid., 384.

75. Mizobe Kazuto, ed., *Dokusan'ni: mō hitotsu no sensō* (Yamaguchi: privately published, 1983), 58.

76. Ibid., 55.

77. Ibid., 63.

78. Ibid.

79. Mori Toshi, *Moritoshi no heitai monogatari* (Tokyo: Aomura shuppansha, 1988), 228.

80. Ibid.

81. Executive Committee for International Public Hearings, ed., "War Victimization and Japan: International Public Hearing Report," vol. 1, 68–70.

82. Kankoku teishintai mondai taisaku kyōgikai and Teishintai kenkyūkai, eds., *Taiwan chiku ianfu hōmon chōsa kobetsu bunseki hōkokusho*, 14–15.

83. Hayashi Hirofumi, "Marei hantō ni okeru nihongun ianjo ni tsuite," *Kantō gakuin daigaku keizai gakubu ippan kyōiku ronshū* 15(July 1993): 77.

84. Ibid.

85. Yoshimi, *shiryōshū*, 374.

86. Ibid., 367.

87. Hayashi Hirofumi, "Shingapōru (Singapore) no nihongun ianjo," *Sensō sekinin kenkyū* 4(June 1996): 34.

88. Fusayama Takao, *Nankai no akebono* (Tokyo: Sōbunsha, 1983), 150.

89. Ibid., 151.

90. Shimotsu Isamu, *Deinei to Kojin* (Nishinomiya: Keizai seichōsha shuppankyoku, 1978), 291–292.

91. Takano butai senyūkai, *Takano butai mindanao tō senjinki* (Sakai, Osaka: Takano butai senyūkai, 1989), 377–378.

92. Hayashi Hirofumi, "Marei hantō no Nihongun ianjo," *Sekai* 579(March 1993): 278.

93. "Firipin (Filipine) 'jūgun ianfu' hoshō seikyū jiken sojō," Part II, 53.

94. Ibid., 54.

95. Shichōhei dai 32 rentai dai 1 chūtai senyūkai hachiboku kai, ed., *Warera no guntai seikatsu* (Tokyo: Shichōhei dai 32 rentai dai 1 chūtai senyūkai hachiboku kai, 1983), 293.

96. "Firipin (Filipine) 'jūgun ianfu' hoshō seikyū jiken sojō," Part I, 23–29, and interview conducted by the author on 18 October 1993 in Tokyo.

97. Ibid., 69–72, and interview conducted by the author on 23 January 1994 in Tokyo.

98. ōmura Tetsuo, "'Genchi chōtatsu' sareta joseitachi," *Sekai* 584(July 1993): 276–277.

99. Nogi Harumichi, *Kaigun tokubetsu keisatsutai* (Tokyo: Taihei shuppansha, 1975), 114.

100. Ibid., 116.

101. Kaigun keiri gakkō hoshū gakusei dai 10 ki bunshū kankō iinkai, ed., *Sōmei* (Tokyo: Kaigun keiri gakkō hoshū gakusei daijūki bunshū kankō iinkai, 1983), 312.

102. Ibid.

4. The Lives Comfort Women Were Forced to Lead

1. Imamura Hitoshi, *Imamura Hitoshi kaikoroku* (Tokyo: Fuyō shobō, 1980), 326.

2. Ibid.

3. Ibid., 328.

4. Nagasawa Ken'ichi, *Kankō ianjo* (Tokyo: Tosho shuppansha, 1983), 44.

5. Ibid., 48.

6. Ibid.

7. Murakami Sennosuke, *Yasen yobi byōin "aru eiseihei no shiki"* (Privately published, 1992), 64.

8. Takano butai senyūkai, *Takano butai mindanao tō senjinki* (Sakai, Osaka: Takano butai senyūkai, 1989), 378.

9. Yoshimi, *shiryōshū*, 388–393.

10. Ibid., 397–401.

11. Horie Yūji, *Shōkei sakusen ni jūgun shita ichigun'i no kaisō* (Ōta, Gunma: Privately published, 1988), 199.

12. Nagasawa Ken'ichi, *Kankō ianjo*, 54.

13. Ibid., 60.

14. Hosokawa Tadanori, *Senjō dōchūki* (Ōmiya: Privately published, 1992), 72.

15. Satō Kanji, *Akai chūrippu (Tulip) no heitai* (Tokyo: Senshūsha, 1978), 77–78.

16. Yanagisawa Masaru, *Ore wa mannen jōtōhei* (Tokyo: Eiji shuppan, 1981), 156.

17. Yamada Seikichi, *Bukan heitan* (Tokyo: Tosho shuppansha, 1978), 86.

18. Yoshimi, *shiryōshū*, 497–499, 515–518.

19. Ibid., 285–287.

20. Ibid.

21. Ibid., 287.

22. Ibid., 288.

23. Ibid.

24. Ibid., 207.

25. Ibid., 291–293.

26. Kankoku teishintai mondai taisaku kyōgikai and Teishintai kenkyūkai, eds., *Shōgen*, 46.

27. Ibid., 48.

28. Interview with Katsuki conducted by the author on 29 July 1993 in Ashiya, Fukuoka Prefecture.

29. Kankoku teishintai mondai taisaku kyōgikai and Teishintai kenkyūkai, eds., *Shōgen*, 77.

30. Nanbara Yukio, *Haruka naru futsuin* (Yokohama: Privately published, 1983), 202.

31. Kankoku teishintai mondai taisaku kyōgikai and Teishintai kenkyūkai, eds., *Shōgen*, 138.

32. Ibid., 125.

33. Nakashina haken kempeitai shireibu, "Rikugun gunjin gunzoku hikōhyō," entries dated November 1941 and February 1942, *Rikushifu dainikki* 6, 9 (1942). Bōeichō bōei kenkyūjo toshokan.

34. Yoshimi, *shiryōshū*, 208.

35. Takasaki Ryūji, ed., *Gun'ikan no senjō hōkoku ikenshū* (Tokyo: Fuji shuppan, 1990), 127.

36. Yoshimi, *shiryōshū*, 322.

37. Marai gunseikan, "Ian shisetsu oyobi ryokan eigyō junshu kisoku," *Gunsei kiteishū* 3(11)(Nov. 1943). Marai (Malay) gunseikanbu.

38. "Firipin (Filipine) 'jūgun ianfu' hoshō seikyū jiken sojō," Part I, 114.

39. Zaidan hōjin Taihokushi fujo kyūen shakaifukuri kikin kai, eds., *Taiwan chiku ianfu hōmon chōsa kobetsu bunseki hōkokusho*, 31.

40. Kankoku teishintai mondai taisaku kyōgikai and Teishintai kenkyūkai, eds., *Shōgen*, 167.

41. Hirosaki Ryū, "Jūgun ianfu ni wa henkan sarenai gunji yūbin chokin," *Shūkan kin'yōbi* 26(May 1994): 25.

42. Hamada Yoshihisa, *Biruma haisenki* (Tokyo: Tosho shuppansha, 1982), 77–78.

43. Yoshimi, *shiryōshū*, 208.

44. Yahōhei dai 3 rentai daisan chūtai shōkei sakusen no omoide henshū iinkai, *Yahōhei dai 3 rentai dai 3 chūtai shōkei sakusen no omoide* (Tokyo: Yahōhei dai 3 rentai daisan chūtai shōkei sakusen no omoide henshū iinkai, 1986), 24.

45. Yoshimi, *shiryōshū*, 325–326.

46. Kankoku teishintai mondai taisaku kyōgikai and Teishintai kenkyūkai, eds., *Shōgen*, 90–91.

47. "Firipin (Filipine) 'jūgun ianfu' hoshō seikyū jiken sojō," Part I, 26–28, and interview conducted by the author on 18 October 1993 in Tokyo.

48. Ibid., 70–71, and interview conducted by the author on 23 January 1994 in Tokyo.

49. Ibid., Part II, 24–27, and interview conducted by the author on 21 July 1994 in Tokyo.

50. Nagasawa Ken'ichi, *Kankō ianjo*, 64.

51. Yoshimi, *shiryōshū*, 460.

52. Kawasaki Masami, *Kanja yusō dai 89 shōtai* (Yamaguchi: Privately published, 1988), 297.

53. Ibid., 296.

54. Dai 11 gun shireikan Anami Korechika, "Tokubetsu hōkoku teishutsu no ken," entry for March 30, 1942, *Rikushifu dainikki* 9(1942). Bōeichō bōei kenkyūjo toshokan.

55. Yoshimi, *shiryōshū*, 277.

56. Imanishi Yoshinori, *Gun'i no shuki* (Amagasaki: Privately published, 1973), 126.

57. Horie Yūji, *Shōkei sakusen ni jūgun shita ichigun'i no kaisō*, 199–200.

58. Yoshimi, *shiryōshū*, 279.

59. Kankoku teishintai mondai taisaku kyōgikai and Teishintai kenkyūkai, eds., *Shōgen*, 124.

60. Ibid., 174.

61. Araki Torao, *Kita shina tōhikō* (Miyazaki: Kōmyakusha, 1982), 81.

62. Watanabe Ryōzō, *Kashū: chiisa na teikō* (Tokyo: Sharōmu tosho, 1994), 58.

63. Kankoku teishintai mondai taisaku kyōgikai and Teishintai kenkyūkai, eds., *Shōgen*, 78.

64. Ibid., 92.

65. Ibid., 176.

66. Ibid., 63.

67. Ibid., 64.

68. Ibid., 233.

69. Ibid., 174.

70. Ibid., 222.

71. Dai 13 shidanchō Uchiyama Eitarō, "Tokubetsu hōkokuchū gunjin henshi no ken," entry for March 21, 1942, *Rikushifu dainikki* 9(1942). Bōeichō bōei kenkyūjo toshokan.

72. Kawata Fumiko, *Kōgun ianjo no onnatachi* (Tokyo: Chikuma shobō, 1993), 119.

5. Violations of International Law and War Crime Trials

1. Kim Il-myon, *Tennō no guntai to chōsenjin ianfu* (Tokyo: San'ichi shobō, 1976), 19.

2. Yoshimi, *shiryōshū*, 102–103.

3. Ibid., 103.

4. Translated in *Treaty Series*, 1912, No. 20 (London: H.M.S.O., 1912), 269–270.

5. International Commission of Jurists (ICJ), *Comfort Women: An Unfinished Ordeal* (Geneva: ICJ, 1994).

6. Abe Kōki, "Guntai 'ianfu' mondai no hōteki sekinin," *Hōgaku semina* 466(Oct. 1993).

7. Sūmitsuin [Privy Council], *Sūmitsuin kaigi gijiroku*, vol. 38 (Tōkyō daigaku shuppankai, 1987), 78.

8. Ibid., 77.

9. Abe Kōki, "Guntai 'ianfu' mondai no hōteki sekinin," 65.

10. Ibid.

11. Yoshimi, *shiryōshū*, 105–106.

12. ICJ, *Comfort Women*, 158.

13. Ibid.

14. Ibid.

15. Abe Kōki, "Guntai 'ianfu' mondai no hōteki sekinin," 65.

16. Ibid.

17. Ibid., 64.

18. ICJ, *Comfort Women*, 158.

19. Abe Kōki, "Guntai 'ianfu' mondai no hōteki sekinin," 65.

20. Ibid., 65–66.

21. Ustinia Dolgopol, comment made at ICJ Report Study Association meeting in Tokyo, 11 March 1994.

22. ICJ, *Comfort Women*, 160.

23. Ibid., 160–161. The regulations in the Hague Convention that consider sexual violence against women as damaging to family honor are problematic because the one whose "honor" is lost in an incident of rape is not the woman who is raped but the person who commits the rape.

24. Abe Kōki, "Guntai 'ianfu' mondai no hōteki sekinin," 66.

25. ICJ, *Comfort Women*, 169–170.

26. Abe Kōki, "Guntai 'ianfu' mondai no hōteki sekinin," 64.

27. "Dutch Government Report." Unofficial translation into English, 24 January 1994, The Hague.

28. Netherlands Institute for War Documentation, Documents on Semarang Forced Prostitution Case Files 1944, 1948.

29. Ibid., and *Asahi Shinbun*, 21 July 1992, page 1.

30. Ibid., and *Asahi Shinbun*, 30 August 1992, page 9.

31. Ibid.

32. "Dutch Government Report," 14.

33. Ibid.

34. Ibid., 14–15.

35. Ibid., 15.

36. Jeanne O'Herne, *Cry of the Raped: A Story to Be Told* (Adelaide, Australia: Privately published, 1992), 3.

37. Ibid., 4–5.

38. Ibid., 6.

39. Ibid., 8.

40. Ibid., 10.

41. Ibid., 9.

42. Ibid., 10–11.

43. Ibid., 13.

44. Ibid.

45. Ibid., 14.

46. Ibid., 15.

47. Ibid.

48. Ibid., 16.

49. Ibid.

50. Ibid., 17.

51. Ibid., 18.

52. The following accounts are based on interviews conducted by the author in Tokyo on 16 July 1994.

53. O'Herne, *Cry of the Raped*, 21.

54. Interview with Ellie van der Ploeg, 16 July 1994.

55. "Hanketsubun," *Asahi Shimbun*, 30 August 1992, page 9; Chaen Yoshio, ed., *BC kyū senpan oranda saiban shiryō zenkan tsūran* (Tokyo: Fuji shuppan, 1992), 107, 120–121.

56. "Dutch Government Report," 13.

57. Ibid.

58. Ibid., 14.

59. Ibid., 16.

60. Ibid., 24.

61. Ibid., 20.

62. Utsumi Aiko, "Senjika no gaikokujin no jinken," *Sensō sekinin kenkyū* 3(March 1994): 13.

63. Tanaka Toshiyuki, *Shirarezaru sensō hanzai* (Tokyo: Ōtsuki shoten, 1993). This book was later translated into English as Yuki Tanaka, *Hidden Horrors: Japanese War Crimes in World War II* (Boulder, Colo.: Westview Press, 1996), 88–92.

64. "Ranryō indo hōrei kōhō," no. 44, *Sensō hanzai saiban kankei hōreishū*, vol. 2 (Tokyo: Hōmudaijin kanbō shihō hōsei chōsabu, 1965), 1–6.

65. Ibid., 320–322.

66. Hōmu daijin kanbō shihō hōsei chōsabu, *Sensō hanzai saiban gaishiyō* (Tokyo: Ministry of Justice, 1973), 249–250.

6. Conditions After the Defeat

1. Awaya Kentarō, ed., *Shiryō nihon gendaishi*, vol. 2 (Tokyo: Ōtsuki shoten, 1980), 149.

2. Hosokawa Morisada, *Hosokawa Nikki* (Tokyo: Chūō kōronsha, 1978), 149 (entry for 26 August 1945).

3. Awaya Kentarō, ed., *Shiryō nihon gendaishi*, 2:149.

4. Ibid.

5. Awaya Kentarō and Kawashima Takamine, eds., *Haisenji zenkoku chian jōhō*, vol. 5 (Tokyo: Nihon tosho sentā, 1994), 206–207.

6. Rōdōshō fujin shōnen kyoku, ed., *Baishun ni kansuru shiryō*, rev. ed. (Tokyo: Rōdōshō, 1955), 12–13.

7. Kobayashi Daijirō and Murase Akira, *Minna wa shiranai: Kokka baishun meirei*, rev. ed. (Tokyo: Yūzankaku shuppan, 1992), 12–14.

8. Ibid., 20.

9. Ibid., 26.

10. Awaya Kentarō and Kawashima Takamine, eds., *Haisenji zenkoku chian jōhō*, 5:108.

11. Hokkaidōchō, "Shōwa 20 nen chōkan jimu hikitugisho," Hokkaidōritsu bunshokan [Hokkaidō Prefectural Archives].

12. Awaya Kentarō and Kawashima Takamine, eds., *Haisenji zenkoku chian jōhō*, 6:122–123.

13. Ibid., 2:96.

14. Awaya Kentarō, ed., *Shiryō nihon gendaishi*, 2:313.

15. Ara Takashi, ed., *Nihon senryō gaikō kankei shiryōshū*, vol. 3 (Tokyo: Kashiwa shobō, 1991), 288.

16. Sumimoto Toshio, *Senryō hiroku*, vol. 1 (Tokyo: Mainichi shimbunsha, 1952), 67.

17. Kaigun shukei 9 ki kai, *5 fun mae no seishun* (Tokyo: Kaigun shukei 9 ki kai, 1979), 930.

18. Ichikawa Fusae, ed., *Nihon fujin mondai shiryō shūsei*, vol. 1 (Tokyo: Domesu shuppan, 1978), 551.

19. Ibid.

20. Tanaka, *Hidden Horrors*, 101–104.

21. Cynthia Enloe, *Does Khaki Become You?: The Militarisation of Women's Lives* (Boston: South End Press, 1983), 27–28.

22. Ibid., 28.

23. Bernard B. Fall, *Street Without Joy* (Harrisburg, Penn.: Stackpole, 1961), 133.

24. Theodore H. White, *In Search of History*, vol. 1 (New York: Harper & Row, 1978), 140.

25. Hosokawa Morisada, *Hosokawa Nikki*, 434 (entry for 21 August 1945).

26. Duus Masayo, *Makkāsā no futatsu no bōshi* (Tokyo: Kōdansha, 1985), 76.

27. Ōhara Makiko, *Kanashimi wa shōkakō ni nagashite* (Tokyo: Niji shobō, 1987), 92–93.

28. Usami Kyōji, *Aa mantetsu* (Tokyo: Kōdansha, 1983), 78–80.

29. Kubota Isao, *Bōkyō: Minami manshū tetsudō* (Sapporo: Kyōdō bunkasha, 1990), 41.

30. Ibid.

31. Hayashi Iku, *Shinpen Taiga nagareyuku* (Tokyo: Chikuma bunko, 1993), 89–90.

32. Franz Seidler, *Prostitution, Homosexualität, Selbstverstümmelung: Probleme der Deutschen Sanitätsführung 1939–1945* (Neckargemünd: Kurt Vowinkel Verlag, 1977), 186.

33. Ibid.

34. Ibid., 187.

35. Ibid., 154.

36. Yoshida Yutaka, *Tennō no guntai to nankin jiken* (Tokyo: Aoki shoten, 1985), 193.

37. Ibid., 195.

38. Ibid., 202.

39. Ibid.

40. Ibid., 203.

41. Inaba Masao, ed., *Okamura Yasuji taishō shiryō: senjō kaisōhen* (Tokyo: Hara Shobō, 1970), 283.

42. Kusado Ryōtarō, *Seito no hate* (Naze, Kagoshima: Privately published, 1992), 245.

43. Naoi Masatake, *Senkon* (Tokyo: Tōsen shuppan, 1973), 111.

44. Shigemura Minoru, "Tokuyōin to iu na no butai," *Tokushū bungei shunjū* 1(Feb. 1955): 223.

45. Yoshimi, *shiryōshū*, 564.

46. Ibid., 581–582.

47. Yun Jong-ok et al., *Chōsenjin josei ga mita "ianfu mondai"* (Tokyo: San'ichi shobō, 1992), 34–35.

48. Kawata Fumiko, *Akagawara no ie* (Tokyo: Chikuma shobō, 1987), 98.

49. Okumura Satoshi, "Chūgoku ni nokosareta kankokujin 'ianfu';" *Sensō sekinin kenkyū* 5(Sept. 1994): 45.

50. Kankoku teishintai mondai taisaku kyōgikai and Teishintai kenkyūkai, eds., *Shōgen*, 284.

51. Ibid., 82.

52. Zaidan hōjin Taihokushi fujo kyūen shakai fukuri jigyō kikin kai, ed., *Taiwan chiku ianfu hōmon chōsa kobetsu bunseki hōkokusho* (Taipei: Taipei Women's Rescue Foundation, 1993), 37.

53. Ibid., 37.

54. Ibid., 38.

55. "Firipin (Filipine) 'jūgun ianfu' hoshō seikyū jiken sojō," Parts I, II.

56. Hirota Kazuko, "Torakku (Truk) tō no jūgun ianfu, geisha 'Kikumaru'," *Joseitachi no taiheiyō sensō*, Bessatsu rekishi dokuhon 34 (Tokyo: Shinjinbutsu ōraisha, 1994), 121.

57. Kankoku teishintai mondai taisaku kyōgikai and Teishintai kenkyūkai, eds., *Shōgen*, 210.

58. Ibid., 282.

59. Zaidan hōjin Taihokushi fujo kyūen shakai fukuri jigyō kikin kai, ed., *Taiwan chiku ianfu hōmon chōsa kobetsu bunseki hōkokusho*, 40.

60. Ibid.

61. Interview with Balajadia conducted by the author on 27 April 1994 in Tokyo.

62. Interview with Henson conducted by the author on 18 October 1993 in Tokyo.

63. "Firipin (Filipine) 'jūgun ianfu' hoshō seikyū jiken sojō," Part I, 23.

64. Kokusai kōchōkai jikkō iinkai, ed., *War Victimization and Japan: International Public Hearing Report*, vol. 1 (ōsaka: Toho Shuppan Inc., 1993), 64.

65. Kankoku teishintai mondai taisaku kyōgikai and Teishintai kenkyūkai, eds., *Shōgen*, 116.

66. Ibid., 267.

67. Ibid., 54.

68. Ibid., 177–178.

69. Zaidan hōjin Taihokushi fujo kyūen shakai fukuri jigyō kikin kai, ed., *Taiwan chiku ianfu hōmon chōsa kobetsu bunseki hōkokusho*, 40.

70. "Firipin (Filipine) 'jūgun ianfu' hoshō seikyū jiken sojō," Part II, 23.

71. Interview with Nacino conducted by the author on 23 January 1994 in Tokyo.

72. Kankoku teishintai mondai taisaku kyōgikai and Teishintai kenkyūkai, eds., *Shōgen*, 69.

73. Ibid., 130.

74. Zaidan hōjin Taihokushi fujo kyūen shakai fukuri jigyō kikin kai, ed., *Taiwan chiku ianfu hōmon chōsa kobetsu bunseki hōkokusho*, 40.

75. Kankoku teishintai mondai taisaku kyōgikai and Teishintai kenkyūkai, eds., *Shōgen*, 69.

Conclusion

1. Kubomura Masaharu, *Dai 11 gun tsūshintai* (Tokyo: Tosho shuppansha, 1987), 97.

2. Kawabata Izuo, *Sunda rettō no kaisō* (Tokyo: Privately published, 1990), 63.

3. Ho 62 kankō 8 kisei shi henshūshitsu, *Ho 62 kankō 8 kisei shi* (Sagamihara, Kanagawa: Ho 62 kankō hakkisei shi kankō jimukyoku, 1992), 189.

4. Konoe hohei dai 5 rentai shi henshū iinkai, *Konoe hohei dai 5 rentai shi*, vol. 1 (Tokyo: Kinpogokai, 1990), 141.

5. Miyachi Masato, *Bakumatsu ishinki no bunka to jōhō* (Tokyo: Meicho kankōkai, 1994), 66–68.

6. Maki Hidemasa, *Jinshin baibai* (Tokyo: Iwanami shoten, 1971), 180.

7. Ibid., 182.

8. Ibid., 194–195.

9. Ibid., 195–196.

10. Yamashita Yong-e, "Chōsen ni okeru kōshōsei no jisshi," in Yun Jong-ok et al., *Chōsenjin josei ga mita "ianfu mondai"* (Tokyo: San'ichi shobō, 1992), 147, 154.

11. Aichiken keisatsushi henshū iinkai, ed., *Aichiken keisatsushi*, vol. 2 (Nagoya: Aichiken keisatsu honbu, 1973), 314–315.

12. Song Yon-ok, "Nihon no shokuminchi shihai to kokkateki kanri baishun," *Chōsenshi kenkyūkai ronbunshū* 32(Oct. 1994): 41.

13. Shigematsu Masashi, "Kōgai kaihatsu ronsō to shisei," *Nihonshi kenkyū* 359(July 1992): 8.

14. Ibid., 10.

15. Ibid.

16. Kitano (Beat) Takeshi, "Jūgun ianfu to chokorēto," *Shūkan Bunshun* 34(5) (Feb. 6, 1992): 49.

Epilogue

1. *Jinmin sensen* 10/11(April 1947): 48.

Bibliography

Place of publication is Tokyo unless otherwise noted.

BOOKS AND ARTICLES

Abe Kōki. "Guntai 'ianfu' mondai no hōteki sekinin." *Hōgaku seminā* 466 (Oct. 1993).

Aichiken keisatsushi henshū iinkai, ed. *Aichiken keisatsushi*, vol. 2. Nagoya: Aichiken keisatsu honbu, 1973.

Ara Takashi, ed. *Nihon senryō gaikō kankei shiryōshū*, vol. 3. Kashiwa shobō, 1991.

Araki Torao. *Kita shina tōhikō*. Miyazaki: Kōmyakusha, 1982.

Asō Tetsuo. *Shanhai yori shanhai e*. Fukuoka: Sekifūsha, 1993.

Awaya Kentarō, ed. *Shiryō nihon gendaishi*, vol. 2. Ōtsuki shoten, 1980.

Awaya Kentarō and Kawashima Takamine, eds. *Haisenji zenkoku chian jōhō*, vols. 1–7. Nihon tosho sentā, 1994.

Chaen Yoshio, ed. *BC kyū senpan oranda saiban shiryō zenkan tsūran*. Fuji shuppan, 1992.

Dai 3 shidan eiseitai kaikoroku henshū iinkai, ed. *Dai 3 shidan eiseitai kaikoroku*. Tabara, Aichi: Dai 3 shidan eiseitai kaikoroku kankōkai, 1979.

Dutch Government. "Report of a study of Dutch government documents on the forced prostitution of Dutch women in the Dutch East Indies during the Japanese occupation." The Hague, 1994.

Duus Masayo. *Makkāsā no futatsu no bōshi*. Kōdansha, 1985. (Originally published as *Haisha no okurimono* by Kōdansha, 1979).

Enloe, Cynthia. *Does Khaki Become You?: The Militarization of Women's Lives*. Boston: South End Press, 1983.

Fall, Bernard B. *Street Without Joy*. Harrisburg, Penn.: Stackpole, 1961.

"Firipin (Filipine) 'jūgun ianfu' hoshō seikyū jiken sojō," Part I, April 1993; Part II, September 1993, Defense Counsel for Former Filipino "Comfort Women's" Compensation Trial.

Fusayama Takao. *Nankai no akebono.* Sōbunsha, 1983.

Hamada Yoshihisa. *Biruma haisenki.* Tosho shuppansha, 1982.

Hara Teruyuki. *Shiberia shuppei: Kakumei to kanshō.* Chikuma shobō, 1989.

Hata Ikuhiko. *Shōwashi no nazo o ou,* vol. 2. Bungei shunjū, 1993.

Hayashi Iku. *Shinpen Taiga nagareyuku.* Chikuma bunko, 1993. (Originally published by Asahi shimbunsha, 1988.)

Hayashi Hirofumi. "Marei (Malay) hantō no Nihongun ianjo." *Sekai* 579 (March 1993).

——. "Rikugun no ianjo kanri no ichisokumen." *Sensō sekinin kenkyū* 1 (Sept. 1993).

——. "Marei hantō ni okeru nihongun ianjo ni tsuite." *Kantō gakuin daigaku keizai gakubu ippan kyōiku ronshū* 15 (July 1993).

——. "Shingapōru (Singapore) no nihongun ianjo." *Sensō sekinin kenkyū* 4 (June 1996).

Hikosaka Tei. *Dansei shinwa.* Komichi shobō, 1991.

Hirahara Kazuo. *Sanpō no shikō sakusen.* Privately (self-)published, 1991.

Hirosaki Ryū. "Jūgun ianfu ni wa henkan sarenai gunji yūbin chokin." *Shūkan kin'yōbi* 26 (May 1994).

Hirota Kazuko. *Shōgen kiroku: jūgun ianfu, kangofu.* Shinjinbutsu ōraisha, 1994.

——. "Torakku (Truk) tō no jūgun ianfu, geisha 'Kikumaru.'" *Joseitachi no taiheiyō sensō,* Bessatsu rekishi dokuhon 34. Shinjinbutsu ōraisha, February 1994.

Hōmu daijin kanbō shihō hōsei chōsabu. *Sensō hanzai saiban gaishiyō.* Tokyo: Ministry of Justice, 1973.

Horie Yūji. *Shōkei sakusen ni jūgun shita ichigun'i no kaisō.* ōta, Gunma: Privately (self-)published, 1988.

Ho 62 kankō 8 kisei shi henshūshitsu. *Ho 62 kankō 8 kisei shi.* Sagamihara, Kanagawa: Ho 62 kankō hakkisei shi kankō jimukyoku, 1992.

Hosokawa Tadanori. *Senjō dōchūki.* Ōmiya: Privately (self-)published, 1992.

Hosokawa Morisada. *Hosokawa nikki.* Chūō kōronsha, 1978.

Ichikawa Fusae, ed. *Nihon fujin mondai shiryō shūsei,* vol. 1. Domesu shuppan, 1978.

Imamura Hitoshi. *Imamura Hitoshi kaikoroku.* Fuyō shobō, 1980. (Originally published under the title *Shiki: ichigunjin rokujyūnen no aikan* by Fuyō shobō, 1970.)

Imanishi Yoshinori. *Gun'i no shuki.* Amagasaki: Privately (self-)published, 1973.

Inaba Masao, ed. *Okamura Yasuji taishō shiryō: senjo kaisō hen.* Hara shobō, 1970.

International Commission of Jurists (ICJ). *Comfort Women: An Unfinished Ordeal.* Geneva: ICJ, November 1994. (Japanese translation: Kokusai hōritsuka iinkai, *Kokusaihō kara mita "jūgun ianfu" mondai.* Akashi shoten, 1995.)

Isozaki Takako. *Sei aru kagiri ruson e.* Kōdansha, 1984.

Kaigun keiri gakkō hoshū gakusei dai 10 ki bunshū kankō iinkai, ed. *Sōmei.* Kaigun keiri gakkō hoshū gakusei dai 10 ki bunshū kankō iinkai, 1983.

Kaigun shukei 9 ki kai. *5 fun mae no seishun.* Kaigun shukei 9 ki kai, 1979.

Kakazu Katsuko. "Okinawaken no ianjo mappu sakusei o tōshite." In *Dai 5 kai zenkoku joseishi kenkyū kōryū no tsudoi hōkokushū,* Zenkoku joseishi kenkyū kōryū jikkō iinkai, 1994.

Kameo Susumu. *Ma no shittangawa.* Ōshisha, 1980.

Kankoku teishintai mondai taisaku kyōgikai and Teishintai kenkyūkai, eds., *Shōgen: kyōsei renkō sareta chōsenjin gunianfutachi.* Akashi shoten, 1993.

Kang Je-on. *Nihon ni yoru chōsen shihai no 40 nen.* Asahi shimbunsha, 1992.

Kawabata Izuo. *Sunda rettō no kaisō.* Privately (self-)published, 1990.

Kawasaki Masami. *Kanja yusō dai 89 shōtai.* Yamaguchi: Privately (self-)published, 1988.

Kawata Fumiko. *Akagawara no ie.* Chikuma shobō, 1987.

———. *Kōgun ianjo no onnatachi.* Chikuma shobō, 1993.

Kempei shireibu, ed. *Saharin haken kempei shi.* Kempei shireibu, date of publication unknown.

Kim Il-myon. *Tennō no guntai to chōsenjin ianfu.* San'ichi shobō, 1976.

Kim Pu-ja and Yang Ching-ja, eds. *Motto shiritai "ianfu" mondai.* Akashi shoten, 1995.

Kitano (Beat) Takeshi. "Jūgun ianfu to chokorēto." *Shūkan bunshun* 34(5)(February 6, 1992).

Kobayashi Daijirō and Murase Akira. *Minna wa shiranai: kokka baishun meirei.* Yūzankaku shuppan, rev. ed., 1992. (Originally published 1961.)

Kokusai kōchōkai jikkō iinkai, ed. *Sekai ni towareru nihon no sengō shori,* vol. 1. Osaka: Tōhō shuppan, 1993.

Konoe hohei dai 5 rentai shi henshū iinkai. *Konoe hohei dai 5 rentai shi,* vol. 1. Kinpogokai, 1990.

Koromo dai 3040 butai kinen jigyō jikkō iinkai, ed. *Kōdo: hokushi haken koromo dai 3040 butai no sokuseki.* Koromo dai 3040 butai kinen jigyō jikkō iinkai, 1977.

Kubomura Masaharu. *Dai 11 gun tsūshintai.* Tosho shuppansha, 1987.

Kubota Isao. *Bōkyō: Minami manshū tetsudō.* Sapporo: Kyōdō bunkasha, 1990.

Kurahashi Masanao. *Jūgun ianfu mondai no rekishiteki kenkyū.* Kyōei shobō, 1994.

Kusado Ryōtarō. *Seito no hate.* Naze, Kagoshima: Privately (self-)published, 1992.

Maki Hidemasa. *Jinshin baibai.* Iwanami shoten, 1971.

Matsuura Takanori, ed. *Owarinaki kaigun.* Bunka hōsō kaihatsu sentā shuppanbu, 1978.

Miyachi Masato. *Bakumatsu ishinki no bunka to jōhō.* Meicho kankōkai, 1994.

Mizobe Kazuto, ed. *Dokusan'ni: mō hitotsu no sensō.* Yamaguchi: Privately (self-)-published, 1983.

Mori Toshi. *Moritoshi no heitai monogatari.* Seison shuppansha, 1988.

Nagamine Hideo. *Zuihitsu: Senjō.* Chigasaki, Kanagawa: Privately (self-)published, 1987.

Nagasawa Hide, ed. *Senjika chōsenjin chūgokujin rengōgun furyo kyōsei renkō shiryōshū,* vol. 3. Ryokuin shobō, 1993.

Nagasawa Ken'ichi. *Kankō ianjo.* Tosho shuppansha, 1983.

Nakayama Tadanao. "Manmō no tabi (3)." *Tōyō* (Nov. 1933), Tōyō kyōkai.

Nanbara Yukio. *Haruka naru futsuin.* Yokohama: Privately (self-)published, 1983.

Nankin senshi henshū iinkai, ed. *Nankin senshi shiryōshū.* Kaikōsha, 1989.

Naoi Masatake. *Senkon.* Tōsen shuppan, 1973.

Nihon bengoshi rengōkai. "'Jūgun ianfu mondai' ni kansuru teigen." Nihon bengoshi rengōkai (Japan Bar Association), 1995.

Nihon no sensō sekinin shiryō sentā. "Kokuritu kokkai toshokan shozō no sensō taikenki butaishi chōsa ni tsuite." *Sensō sekinin kenkyū* 3(March 1994).

——. "'Jūgun ianfu' seido ni yoru giseisha no higai kaifuku ni tsuite no teigen." *Sensō sekinin kenkyū* 4(June 1994).

Nishino Rumiko. *Jūgun ianfu.* Akashi shoten, 1992.

——. *Jūgun ianfu to 15 nen sensō.* Akashi shoten, 1993.

Nogi Harumichi. *Kaigun tokubetsu keisatsutai.* Taihei shuppansha, 1975.

Ogino Fujio. "Toyamaken ni okeru 'rōmu ianfu' ni tsuite." *Sensō sekinin kenkyū* 6(Dec. 1994).

Ōhara Makiko. *Kanashimi wa shōkakō ni nagashite.* Niji shobō, 1987.

O'Herne, Jeanne. *Cry of the Raped: A Story to Be Told.* Adelaide, Australia: Privately published, 1992.

Okabe Naosaburō. *Okabe Naosaburō taishō no nikki.* Fuyō shobō, 1982.

Okumura Satoshi. "Chūgoku ni nokosareta kankokujin 'ianfu.'" *Sensō sekinin kenkyū* 5(Sept. 1994).

Ōmura Tetsuo. "'Genchi chōtatsu' sareta joseitachi." *Sekai* 584(July 1993).

Rikujō jieitai eisei gakkō, ed. *Daitōa sensō rikugun eiseishi,* vol. 1. Rikujō jieitai eisei gakkō [Ground Self-Defense Force Medical School], 1971.

Rōdōshō fujin shōnen kyoku, ed. *Baishun ni kansuru shiryō,* rev. ed. Ministry of Labor, 1955.

Sakurada Takeshi and Shikanai Nobutaka. *Ima akasu sengo hishi,* vol. 1. Sankei shuppan, 1983.

Sanbō honbu [General Staff Office], ed. *Taishō 7 nen naishi 11 nen shiberia* (Siberia) *shuppei shi*, vol. 4. Sanbō honbu, 1933.

Satō Kanji. *Akai chūrippu* (Tulip) *no heitai*. Senshūsha, 1978.

Seidler, Franz. *Prostitution, Homosexualität, Selbstverstümmelung: Probleme der Deutschen Sanitätsführung 1939–1945.* Neckargemünd: Kurt Vowinkel Verlag, 1977.

Senda Kakō. *Jūgun ianfu: Keiko*. Kōbunsha, 1981.

——. *Jūgun ianfu*, vols. 1–2. San'ichi shobō, 1978. (Originally published by Futabasha, 1973.)

Shigematsu Masashi. "Kōgai kaihatsu ronsō to shisei." *Nihonshi kenkyū* 359 (July 1992).

Shigemura Minoru. "Tokuyōin to iu na no butai." *Tokushū bungei shunjū* 1 (Feb. 1955).

Shichōhei dai 32 rentai dai 1 chūtai senyūkai hachiboku kai, ed., *Warera no guntai seikatsu*. Shichōhei dai 32 rentai dai 1 chūtai senyūkai hachiboku kai, 1983.

Shimada Toshihiko. *Kantōgun*. Chūō kōronsha, 1965.

Shimotsu Isamu. *Deinei to Kojin*. Nishinomiya: Keizai seichōsha shuppankyoku, 1978.

Shinkyō rikugun keiri gakkō dai 5 kisei kinen bunshū henshū iinkai jimukyoku, ed. *Tsuioku*, vol. 1. Shinkyō rikugun keiri gakkō daigokisei kinen bunshū henshū iinkai jimukyoku, 1985.

Song Yon-ok. "Nihon no shokuminchi shihai to kokkateki kanri baishun." *Chōsenshi kenkyūkai ronbunshū* 32 (Oct. 1994).

Sumimoto Toshio. *Senryō hiroku*, vol. 1. Mainichi shimbunsha, 1952.

Sūmitsuin [Privy Council]. *Sūmitsuin kaigi gijiroku*, vol. 38. Tōkyō daigaku shuppankai, 1987.

Suzuki Takushirō. *Kempei kashikan*. Shinjinbutsu ōraisha, 1974.

Suzuki Yūko. *Chōsenjin jūgun ianfu*. Iwanami shoten, 1991.

——. *"Jūgun ianfu" mondai to seibōryoku*. Miraisha, 1993.

Takano butai senyūkai. *Takano butai mindanao tō senjinki*. Sakai, Osaka: Takano butai senyūkai, 1989.

Takasaki Ryūji, ed. *Gun'ikan no senjō hōkoku ikenshū*. Fuji shuppan, 1990.

Tamai Noriko. *Hinomaru o koshi ni maite*. Gendaishi shuppankai, 1984.

Tanaka Tsuneo, ed. *Tsuioku no shisen*, vol. 2. Yokohama: Ōrupurainingu, 1989.

Tanaka Toshiyuki. *Shirarezaru sensō hanzai*. Ōtsuki shoten, 1993.

Usami Kyōji. *Aa mantetsu*. Kōdansha, 1983.

Utsumi Aiko. "Senjika no gaikokujin no jinken." *Sensō sekinin kenkyū* 3 (March 1994).

Watanabe Ryōzō. *Kashū: chiisa na teikō*. Sharōmu tosho, 1994.

White, Theodore H. *In Search of History*. New York: Harper and Row, 1978. Translated by Hori Taoko as *Rekishi no tankyū*, vol. 1, The Simul Press, Inc., 1981.

Yahōhei dai 3 rentai daisan chūtai shōkei sakusen no omoide henshū iinkai. *Yahōhei dai 3 rentai dai 3 chūtai shōkei sakusen no omoide*. Nagoya: Yahōhei dai 3 rentai daisan chūtai shōkei sakusen no omoide henshū iinkai, 1986.

Yamada Sadamu. *Kempei nikki*. Surugadai shobō, 1985.

Yamada Seikichi. *Bukan heitan*. Tosho shuppansha, 1978.

Yamaguchi Hikozō. *Rakujitu no fu*. Higashimatsuyama, Saitama: Matsuyama shobō, 1987.

Yamazaki Tanshō. *Gaichi tōchi kikō no kenkyū*. Takayama shoin, 1943.

Yamashita Yong-e. "Chōsen ni okeru kōshōsei no jisshi." In Yun Jong-ok et al., *Chōsenjin josei ga mita "ianfu mondai."* San'ichi shobō, 1992.

Yanagisawa Masaru. *Ore wa mannen jōtōhei*. Eiji shuppan, 1981.

Yasuhara Keiko. "Kakkoku ianfu no sengo to genzai." *Sensō sekinin kenkyū* 3(March 1994).

Yoshida Yutaka. *Tennō no guntai to nankin jiken*. Aoki shoten, 1985.

Yoshimi Yoshiaki, ed. *Jūgun ianfu shiryōshū*. Ōtsuki shoten, 1992.

——. "Rikugun chūō to 'jūgun ianfu' seisaku." *Sensō sekinin kenkyū* 1(Sept. 1993).

——. "'Jūgun ianfu' seisaku no shiki meirei keitō." *Shōgaku ronsan* 35(1–2). Chūō daigaku (March 1994).

Yun Jong-ok et al. *Chōsenjin josei ga mita "ianfu mondai."* San'ichi shobō, 1992.

Yun Myong-suk. "Nitchū sensōki ni okeru chōsenjin guntai ianfu no keisei." *Chōsenshi kenyūkai ronbunshū* 32(Oct. 1994).

Zaidain hōjin Taihokushi fujo kyūen shakai fukuri jigyō kikin kai, ed. *Taiwan chiku ianfu hōmon chōsa kobetsu bunseki hōkokusho*. Taipei: Taipei Women's Rescue Foundation, 1993.

MANUSCRIPTS AND GOVERNMENT DOCUMENTS

Chōsengun rinji heitan shireibu Jinsen shibu. "Dai 20 shidan tenzoku jinba yusō gyōmu shōhō," entry for January 1938. In *Mitsu dainikki* 11 (1938). Bōeichō bōei kenkyūjo toshokan [Defense Agency's Defense Research Institute Library].

Dai 11 gun shireikan Anami Korechika. "Tokubetsu hōkoku teishutsu no ken," entry for March 30, 1942. In *Rikushifu dainikki* 9(1942). Bōeichō bōei kenkyūjo toshokan.

Dai 13 shidanchō Uchiyama Eitarō. "Tokubetsu hōkokuchū gunjin henshi no ken," entry for March 21, 1942. In *Rikushifu dainikki* 9(1942). Bōeichō bōei kenkyūjo toshokan.

Daihon'ei rikugunbu kenkyūhan. "Shina jihen ni okeru gunki fūki no kenchi yori kansatsuseru seibyō ni tsuite," dated October 1940. Bōeichō bōei kenkyūjo toshokan.

Hagiwara Hikozō takumushō chōsen buchō. "Kankō e no tokōsha torishimari ni kansuru ken," entry dated February 20, 1939. In *Shōwa 13, 14 nen ryoken reiki (tōyō)*, produced by the Chōsen sōtokufu gaimuka. Korean National Archives, Pusan Branch.

Hokkaidōchō. "Shōwa 20 nen chōkan jimu hikitugisho." Hokkaidōritu bunshokan [Hokkaidō Prefectural Archives].

Hokushi keimubu. "Hōjin shokugyō betsu jinkō tōkeihyō," dated July 1, 1939. Gaimushō gaikō shiryōkan [Ministry of Foreign Affairs Archives].

Kantōgun sanbōbu senden sankō. "Kanminzoku no tokushitsu" (July 1933). In Rikugunshō, ed., *Manshū jihen rikugun eiseishi*, vol. 8. Rikugunshō, 1938.

Kinbara Setsuzō. "Rikugunshō gyōmu nisshi tekiroku," Part I: 14 vols.; Part II: 24 vols. (Jan. 1940–Jan. 1942). Bōeichō bōei kenkyūjo toshokan. The original is in the collection of the Rikujo jieitai eisei gakkō [Ground Self-Defense Force Medical School].

Kitashina hōmen gun shireibu. "Kyōsantō no waga guntai ni taisuru shisōteki gakai kōsaku no shinsō to kore ga bōatsu hōsaku" (April 5, 1939). Kokuritsu kōbun shokan [Japanese National Archives].

Konsei dai 14 ryodan shireibu. "Eisei gyōmu junpō," 1933. Kokuritsu kōbun shokan.

Mandaree chūtonchi shireibu. "Chūtonchi ianjo kitei," dated May 26, 1943. UK Imperial War Museum. Courtesy of Hayashi Hirofumi.

Marai gunseikan. "Ian shisetsu oyobi ryokan eigyō junshu kisoku." In *Gunsei kiteishū* 3(Nov. 11, 1943). Marai (Malay) gunseikanbu. Bōeichō bōei kenkyūjo toshokan.

Marai gunseikan. "Ian shisetsu oyobi ryokan eigyō torishimari kitei." In *Gunsei kiteishū* 3(Nov. 11, 1943). Marai (Malay) gunseikanbu. Bōeichō bōei kenkyūjo toshokan.

Morikawa butai (Dokuritsu san hōhei daisan rentai). "Morikawa butai tokushu ian gyōmu ni kansuru kitei," dated November 14, 1939. In *Jinchū nikki* (Nov. 1939). Dokuritsu san hōhei dai 3 rentai. Bōeichō bōei kenkyūjo toshokan. Courtesy of Matsuno seiya.

Naimu daijin seigi. "Chōsen sōtokufu bunai rinji shokuin setchiseichū kaisei no ken," entry dated June 27, 1944. In *Kōbun ruishū* 68(25)(1944) [kanshokumon, kansei 25, chōsen sōtokufu 4]. Kokuritsu kōbun shokan.

Nakashina haken kempeitai shireibu. "Rikugun gunjin gunzoku hikōhyō," entries dated November 1941 and February 1942. In *Rikushifu dainikki* 6 and 9 (1942). Bōeichō bōei kenkyūjo toshokan.

Netherlands Institute for War Documentation. Documents on Semarang Forced Prostitution Case Files 1944, 1948. Courtesy of the Asahi Shimbunsha.

"Ranryō indo hōrei kōhō," no. 44, in *Sensō hanzai saiban kankei hōreishū*, vol. 2. Hōmudaijin kanbō shihō hōsei chōsabu, 1965.

Rikuamitsu dai 1283. "Rikugun kankeisha nanpō senryōchi (Hukumu Hong Kong) shinshutsu tetsuzuki ni kansuru ken," entry dated April 23, 1942. In *Rikuamitsu dainikki* 18(1942). Bōeichō bōei kenkyūjo toshokan.

Rikuamitsu dai 1398. "Tokō tetsuzuki ni kansuru ken," entry dated November 18, 1942. In *Rikuamitsu dainikki* 55(1942). Bōeichō bōei kenkyūjo toshokan.

Index

Prostitution (*continued*)
  and recruitment, 100–103,
  110–111; and sexually transmitted
  disease prevention, 47–48, 70; and
  Shanghai Incident, 43–44. *See also*
  Trafficking treaties
PTSD. *See* Post-traumatic stress
  disorder
Public opinion, 27–28

Rape in comfort stations, 11, 29,
  139–140; anti-apology activists on,
  10; Semarang case, 167, 168–169,
  170; Southeast Asia, 124
Rape prevention, 9–10, 65–68; Asia
  Pacific War, 78–80; China War,
  45, 49, 52, 54–55; and comfort
  stations for Allied forces, 179–184;
  Semarang case, 164
Rapes: by Allied forces, 183–184;
  Asia Pacific War, 78–79; China
  War, 52, 80; in comfort stations,
  11, 29, 139–140, 167, 168–169,
  170; condoning of, 10, 68,
  190–191; gang rape, 122; and
  international law, 161, 162;
  numbers of, 29, 30; punishment
  for, 66; by Soviet forces, 188
Reasons for comfort stations. *See*
  Espionage prevention; Morale;
  Rape prevention; Sexually transmitted disease prevention
Recruitment: China, 118–123; and
  civilian prostitutes, 100–103,
  110–111; conscription plans,
  109–110; debt slavery, 29, 106;

deception, 29, 103–105, 116–117,
  125–126; governments-general
  involvement, 63–64, 107–108,
  109, 111–112, 113–115; illegality
  of, 111–112; Japanese military
  involvement, 10, 59, 64–65; and
  patriotism, 101; sale of women,
  105–106; Southeast Asia, 123–128;
  Taiwan, 63–64, 115–117. *See also*
  Coercive recruitment
Remuneration, 142–144, 206
Reparations. *See* Compensation
Research on War Responsibility, 27
Respite, 141–142, 169
Roh Te-woo, 33
Rwanda, 19
Ryōriten shakufu system, 44

Sakabe Yasumasa, 128
Sakhalin, 46–47
Salinog, Tomasa, 194
Sams, C. F., 184
San Francisco Peace Treaty (1951),
  162, 176
Sasagawa Ryōzō, 182
Sasaki Takayoshi, 101–102
Self-Defense Agency. *See* National
  Institute for Defense Studies
  Library
Semarang case, 163–173; coercive
  recruitment, 165–166; comfort
  station closings, 171; "Dutch
  Government Report," 173–174;
  O'Herne, 166–167, 171; planning,
  164–165; ruling, 171–173; sources,
  163–164; testimony, 169–170; van

Yasuda Tsuneo, 84
Yorichi, Alex, 106, 110
Yosano Hikaru, 184
Yoshida Yutaka, 190

Yoshimi Yoshiaki, 6–7, 10–11, 27
Yun Jung-ok, 192
Yun Myong-suk, 113